Cornering the Market

Cornering the Market

Independent Grocers and Innovation in American Small Business

SUSAN V. SPELLMAN

OXFORD
UNIVERSITY PRESS

OXFORD

UNIVERSITY PRESS

Oxford University Press is a department of the University of Oxford. It furthers
the University's objective of excellence in research, scholarship, and education
by publishing worldwide. Oxford is a registered trade mark of Oxford University
Press in the UK and certain other countries.

Published in the United States of America by Oxford University Press
198 Madison Avenue, New York, NY 10016, United States of America.

© Oxford University Press 2016

First issued as an Oxford University Press paperback, 2020

Library of Congress Cataloging-in-Publication Data
Spellman, Susan V., 1971– author. Cornering the market : independent grocers and innovation in
American small business / Susan V. Spellman.
    pages cm
Includes bibliographical references and index.
ISBN 978–0–19–938427–3 (hardback) — ISBN 978–0–19–754599–7 (paperback) —
ISBN 978–0–19–938428–0 (electronic) — ISBN 978–0–19–938429–7 (electronic) —
ISBN 978–0–19–049550–3 (electronic) 1. Grocery trade—United States—History.
2. Small business—United States—History. I. Title.
HD9321.5.S64 2016
381'.4564130973—dc23
2015033601

For my mother and in memory of my father

Contents

Acknowledgments

It is tempting employ the style and form of a grocer's ledger to detail the many obligations I have incurred while writing this book. The only problem is that double-entry bookkeeping demands that both debits and credits balance at the end of the day, an impossible task given my substantial and prolonged withdrawals of wisdom, time, and money from scholars, institutions, friends, and family. After all, this project had its beginnings nearly twenty-five years ago when, instead of immediately pursuing college, I chose to take a full-time job in a grocery store. Over the next six years, I learned the trade working for various chain supermarkets as a cashier, bagger, stocker, and produce clerk. My debts, therefore, begin with my father, Dana Spellman, who pointed me toward this job when an old friend opened a Giant Eagle franchise in his hometown, unknowingly setting me on the path to my future scholarly career.

In the course of my academic life, I've had the good fortune of working closely with three extraordinary individuals. Scott Sandage has been a champion of this project from its conception as a second-year seminar paper at Carnegie Mellon. For more than a decade, he has been an unstinting advisor and counselor, giving more of his time and attention than I probably deserved and reading far too many revisions to count. Above all, Scott has been a good friend and confidant, his warmth and wit making this journey bearable and downright fun at times. It is a rare treat to become colleagues with a former advisor, especially one as kind and supportive as Allan Winkler. Allan first directed my master's thesis at Miami University before serving as my faculty mentor. His generosity and guidance have propelled this book in directions I never thought possible and I am forever grateful. I am likewise thankful for

Shirley Wajda's unflagging encouragement and friendship. Her keen insights, editorial eye, and genuine interest in my work have been tremendously valuable since my days as an undergraduate.

It is true that despite many lonely hours spent in the archives and in front of a computer screen, nobody writes a book alone. David Hounshell, Kenneth Lipartito, and Joel Tarr provided valuable methodological and analytical contributions as dissertation committee members. Both Pamela Laird and Stephen Mihm have cheered on this project and offered welcomed critiques at various stages. Fellow grocery scholars Marc Levinson, Tracey Deutsch, and Susan Tolbert welcomed me and provided important insights. I found early backing from faculty members of the Business History Conference's Newcomen Dissertation Colloquium (now Oxford Journals Doctoral Colloquium) including JoAnne Yates, David Sicilia, Mary O'Sullivan, William Hausman, and W. Bernard Carlson. Rosanne Currarino, Sarah Elvins, Walter Friedman, Vicki Howard, Jan Logemann, Uwe Spiekermann, Jocelyn Wills, and an anonymous reviewer, in addition to many enthusiastic conference panelists and audience members shared insights and ideas for fresh directions and sources. Paul Fischbeck and Katherine Lynch helped me make sense of the data I gathered on cash registers. I thank them all for taking the time to encourage me and to improve my work.

Several institutions provided financial and material resources that made researching and writing not only possible but a far more enriching experience. The American Historical Association in cooperation with the Kluge Center and Library of Congress awarded me the J. Franklin Jameson Fellowship and the opportunity to spend several months immersed in their collections, as did the Smithsonian Institution's National American History Museum Predoctoral Fellowship. The New England Regional Fellowship Consortium through the Massachusetts Historical Society provided funds to visit the Schlesinger Library and Maine Historical Society, as well as Baker Library at the Harvard Business School. I was able to return to Baker Library with the help of a Chandler Traveling Fellowship from the Business History Conference. I received additional assistance from the American Historical Association's Littleton-Griswold Grant, along with support from the Miami University Department of History Research Fund Grant, Miami University Hamilton Campus Faculty Research Grant, Carnegie Mellon University Graduate Small Project Help (GuSH) Grant, and Susan Van Horn Fund.

I have benefited from the assistance of many archivists, curators, and librarians in the years it took to piece together small grocers' businesses and lives. At the National Museum of American History, Peter Liebhold was a kind and willing advisor, while Rueben Jackson, Susan Strange, Vanessa Broussard

Simmons, Fath Ruffins, and Peggy Kidwell pointed me toward good collections and better ideas. Jeff Flanery, Abby Yochelson, and other Library of Congress staff, along with Jeff Opt, National Cash Register archivist at the NCR Archive at Dayton History provided indispensable help in navigating their collections and directing me to other resources. Laura Linard and her team at Baker Library welcomed me even when the archives were closed for renovations. Dale Rosengarten, Curator of Special Collections at the Addlestone Library, College of Charleston, patiently answered my questions. I am equally grateful to librarians and archivists at the Jewish Heritage Collection at the College of Charleston; Maine Historical Society; Massachusetts Historical Society; Minnesota Historical Society; Schlesinger Library at the Radcliffe Institute for Advanced Study, Harvard University; South Caroliniana Library at the University of South Carolina; Wisconsin Historical Society; and the Jewish Historical Society of Greater Washington.

I am exceedingly fortunate to have profited twice from Miami University's community of scholars. Rob Schorman was a particularly supportive dean, as was Lee Sanders. Likewise, department chairs Charlotte Goldy, Mary Kupiec Cayton, Carla Pestana, and Wietse de Boer, and coordinator Sree Subedi have been excellent advisors. Drew Cayton offered a sympathetic ear and critical eye on numerous occasions. I also thank John Forren and Helen Sheumaker for their encouragement and friendship. Farther south at the warmer University of Miami, Mary Lindemann has remained a wise and encouraging mentor. Nancy Toff at Oxford University Press has shepherded me through the publishing process while sharing her own family's grocery store history. Indeed, one of the most rewarding aspects of working on corner grocers has been hearing from countless strangers and friends about their families' neighborhood shops. The highlight of these experiences came in May 2008 when I traveled to rural Maine to meet Rachel L. Newcomb, Edmund Fuller's great-granddaughter. Rachel opened her home and personal archive to me, sharing the better part of a day along with her extensive research. She later provided helpful comments on chapter 1.

A small, but close cadre of friends has sustained me throughout this long journey. Michelle Abraham has been a wonderful colleague and trivia partner. Our weekly routine kept me from sweating the setbacks that come with publishing, while enriching my social life and pocketbook. I am grateful for her friendship and for sharing her family with me. Lee Vinsel is the smarter, younger brother I never had. He has remained a trusted ally and sounding board since graduate school. Angela O'Neal shared her home and friends with me on numerous occasions, reminding me that there is life and fun outside of academe.

My greatest debts are owed to my father and my mother Vivian Spellman, extraordinary parents who instilled in me a strong work ethic and independent spirit. My mother in particular has been a tremendous source of strength, listening to me kvetch, comforting me when things went sideways, and rooting me on to the end. Words alone could never express how truly grateful I am for her unending support. I began and will conclude by thanking my father. Through his own life, he showed me how to make the most of modest beginnings, while giving me a valuable bit of life advice: always get a second opinion. My only hope is that I would have made him proud to see how far I have come. It is to him and to my mother that this book is lovingly dedicated.

Cornering the Market

Introduction

Corner Store Folklore

A few days before Christmas 1896, the *Oakland Tribune* named August Bjorkman "Proprietor of the Most Modern Grocery Store" in San Leandro, California. The sixty-year-old Swedish immigrant ran a "very large business" in the up-and-coming town, just east across the bay from San Francisco. Bjorkman competed with eight other San Leandro grocers for recognition as one of the city's "Go-Ahead" businessmen. "Mr. Bjorkman's store if lifted up and carried off to San Francisco," the editors boasted, "would be in perfect harmony with one of the best equipped stores in that city." Bjorkman bought and sold goods as cheaply as merchants in nearby Oakland, and his cosmopolitan trade sent his wagons for the freshest and best merchandise to places such as Fruitvale and Haywards, destinations anywhere from five to fifteen miles from the grocer's shop. Personalized service distinguished Bjorkman from his rivals: "He attends to the wants of his customers," observers acknowledged, "sees to it that they get exactly what they order," and offered amenities that were "prompt and satisfactory always."[1]

What was it that made Bjorkman's business modern in 1896? Very little about the grocer or his store seems particularly fresh. Absent from the newspaper's accolades are mentions of "bigness" and "efficiency," hallmarks of today's "modern" trade. Just one year earlier, the *Fresno Weekly Republican* detailed a similar visit to local grocer Budd T. Scott's store, noting that Scott had "kept pace with all the modern innovations of the trade." He carried a "thousand delicacies gathered from every country and clime" displayed "in an attractive manner," and served shoppers in a "careful and painstaking" fashion. Scott did business solely for cash, which allowed him to sell "at the lowest possible margin of profit." These terms and language might easily describe chain grocers of the 1920s and 1930s, yet the newspaper applied the term "modern" no fewer than four times to Scott and his nineteenth-century operation.[2]

For the newspapers to call Scott and Bjorkman "modern" tells us that they and their contemporaries saw grocers as forward-thinking businessmen, not as barriers to progress. From the Civil War through the Great Depression, small proprietors anchored the United States' grocery trade. Stores like Bjorkman's and Scott's appeared in every large city, small town, and rural outpost. One trade journal estimated that in the early 1900s the number of retail grocers in New England alone approached nearly ten thousand, "not including those who have cellar stores and keep in stock only a pound or two of sugar, a jar of confectionery, or a loaf of bread." Counting these shops, "the number might be trebled." By 1930, the first year the U.S. Census published retail store numbers, there were more than 300,000 groceries in America, 83 percent run by independent dealers—that is, they were not part of a chain organization. As late as 1948, these establishments accounted for more than 60 percent of retail grocery sales in the United States, making independent firms and their innovative contributions to retailing, wholesaling, and distribution a key and understudied factor in the story of American commercial and industrial development.[3]

In the 1890s, when journalists could credibly label small grocers "modern," Gilded Age America was awash with transformations, among them the shift from agricultural to mass production and from locally fixed commerce to national, large-scale business. This was a period rife with modernizing impulses—the push for systemization, rationalization, and bureaucratization altering not just manufacturing but government, labor, and culture as well. Magnates, tycoons, and financiers led the charge, with men like Andrew Carnegie, John D. Rockefeller, and J. P. Morgan centralizing resources, instituting new analytical tools, and initiating organization structures to coordinate and control behemoth operations. Theirs became the most visible route through industrial capitalism, the sheer size and prominence of their undertakings simultaneously expanding and concentrating American capital while unleashing middle managers, a new form of businessman. Size mattered and "bigness" quickly became historians' code for "modern."[4]

Questions about the great industrialists' aptitude for and the centrality of their methods, however, have shifted attention to business operations—ground-level functions of large and small firms. Doing so has reoriented accounts of economic development. Disorganization, ambiguity, and dysfunction, for example, typified transcontinental railroad corporations, the ineptitude of their operators resulting in bloated operations, unnecessary tracks, and fabulously wealthy capitalists. Bureaucratic incompetence and not Weberian rationality was a sign of progress, system-building run amok. Others found in small-scale manufacturing's "endless novelty" the impulse for organizational innovation and transformative production techniques outside of corporate boardrooms. Even without the latest technological, administrative, and managerial advances, batch and custom producers nonetheless accounted for the vast majority of the nation's industrial capacity. Might, it seems, was not always right. Yet the Gilded Age's "gilders"—capitalism's big winners—and manufacturing firms still headline. The countless small-scale intermediaries and storekeepers who dominated nineteenth-century distribution and retailing have lingered in the background, despite their significance to the American economy. Our portrait of American industrialization, therefore, remains limited in its scope and imprecise in its emphasis on big men and big businesses as the primary modernizers.[5]

The era's awakening giants get top billing even in narratives about retailing. Department stores and their moguls have been the focus of most studies about nineteenth-century consumption. Marshall Field's and John Wanamaker's "consumption palaces" resembled producers' giant corporations more than they did corner storefronts. Mail-order houses and chain stores too received greater attention for their similarity to colossal manufacturing firms. Small retailers, when they made appearances, often did so as barriers to "progress," men and women who bemoaned changes taking place in their neighborhoods and shops. This was especially true in studies of the chain-store era, where nineteenth-century storekeepers made a convenient (if inaccurate) counterpoint to the twentieth-century vertically integrated Great Atlantic and Pacific Tea Company (A&P). In the telling, Gilded Age grocers' "inefficiently run" small shops, where "confusion and disorganization" reigned, lacked "most of the tools at the command of today's retailer." With chains rising to prominence in the 1920s and 1930s, these seeming relics of an earlier age spoke out only as "the voice of the past crying out against the present." August Bojorkman and Bud Scott had become antiquated expressions of yesteryear instead of industrialists' contemporaries.[6]

Capitalism's complexity and dynamism has been obscured in the search for order, which tended to equate big firms' corporate dominance with modernization, making small businessmen bit players in industrialization's drama. Efforts to resolve perceived tensions between community aspects of early retailing versus the capitalistic system in which it is embedded have cast grocers in our popular imagination as genial men who puttered along, plucking pickles from the briny depths of barrels and spinning yarns with locals. Not until chain stores appeared did storekeepers' humble fortunes shift, according to these accounts. The problem with this view is that it ignores the ways in which local retailers helped structure the nineteenth-century economy by consciously shaping mass distribution, retailing, and consumption. They were the driving force behind new networks, technologies, and systems that moved food to the predominantly rural nation's countless backwoods towns. It was in their Main Street shops and banks and not in urban department stores, boardrooms, or commodity markets where most Americans witnessed and experienced the effects of the new corporate economy.[7]

As small retailers carved a route through industrial capitalism, they combined personal services with profit motives to create a powerful and (for many) lucrative method of selling. Private thoughts from storekeepers' diaries, nib and ink calculations, and notations found in business ledgers and documents tell this story from their perspective, along with the protests, boasts, and commiserations grocery retailers, wholesalers, traveling men, and consumers detailed in their letters. Grocery proprietors generally were male and female owner-operators of a single store—the core of an emerging middle class that by the reform years of the Progressive Era would become outspoken repudiators

C. R. Robertson's modern business style and slogan belie the hodgepodge of baskets, produce, signs, and loiterers outside his store. Nineteenth-century grocers like Robertson pioneered and employed commercial practices most commonly associated with twentieth-century big businesses. Author's collection.

of a corporatizing America. Yet through their own actions, sales records, credit reports, and legislative efforts to regulate chain stores, they contributed from the bottom up to the transformation under way in the nation's infrastructure and political economy. The difficulty of piecing together their experiences explains in part why historical studies about this sector have tended to rely on common misperceptions. Indeed, neighborhood grocers have become little more than Norman Rockwell paintings, symbols of a lost era when business was supposedly more personal and less about the bottom line, perpetuated by sentimental stories about "the old country store." As history has shown, however, close relations and profits are not mutually exclusive in either theory or practice.[8]

The paradoxical character of American small business further clouds this portrait. Americans generally have celebrated small business owners' entrepreneurial spirit as part of the "American dream" but at the same time have criticized their businesses for their apparent lack of economic productivity and perceived resistance to "progress." Small grocers embodied Americans' quest for economic independence. Since Thomas Jefferson's time, the republican ideal of personal liberty and the desire for financial stability inspired thousands to open their own stores. That dream was still alive in the 1910s when German immigrant and prospective grocer Richard Brune used capitalist logic to articulate his reason for becoming an independent grocer. "Why shouldn't I collect not only my own wages, and profits but the profits from the labor of others?" The precarious nature of small business, though, often entangled these men and women (many of whom lacked commercial experience) in the crosswinds of market forces. The thousands who entered the ranks of independent entrepreneurship did so in the classic sense of the term, running their own businesses, assuming all risks and profits, and bearing heavy burdens when they failed in their pursuit of happiness. Brune, though, had good fortune in Connecticut where he captured the attention of the Burroughs Adding Machine Company, which told his story in a 1915 promotional book. Those who succeeded only confirmed for others that American ingenuity, "thinking powers," and "courage," qualities that made Brune a model entrepreneur according to the technology firm, were enough to get ahead. Many more, though, would discover that virtues alone would not suffice.[9]

In Richard Brune's day, calling someone a "corner grocer" was no slight to the size of his store or the kind of business he conducted. It was, rather, a nod to a merchant's shrewdness and competitive spirit. In the 1850s, the term denoted the advantageous placement of a retail shop at the intersection of two roads. John Russell Bartlett's 1859 *Dictionary of Americanisms* defined the "corner-grocery" as "a favorite location for such establishments in American towns," making the expression peculiar to this nation and therefore a touchstone of its culture. When Charles Slack put his Chicago store up for sale in 1883, he advertised it as "one of the largest, finest and best paying corner Groceries," presuming interested parties would recognize the beneficial setting. Just before the turn of the twentieth century, the term began carrying what would become the twin stigmas of smallness and parochialism. "The corner grocery is an institution of established recognition; it stands for thrift, integrity, and social honor," one novelist claimed in 1897, adding that such shops had become more a "matter of description than location."[10]

The thrift, integrity, and social honor that once exalted small businessmen in the nineteenth century became drawbacks by the twentieth. Frustrations emerged within the trade over grocers who refused to clean up their shops, track sales, account for money coming in and going out, or maintain fresh stocks. Such storekeepers, many believed, brought down the whole trade, making all look bad to consumers. Progressive women's journals decried the "dirty grocery store," where "the windows needed washing," "barrels were uncovered," and boxes of crackers and other goods were "piled in hopeless confusion." Driven in part by the Pure Food and Drug Act (1906), shoppers took to the stores to protest grime and grunge in the name of health. By the 1930s, the corner grocer and his neighborhood store were a target for economists, lawmakers, politicians, and the public for failing to meet the new merits of efficiency, rationalization, and standardization that had come to symbolize "modern" business.[11]

Historians have adopted this general view, depicting the battle between independent grocers and chains as a David and Goliath struggle of "tradition" versus "modernity," a war between two separate business systems. In this interpretation, Joseph Schumpeter's 1942 theory of "creative destruction" explains how "more efficient" chain stores evolved to supplant small retailers. "The fundamental impulse that sets and keeps the capitalist engine in motion," Schumpeter argued, "comes from the new consumers' goods, the new methods of production or transportation, the new markets, the new forms of industrial organization that capitalist enterprise creates." When it comes to the grocery trade, most historians and critics cast chain stores both as architects and beneficiaries of those forces. "Most small businesses neither grow nor innovate," suggested one historian of the Great Atlantic and Pacific Tea Company (A&P), founded as a single-store tea business in 1859, which grew into the trade's first and largest national chain. Schumpeter's notion that old forms are incessantly destroyed in favor of new ones makes it easy to write small grocers out of the picture by the 1950s, when chains and supermarkets came to dominate nationally.[12]

In spite of such characterizations, nineteenth-century corner grocers stood at the crossroads of extraordinary structural changes that matured in commercial capitalism following the Civil War. They experienced firsthand the revolutions in transportation, communications, mass production, distribution, and marketing, along with the growth of regional and national markets and the introduction of new organizational and business methods. How different might the story be if we also cast small businessmen as pursuers of capitalism's "fundamental impulses," making them innovators and initiators of the kind of centralized, rationalized, and standardized methods most commonly associated with large-scale corporations? Historian Thomas Schlereth briefly considered this possibility, alluding to the potential for invention in nineteenth-century shops: "Paeans are sung to its legendary front porch, its inspirational cracker barrel, and its hospitable potbellied stove rather than its innovative merchandising displays, special bargain packaging, or widespread use of national-brand advertising." Today we know very little about these early grocers or their corner stores and even less about their major contributions to the making of "modern" commercial enterprise in the United States.[13]

Part of this oversight stems from journalistic representations of "mom-and-pop" grocers, a sentimental epithet first used in the 1930s to illustrate the plight of family-owned retail shops. The expression quickly came to symbolize a "golden age" in local business. In the 1940s and 1950s, popular works propagated yarns about corner grocers and their antiquated peculiarities, corresponding in time with the ongoing decline of independent retailers and the rise of chains and supermarkets following World War II. Advertisers and authors alike looked back mawkishly on the bygone days of small, local business. A 1940s poster-sized advertisement from Chase and Sanborn Coffee distributed to countless stores and published in numerous magazines, titled "The Old New England Grocery," did much to cultivate this image. Featuring an 1897 Abbott Graves painting that depicted a scene "typical of the many stores that once served villages and town," the ad relied on the Maine artist's picture to illustrate the charm and intimacy, supposedly lost, of rural storekeeping. A bearded grocer, a mishmash of merchandise, and rudimentary fixtures provided the setting for four characters crowded around a potbellied stove. Focused on retailing's social facets, the copy imparted folksy descriptions of the men seated on wooden settles and overturned buckets, and recounted the store's importance as a public space for airing ideas about "theology, politics, adventure, farming, history, reform." The backdrop for these conversations, however, also contained lithographed advertisements, canned and packaged goods, and signs for "Japan Tea" and "Fresh Butter," indications of the counterman's international and regional market activities. Business dealings, though, played little role in Chase and Sanborn's characterization, short of urging all to "gratefully remember" storekeepers for "working so faithfully in the day of small things."[14]

Suspending rural storekeepers in time, popular literature of the mid-twentieth century perpetuated these impressions. Accounts by New England merchants proved particularly potent, the spirit of Yankee enterprise—symbolic of independence and self-rule—weighed down by checkerboards and spittoons. Down-home exchanges with odd characters eclipsed the fundamental business functions of giving and getting credit, advertising, and merchandising, concealing commerce "within the lore of the storekeeper." Stories about "goose-pokes" (a yoke placed around the neck of a goose, intended to keep the bird from slipping through a fence) and amiable idlers portrayed merchants as "character[s] in folklore" rather than as businessmen. One long-time grocery store owner-turned-author employed colorful anecdotes about slick grocers and slippery customers to liven up his 1961 work on country storekeeping, despite having transformed his own small shop into a supermarket. Tall tales and local legends fed the reading public's expectations and desire to reminisce about "simpler" times when local grocers were central to town life in a way that chains and supermarkets struggled to replicate. As a result, "mom-and-pop" came to signify the kind of community-centered exchanges many people believed had been lost in the commercialization of American life.[15]

Comparing independent groceries to chain stores, in both popularized and scholarly accounts flattens the many complicated ways in which the two business forms intersected and overlapped. Distinctions between proprietary and corporate capitalism in the grocery business did not fully emerge until the 1910s and 1920s, years after most historical accounts of industrialization exclude small retailers from the process, making it seem as if they had no hand in the transformation. Yet for most contemporaries, the transition was never as self-evident or straightforward as some suggest. Consumers especially had difficulty distinguishing between the two systems. Stepping into almost any corner shop—independent or chain—between 1890 and 1925, shoppers encountered similar scenes: shelves stocked with bulk and packaged goods from around the world purchased from and distributed by independent wholesalers; display windows and cases of canned goods and delicacies; clerks who selected and wrapped customer orders for home delivery; and a greater number of stores encouraging cash payment over credit in an effort to reduce losses from bad debts.[16]

Sometime between the end of the Civil War and the beginning of the 1890s, every one of these methods was innovative and new. Even self-service and cash-and-carry schemes first appeared in independents' small shops before becoming quintessential chain store techniques. Early grocers' customary practices did not become "backward" or problematic until chains grew into "big businesses," employing different (but not necessarily new) distribution and marketing strategies. Taking this view, the line between small business's so-called "traditional" practices and corporations' "modern" forms begins to blur.

Contrasting independent grocers with chain stores has become for some a dichotomy of convenience. Economic measures—productivity, transaction costs, turnover, and profit margins—inherently place nineteenth- and early-twentieth-century grocers at an analytical disadvantage, making them appear inefficient in relation to chains. The diffuse nature of the perishable goods business and its corresponding distribution challenges made it difficult for early grocers to adopt vertical integration strategies and corporate organizational forms that emerged in the 1890s in manufacturing and retail department stores. "Substantial economies of scale," historians have remarked, "were virtually unrealizable" when it came to moving agricultural and manufactured foodstuffs. Grocers, however, were neither ignorant of these problems nor afraid to point out their concerns. New York dealers in 1875 sympathized with the new distribution scheme's imperfections. "Springing into existence as it has, it would be strange if there were not defects and inequalities in our transportation system." Steam, rails, and electricity had "completely revolutionized commerce by extending its area, and facilitating the exchange of the World's products," they noted, but "as yet it is crude and comparatively inefficient." Such haphazard yet radical structural challenges "take many years to solve," grocers acknowledged, even as they remarked how "the old methods of transacting business have been almost entirely superseded." Focusing on the "long term outcomes" of this evolutionary process has obscured the outgrowth of American industrial capitalism in the small corner stores that comprised the first 150 years of retailing and distribution.[17]

Shifting attention from economic factors to business practices tells a different story, one where small businessmen led the modernization process instead of reluctantly trudging behind giant companies. The first grocers to purchase and use cash registers in the 1880s, for example, were corner dealers who operated firms often valued at less than $500. They nevertheless became early adopters of the latest retail technology, making routine the kinds of commercial and informational controls and practices we now take for granted every time we go through a checkout line. Small grocers developed fresh ways to acquire, distribute, and market goods, radically altering the ways in which businessmen and consumers alike came to understand retail stores and shopping. In short, they actively engaged in the larger process of determining the shape of both the modern market economy and the grocery trade. The irony, however, is that many of the methods and practices these men pioneered ultimately drove independent grocers from the marketplace they helped construct.

This book explores the grocery trade's development from the Civil War through the 1940s and considers the multiple ways grocers responded to and pioneered changes in nineteenth- and twentieth-century capitalism. Before 1869, the year the trade's first journal began publication, grocers' roots in liquor stores and groggeries coupled with a lack of specialization did not hamper them from becoming the primary movers of farm products and manufactured goods between frontier towns and commercial hubs. In the following decade, efforts to professionalize storekeepers' practices came from within, as grocers began creating and looking for new and better ways to conduct business. Responding to challenges brought about by fundamental shifts in commerce and the economy, early grocers unveiled new merchandising, accounting, and distribution techniques and established foundational elements of retailing.

Building on these components, grocers became part of the larger "control revolution" taking place in late nineteenth-century business. Beginning in the 1880s, they transitioned from handwritten ledgers, daybooks, and customer passbooks to register keys, paper receipts, and cash-drawer bells, generating greater command over everyday trade, routinizing nonstandard operations, and shaping the informational and technological transformations that defined retailing in the twentieth century. In addition to these technological changes, modifications in grocery production, marketing, and distribution brought the need for greater coordination between all branches of the grocery business. Wholesale grocers (chief distributors) developed innovative methods to address spatial and structural problems that limited expansion of their trade and movement of goods. One solution came in the 1870s and 1880s by way of traveling salesmen—agents who established commercial networks and relationships of trust by shoring up long-distance dealings between wholesalers and retailers. The experiences of men like South Carolina "drummer" Samuel Iseman illustrate how trade networks transcended and redefined regional boundaries to build a mass grocery distribution system at the end of the nineteenth century.

Yet by the turn of the twentieth century, retailers looked for ways to avoid distribution networks established by traveling salesmen. Wholesale grocers had begun forming strong commercial and financial alliances with manufacturers through cartels and other cooperative organizations. Groups like the Boston Wholesale Grocers' Association (BWGA) attempted to centralize and consolidate their businesses while fixing prices and limiting goods to retailers, refusing to acknowledge how changes in other trades such as dry goods and clothing might transform grocery distribution. Small retail grocers responded by organizing buying exchanges, bypassing wholesalers and dealing directly with manufacturers, thus disrupting established distribution channels and suggesting alternative paths along which goods might travel. By the 1910s, both wholesalers' attempts to dominate distribution and retailers' efforts to eliminate the middleman opened the door to new organizational and operational possibilities in the distribution of groceries.

Chain stores helped realize some of that potential. The "chain store question" of the 1910s and 1920s pitted independent grocers against chain moguls as each sought to become the model for both grocery retailing and American enterprise. Neighborhood grocers fought to show chain organizers how so-called backward methods built around notions of "thrift, integrity, and social honor" could also point the way to "progress." The very definition of the "American dream" as well as market dominance was at stake in this struggle. Owning and operating a small business—"entrepreneurial spirit"—had long been a route to the kind of independence inherent in America, but that opportunity seemed to be disappearing as national chain store moguls and managers threatened to become new archetypal entrepreneurs and businessmen. Yet even by the 1930s, the outcome was undetermined; neither chains nor independents could claim industry dominance nor be assured of their future within either the grocery trade or American business.

The national study presented in this book draws examples from all regions and from grocers representing multiple facets of the trade. Notwithstanding this wide scope, few women and ethnic grocers appear. This lacuna stems in part from a lack of their surviving archival records and from their absence in the print culture of trade journals, newspapers, and weeklies. African American and women grocers in particular are difficult to track in business and commercial records, especially before the twentieth century. They often operated much smaller stores with trade that ebbed and flowed even more delicately with economic shifts than did those of their white, male counterparts. Records from either black or female grocers, therefore, are scant, or at least difficult to identify as such. Finding women grocers carries with it the additional burden of distinguishing ownership. While countless female names appear in city directories, many more conducted trade under their husbands' names. But whenever possible, their voices enrich this book's arguments and assertions about "businessmen" and remind us that small grocers represented a vastly divergent group of men and women.

Recovering independent grocers' stories refocuses the narratives of business and cultural history onto real people who built the trade and struggled with the day-to-day problems, challenges, and tasks associated with running a small shop. Too often we have concentrated on the structures of commerce and relied upon well-worn stereotypes of "corner grocers" to tell the story of small retailers, forgetting to ask questions of the men and women who made the independent grocery trade possible and made it work. Rural shopkeeper Edmund Fuller, one of many typical New England merchants, wrote keenly in his diary not only about his experiences but also his responses to large-scale shifts in American commerce. From behind the counter of his Maine store, Fuller remarked in the 1870s and 1880s on the slew of traveling salesmen whose visits replaced the regular stock-buying trips he once made to Boston. Around the time Fuller began trading eggs in Boston, he installed a telegraph wire in his shop to monitor prices and conditions in the distant market. When he caught wind that his customers wanted one of the latest advertised goods, Fuller hopped a train to the next town to learn more before sending a telegram to place his order. Shortly after Bell invented the telephone in 1876, Fuller put one in his store to stay in contact with customers and family. Changes in the commercial economy brought corresponding and innovative solutions.[18]

Although Edmund Fuller never lived to see the twentieth century, he would have found something familiar in the chain stores and supermarkets that now appear on city streets and in suburban neighborhoods. It was in the shops of men like Fuller where ideas, methods, and models for a national grocery trade percolated. While others used these tools to build bigger stores and businesses, independent grocers in the nineteenth and early twentieth centuries laid the foundation for their eventual success and found innovative ways to address challenges and obstacles. Many of the men who appear in the following chapters never saw their names splashed across the front of more than one small store or ever became operators of "big businesses," yet they are no less a part of the story of "modern" American business and retailing than their corporate counterparts. Indeed, they are the story.

1

From Grog Shops to Grocery Stores

On September 15, 1869, John Darby, an Alabama chemistry teacher turned New York City publisher, announced the publication of *American Grocer*, a new monthly that would serve as "an organ of communication between buyers and sellers, between producers and consumers." The former educator had little experience turning out periodicals, having earned his name as manufacturer of Darby's Prophylactic Fluid, a popular treatment for the prevention of gangrene in Civil War battle wounds and dental abscesses. His *American Grocer*, however, became the trade's first comprehensive paper, marking an important turning point. In years prior, storekeeping had developed a reputation for harboring drunkards and other nefarious types owing to its earliest connections with primitive grog and liquor shops. This image was anathema to *American Grocer*'s readers, relics of a past to be vanquished by businessmen with inventive ideas and an eye toward professionalizing retail entrepreneurship. The journal reflected this new grocer, one keen for up-to-date market reports, advice columns, and tips on store organization, operation, and appearance. By the time the fourth issue appeared in November 1869, insiders forecasted monumental changes. "The grocery business is increasing in magnitude—competition and science are already bearing down and crushing antiquated notions," declared an experienced merchant; "every one of us must move with the times, or be outdistanced and isolated—say which shall it be?"[1]

Between 1860 and 1880, grocers challenged themselves to innovate, to transform an old trade into a modern industry. Their small firms dominated American retailing, making them representative nineteenth-century businessmen. Despite their often limited means, they established commercial methods and networks that provided goods and services to local, regional, and eventually national markets. By the time *American Grocer* appeared, they had begun wrestling with major adjustments brought about by industrial, communications, and transportation revolutions that were transforming their everyday business routines and the nation's everyday life.[2]

American Grocer's near-immediate popularity spoke to enterprising businessmen's thirst for new approaches to long-standing practices. Within one year, the paper shifted from semi-monthly to weekly publication, with upward of five thousand subscribers in 1872 paying $3 annually to have it delivered directly to their stores. Part of the journal's easy acceptance stemmed from the collaborative nature of its correspondence column. Grocers penned letters seeking guidance from others while offering their own remedies. Editors collated these suggestions into a sort of storekeeper's playbill, acknowledging key parts while highlighting coming attractions. Advertisements for Atmores Mince Meat, F. Evans & Co. Concentrated Cocoa, and George C. Naphey's & Son Pure Leaf Lard heralded the latest canned and branded goods. Notices for Hyde's Portable Coffee Roaster, Buoy's Counter Scale, and Haviland & Son's Swift Mill plugged state-of-the art technologies and fixtures. News of financial failures and store closings, meanwhile, served as cautionary tales for frontrunners and laggards alike. *American Grocer*, in other words, was both signpost and roadmap for inventive storekeepers and their ideas.[3]

Grocers' initial efforts at elevating their businesses focused on store basics. Which fixtures were essential? How should a store be arranged? What records ought to be maintained? Should trade be conducted on cash or credit? The answers changed over time as grocers created and analyzed innovative retailing forms to keep pace in the competitive marketplace. By 1880, merchants from Maine to California had weighed in on the pages of *American Grocer* as well as in their correspondence to one another and in their personal diaries, each playing his or her part to recast the business in a different light. The solutions they proposed and employed helped dissociate grocers from their dubious past and put them on the path to creating a modern trade.

Grocery Storekeeping before 1869

Grocery shops lacked any great distinctiveness from general stores and other retail consumer goods businesses prior to the 1860s, save for their sordid connection to liquor sales. By the 1830s, most of the nearly 58,000 businesses selling food could be classified as country outlets, their primary economic function to buy and sell goods from local farmers, wholesalers, and importers.

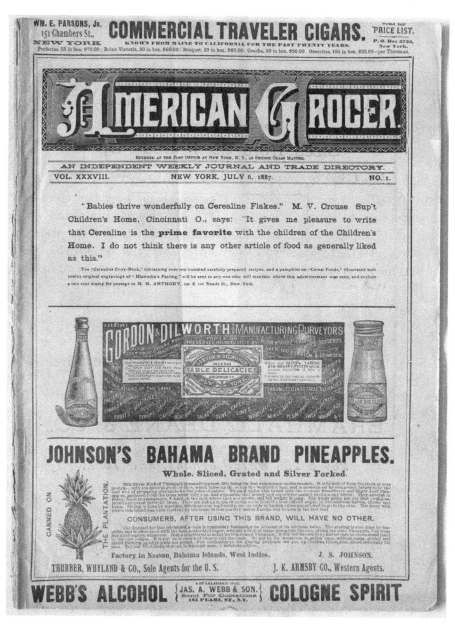

First published in 1869, *American Grocer* became the trade's primary source for information; it included advertisements detailing a growing proliferation of manufactured and branded products. News and information about a burgeoning national trade helped unite grocers and promote their ideas and methods. Author's collection.

Though the earliest origins of the term "grocer" referred to the large quantities or "gross" of goods these traders bought and sold, eighteenth- and early-nineteenth-century American usage instead linked grocers with groggeries, taverns, saloons, and tippling houses. In an 1838 address to his Connecticut parishioners, Leonard Bacon remembered matter-of-factly, "A few years ago, every grocer was of course a dealer in all sorts of alcoholic liquors," including rum, brandy, gin, and other spirits sold by the bottle and the glass. Americans of all ages, classes, genders, and races consumed liquor for both pleasure and practicality given the unhealthy state of water supplies. Alcohol's ubiquity made it a popular and potentially lucrative retail market. One 1837 observer of Detroit's drinking scene claimed that the city's two hundred liquor establishments collectively took in $1,000 a day. Per capita consumption peaked in the 1830s, climbing to over five gallons and inciting alarm from moralists and health advocates alike who saw in a nation of drinkers the decline of America's welfare and virtue. Retail stores quickly became primary targets of temperance crusaders.[4]

Temperance reform prompted the passage of state and municipal legislation to regulate liquor sales and in the process began redefining grocery stores. In the aftermath of the Second Great Awakening's religious revivals, which swept the northern United States in the early 1830s, church leaders, politicians, and scores of others sought to banish demon rum and other liquor from their cities and towns. Revivalists in a sense helped businessmen navigate and shape a budding market economy by imposing structure through morality, with some calling for prohibition and others demanding legal oversight of liquor sales. In 1832, Indiana began requiring prospective grocers to apply for licenses, a process that included certification from at least twenty-four "respectable freeholders of the town" attesting to the applicant's "good moral character." The law further prohibited the selling of spirits on credit in amounts greater than $1, along with vending to minors or the intoxicated. Iowa territorial laws described grocery stores in 1839 as "any house or place where spirituous or vinous liquors are retailed by less quantities than one gallon," to distinguish them from wholesalers and importers who took over primary responsibility for handling larger measures. They likewise barred "unlawful gaming or riotous conduct" in grocery shops to differentiate them from taverns and saloons where such behavior typically took place.[5]

Reformers pointed the finger at all who sold alcohol but at grocers in particular, their large numbers and central economic function making them prominent marks. Temperance agitators saddled them with being "the corrupter of youth" and "the primary cause of all our poor-houses being filled," as a cantankerous Virginian announced in 1839, while also charging storekeepers with being "the origin of every crime or offence in which our courts of justice are called on to interpose their authority." Those looking to separate themselves from liquor dealers did so using reformers' language and ideas. Announcements heralding "temperance grocery stores" touted proprietors' adherence to the movement's principles and the desire to "banish the monster, Ardent Spirits" from their businesses, a phrase Hayden, Upham, and Company of Boston, Massachusetts, used in its 1831 advertisement. Some employed the term "family grocery" to identify their stores as places where women and children could shop undisturbed by imbibing men.[6]

Not long after regulatory measures took effect, grocers challenged their constitutionality claiming restraint of trade and violation of property rights, their pleas further delineating grocery stores from drinking establishments. "Why a man who retails innocent beef, pork, candles, and molasses, is to be mulcted in a penalty for having on his premises what half his fellow-citizens not only keep, but use too, is passing strange," one litigator argued in South Carolina's Supreme Court when his client was fined in 1849 for selling gin, whiskey, and brandy in the back room of his Charleston grocery store without a license. Charleston's ordinance was particularly strict, barring grocers from selling any liquor "where meat, grain, fruit, provisions, or other articles are exposed for sale" in an attempt to limit its consumption, especially among slaves. Grocers' protests for the most part went unheeded. State licensing laws remained on many books throughout the 1850s and 1860s even as Americans' per capita alcohol consumption declined to less than two gallons per year by the 1850s. In 1867 when the Reverend Stedman W. Hanks, district secretary of the American Seaman's Friend Society, took the stand in a special hearing conducted by Massachusetts legislators to evaluate the state's licensing law, he reported that during the past twenty years in his hometown of Lowell, "the change has been perfectly enormous. . . . The sale of liquor at the grocery shops is stopped."[7]

Hanks was optimistic perhaps, but efforts to regulate alcohol distribution and consumption prompted the definition of grocery stores as establishments primarily for marketing foodstuffs, even as they continued dispensing spirits and other goods, in addition to serving as post offices, hotels, and meeting houses in many places. In the absence of specialization among retail trades, most stores continued to carry everything from potatoes to potash. An 1857 sheriff's sale for a Chester, Pennsylvania, store listed under the heading of "groceries" items such as spices, tobacco, oils, sperm candles, tubs, buckets, hats, caps, and brushes, with hardware, queensware, and fabrics occupying other distinct classes of goods. Westward expansion in the 1850s likewise encouraged storekeepers to amass large varieties of goods to serve travelers as well as settlers from the multiple towns and surrounding communities their stores generally served. Some large cities, meanwhile, boasted thousands of grocers, as did New York City in 1859, with more than 2,500 retailers listed in the burgeoning metropolis's directory. Many of these shops, however, still functioned as makeshift liquor stands, selling glasses of spirits alongside edibles and assorted goods in front rooms of houses and makeshift shanties in addition to more substantial corner storefronts.[8]

The frontier merchants and urban storekeepers who populated early trade played a generally unacknowledged role in the nineteenth-century market revolution. These businessmen directed and facilitated the economic and distribution systems that moved groceries and other agricultural and manufactured products between rural farms and East Coast commercial centers. Farmers typically supplied grocers with local produce, their harvests often serving as barter payment for store purchases. Shop owners then hauled these goods to port cities such as Boston, Charleston, or Philadelphia and other exchange centers where they traded for manufactured and imported articles, returning home to sell these articles in their shops. Merchants' success or failure in establishing and employing these routes to competitive advantage often dictated which rural towns and cities developed faster as the century progressed, with places like St. Louis and later Chicago emerging as wholesale hubs. Assuming the roles of procurer, distributor, banker, and transporter, storekeepers played a vital part in the nation's nascent economy, expanding rural and urban development through their fundamental distribution chains.[9]

It was no easy task, though, given the vagaries of early overland and water travel. Maria Brown recalled the difficulties her husband Daniel encountered in the 1840s shipping farm products from his store in Amesville, Ohio, to New Orleans. Every fall he, along with his business partner, would fell logs to build a flatboat and load it with wool, dried fruits, and other local products. Oxen pulled the boat through the mud to a nearby creek, where they waited for spring floods to carry it to the Hocking River, down the Ohio River, and into the Mississippi. As they floated downriver, the merchants traded their wares at riverside plantations and posts. Stopping in Cincinnati, they sold off some grain and tobacco. Further down the Mississippi, they traded bacon for molasses. Once in New Orleans, Daniel swapped the molasses for refined sugar, sold his boat, and pocketed Mexican silver in return. He journeyed back to Amesville along with his purchases via steamboat, the latest and fastest water transportation. The storekeeper then took his $2,000 profit either to the manufacturing center of Pittsburgh "to invest in hardware" or the importing wharves of Philadelphia "to buy general merchandise," which Brown sent home by freighters, "immense wagons, each with six horses."[10]

Daniel Brown and countless others repeated this "long and laborious process" sometimes twice yearly, collecting and bartering northern goods for southern and foreign products and currency to be exchanged in eastern markets. They speculated in commodities like bacon, molasses, and sugar without benefit of up-to-date market information, reliable transportation, or the ability to store and hold perishable goods until conditions and prices improved. Steamboats, canals, and wagons helped this commercial current flow, but frozen waterways and other hazards often intervened. Newspapers and letters carried commercial reports, yet offered little insurance against changes in market conditions. In July 1844, two months after Samuel Morse demonstrated the telegraph, merchant John Burrows loaded 2,500 bushels of potatoes into his Davenport, Iowa, boat bound for New Orleans where wholesalers were paying $2 a bushel. Making his way down the Mississippi, he tried first to offload the tubers in Memphis but found the market glutted. "The best offer I got was twenty-five cents a bushel," half of what Burrows had paid, "so I pulled out." Six weeks later, after being "windbound two or three days at a time," he arrived in New Orleans "to find a dull market," and ended up selling his potatoes for eight cents a bushel, taking coffee instead of cash for payment. Without current market information and quick shipping, buying and selling perishable commodities was always a highly speculative venture.[11]

Despite these perils and uncertainties, once goods arrived at a store, merchandising was straightforward. No universal guidelines existed for marketing or arranging items in an attractive or enticing fashion. Most grocers displayed their wares in the functional custom of the day, filling shelves, barrels, bins, and hooks around the shop. For rural storekeepers in particular, there was little competitive incentive to draw customers through creative means—their prominence in remote locations locked in area trade. They instead promoted their inventories in pragmatic newspaper announcements. "Ford & Drouillard have just received a large and well selected stock of Fresh Groceries," the Gallipolis, Ohio, firm advertised in April 1853, listing only eleven food items including rice, raisins, and coffee in addition to washboards, cigars, glassware, and two dozen other articles. The partners invited customers to "Call and examine for yourselves" at their "cheap Grocery Store."[12]

Yet not all early shops were austere. Not far from Ford and Droulliard, the African American retailer and wholesaler Samuel T. Wilcox operated a grand store. Unlike many black and white proprietors who struggled to accumulate capital in these early days, Wilcox started his Cincinnati business in 1850 with $25,000 cash, earned from real estate investments. He opened a store that black abolitionist and journalist Martin Delany described as "really beautiful" and resembling "more an apothecary store, than a Grocery House." Inside,

Wilcox carried brandied fruits, "Yankee Vegetables, hermetically sealed," foreign and domestic preserves, imported cigars, "Superior Wines and Brandies," and other fancy, or fine-quality groceries. He recorded annual sales for one year of $140,000 and ran up "constant and heavy bills in eastern houses," despite his claim that he had "never yet been east after his goods," probably to conceal his race from creditors, most of whom he believed "never . . . knew he was a colored man." Wilcox instead ordered goods sent to his store in the city's downtown, just across the Ohio River from Kentucky, where slavery kept most blacks from engaging in entrepreneurial activities until well after the Civil War.[13]

Wilcox's ample and showy stocks were quite different from most early grocers' offerings. Before canned goods revolutionized food packaging in the last half of the nineteenth century, most shopkeepers typically stocked only one or two product varieties to satisfy demand. Even sugar, a popular seller, existed in only a few forms—granulated, crushed, and powered among them. Early processed and bulk goods generally shipped without brand names, identified solely by the contents labeled on their wooden crates. Their unmeasured quantities required storekeepers to keep a range of fixtures and technologies for breaking them down into smaller parcels for consumption. Scales weighed unpackaged staples; sugar grinders broke up hardened chunks into fine sprinkles; hand-cranked coffee mills ground beans; and cellar storehouses kept cheese, eggs, butter, and other perishables cool without the assistance of refrigeration. In 1852, inventor Francis Wolle obtained a patent for a machine that manufactured 1,800 paper bags per hour, but most storekeepers still wrapped bundles in cheap paper drawn from large rolls and tied them with string pulled from overhead spindles before placing them in customers' hands.[14]

Merchants generally did this work alone, the vast majority of nineteenth-century grocery businesses running as family affairs, with husbands and wives, children, and relatives lending a hand as needed. By midcentury, though, some larger operations started employing a range of porters, clerks, and other ancillary workers to assist with the headwork of bookkeeping and handwork of shifting and displaying stock, tending to customers, mopping the floors, and cleaning the windows. Porters in particular bore the brunt of a store's drudgework. Using two-wheeled carts or wagons, they loaded and hauled heavy crates and barrels from the wharf-side boats that carried imported goods to America and transported firkins of butter, cheese, and other farm products from wholesalers' warehouses to retail grocery storerooms. The lines between porter and clerk often blurred, as one young man hoping to secure a porter's job acknowledged in 1854 when he posted an advertisement seeking work, alerting potential employers to his desire to "make himself generally useful" both with his brawn and his ability to write with "a good hand." A large number of such men came from overseas, with many taking positions in the ethnic shops of family and friends. Some, however, encountered discrimination, with nativist grocers seeking help from "none but an American," as one 1866 New York ad for a grocery clerk proclaimed, indicating that xenophobia and racism was growing in conjunction with wage labor. By 1869, almost 200,000 retail employees worked in all varieties of trades, their numbers mounting as industrial capitalism took hold and commercial opportunities grew.[15]

Those who found jobs discovered that grocery store work tended to be irregular, with buying and selling cycles paralleling agricultural seasons and hence work intervals. Strivers eager to learn the retail business often found the path blocked both by the sporadic nature of trade and the prolonged association of grocery stores with liquor. "A very large proportion of these clerks are boys and young men, whose education is yet incomplete," an 1850 New York editorial opined. "Nightly duty at the grocery bar," they averred, "deprives the Grocery Clerk of intellectual privileges, such as Dry Goods Clerks are beginning to enjoy." The anonymous letter writer doubtlessly believed that halting evening sales (as some of New York's dry goods shops had done) would allow grocery clerks to spend more time with books rather than behind the counter. For those "on the make," though, increased specialization in other trades had begun opening new economic prospects and chances for social mobility, far removed from the licentiousness of alcohol. Grocery clerks would find greater prospects in the last quarter of the century when stores further distanced themselves from their spirituous pasts. Meanwhile, a few fledgling upstarts purposefully sought positions in grocery stores, as did one sixteen-year-old Cincinnatian eager to find employment in 1859. His goal was to "gain a thorough knowledge of business," an increasingly popular way to ascend social and economic ranks to independent proprietorship.[16]

The growing infusion of clerks and other wageworkers into retail trades signaled a nascent shift from subsistence selling—making ends meet—that was prevalent among family-run businesses, to the specialized, commercial enterprises that came with market expansion. The young men (and some women) who staffed counters, desks, and storerooms administered with their pens, ledgers, and carts the movement of goods through new market channels. Inspiration for those who saw big payoffs in retailing undoubtedly came from men like Stephen Whitney who had succeeded in progressing through the clerking ranks to become one the "merchant princes" of New York City. Born in Connecticut in 1776, Whitney moved to the metropolis as a youngster, eventually climbing from clerk to groceryman and finally to shipping merchant, his vast fortune (one 1860 estimate placed it at $8 million) helping to fund construction of the Merchants' Exchange Building, home to New York's stock exchange. Upon his death, one eulogist credited Whitney's success to "simply keeping an eye to the main chance."[17]

Clerks eager to make their own opportunities occasionally posted announcements in city newspapers advertising their "honest and industrious" characters and skills as a "good Penman" or "accountist." One New Yorker went so far as to claim "wages no great object for the first three months," committed instead to gaining entrance into the trade. Store owners likewise placed want ads requesting "a young man to take charge" or a "boy—one who has had some experience," youth and confidence seemingly prerequisites to clerking. One study indicates that of those aspiring 1850s New York clerks who sought independence through business ownership, nearly 30 percent achieved their goal, with just as many remaining in clerkships, their ambitions tempered by a lifetime of salaried employment. Those who "made it" and opened their own shops, however, would find the road through proprietorship an ever-changing route.[18]

A New Era in Storekeeping

In January 1869, a self-described "looker on" in Vincennes, Indiana, a town of 5,500 on the Wabash River, sought to motivate locals by describing ongoing transformations in eastern retailing. "A radical change from the present village mode of doing business" (where "piles of heterogeneous goods" cluttered stores) "to one more city like," the local man urged, "could be better effected by separating the different lines of trade and concentrating them in other stores." Other proposals included adopting "the one-price system," which "prevails in all the Eastern States," along with establishing a large wholesale house. Goods could be "distributed from it to several retailers as wanted," taking advantage of "manufactories and railroads so much talked about." These changes were necessary, the writer claimed, "if it only be to keep pace with the fashion of the times." In 1869—months before the transcontinental railroad stood poised to open the West to commercial trade and travel, the "Black Friday" panic crippled financial markets, and *American Grocer* debuted—at least one Indiana merchant worried about straggling, as did the New York tea man who urged all to "move with the times" that same year. As both small-town dealer and big-city merchant fretted about being outrun by business and economic developments, one thing was clear: each sensed momentum for change.[19]

Transformation was palpable by the 1870s, even if things appeared familiar on the surface. Places like Vincennes with easy access to water and rail transportation, large populations, and readily available goods attracted greater demand for specialized retailing. Yet these enhanced market advantages did not necessarily bring about the growth of individual enterprises; most remained small affairs. Even by 1885, 55 percent of the nearly eight hundred Boston grocery retailers rated by the Mercantile Agency (precursor to the credit-reporting firm of Dun and Bradstreet) had estimated capital and credit combined of less than $1,000, with 10 percent of those grocers only having more than $500. The situation was similar in western and southern towns. More than 40 percent of Cedar Rapids, Iowa, grocers operated with capital resources of less than $1,000; the same was true farther south in Vicksburg, Mississippi. The growth of railroads may have moved goods and people faster and more efficiently, but for most retailers, they did not signal a demand for larger or more sophisticated organizational structures. Small operations, for most of these businesses, were the best way to sell goods and services in a market dominated by local trade and perishable products.[20]

Low entry barriers also made the grocery business one that enterprising men found attractive. A few hundred dollars covered initial overhead expenses such as rent and fixtures, while wholesalers' credit provided for additional stocks and supplies. American and immigrant aspirations for economic independence and mobility prompted former wage earners to go into business as soon as they acquired the minimum necessary funds, even if they had no prior business experience. Edward Bugbey invited *American Grocer* editors in 1876 to visit him in Springfield, Ohio, to see "the amount of business that is done here by men who were never raised to the mercantile business, and on how little capital." One partnership formed between two farmers, "neither one of them knowing any thing *practically* of the business." Each invested $1,000 and rented a store for $80 a month. Within thirty days, the farmers cum grocers had stocked their shop with upward of $10,000 in merchandise, all bought on credit. "They have been floating with the trade ever since," Bugbey admonished, "but sooner or later they must sink."[21]

The same low entry barriers that made the grocery business appealing also made it volatile. Nobody knows just how many nineteenth-century grocers failed; studies of the early twentieth-century trade, however, suggest that 60 percent closed within two years of opening. Trade journals published regular lists of grocers who tried their hand at storekeeping but fell short. For one week in October 1883, *American Grocer* reported thirty-four grocery store failures nationwide, doubtlessly bogged down by the previous year's economic recession that depressed prices until 1885. One such proprietor, Henry Houghton, called a meeting of his creditors to break the news; another, James P. Skerry, was "financially embarrassed." In November 1885, the regional trade journal *New England Grocer* reported seven of the area's grocers insolvent. "Entering business before one possesses funds adequate to conduct his affairs," one black merchant chided, led many to fail, as did a "lack of a reserve to meet unforeseen demands." Any combination of limited capital, lack of business skills and credit, or poor market conditions closed shop doors and sent thousands back into the ranks of wage earners; the situation for many worsened in the economically turbulent Reconstruction years of the 1870s.[22]

Yet the volatility of the grocery business also encouraged a kind of Schumpeterian revolving door: a constant influx of new men with ideas, a drive to learn the trade, and a willingness to change it from within. These were the men *American Grocer* targeted. They mocked the unambitious "Nehemia Dozy" and his "Old-Fashioned Store" in the "go-ahead times" of 1876, when "one can rarely find a real old-fashioned man" in the grocery trade. "Vim and energy and a thorough knowledge of one's business in all its details and branches" were now the tools necessary for success. And they poked fun at the pseudonymous George Washington Dusenbury, who that same year attacked imaginary enemies from his shop in the equally pseudonymous Windmill Point, Idaho, because it was all *"business, business, business"* in other stores. A recent visit to a large New York grocery wholesaler had sent Dusenbury into a tizzy. "Forty or fifty book-keepers, telegraph office, all busy, everybody driving as if mad." Ambition pushed men and capitalism as much as it did business methods and means, even if not all felt the same motivation to move with the times. "Away with your paper and high-pressure modern ways," Dusenbury grumbled, "and let us sail along in the *good old way*."[23]

American Grocer, however, had little interest in promoting outdated methods. The journal instead facilitated fresh discussions about local, regional, and countrywide business, uniting grocers in their common interests well in advance of formal trade associations, which did not materialize until the 1880s and 1890s. The journal's title alone reflected editors' expansive thinking and their vision for a nationwide alliance, encouraging collective innovation, information sharing, and problem solving. Thousands of small businessmen scattered across the country could turn the pages to gauge conditions and developments in both rural and urban communities, keeping abreast of the latest commercial trends, political happenings, and trade gossip. All agreed that *American Grocer* was not for the Dusenburys of the world, "but for the bright, active grocery men who are going to do the business of the future."[24]

What's in Store?

James Hovey was one of those grocers of the future. In March 1876, he grew impatient when his prune order had not yet arrived at his Marietta, Ohio, store from H. K. and F. B. Thurber and Sons, the very New York wholesaler Dusenbury detested. Hovey placed his request on the sixth, but one week later was still waiting. "We needed them bad," the grocer complained, "or we would not have ordered them by telegraph." At fifty-three years old, Hovey was no overanxious whippersnapper. Rather, he had grown accustomed to receiving lightning-fast shipments across the five hundred miles that separated Marietta and New York and grew agitated when his timing seemed out of sync with the big-city wholesalers. Thurber and Sons, for their part, acknowledged they had been "slower than usual." In a new age of electronic communications and high-speed travel, "patience ceased to be a virtue" in Hovey's estimation.[25]

In the grocery trade, as small businessmen took on the task of coordinating the flow of farm and manufactured goods, they did so without the aid of vertically integrated corporations, managerial hierarchies, or corporate power. The great mass distributors who concentrated production in the 1870s in the steel, sewing machine, and processed meat industries did not arise in canned and packaged foods manufacturing until after the turn of the century. Middlemen wholesalers like Thurber and Sons instead synchronized production demands with manufacturers, scheduled shipments to thousands of rural outposts, and similarly benefited from the communication and transportation advantages industrial producers enjoyed. While no organizational revolution materialized in the nineteenth-century grocery trade, a modern distribution and production system nevertheless took root. In 1876, James Hovey's demand for faster service was not that of a loafer looking backward but of a businessman eager to keep step with fast-moving commercial developments.[26]

The same advances that brought goods to Hovey more quickly accelerated the growth of all retail businesses across the country. Nearly 430,000 retail proprietors and 196,000 employees operated stores of all kinds nationwide in 1869, jumping to just over 600,000 owners and 349,000 clerks, stockers, and deliverymen ten years later. Large-scale, city dry goods retailers such as Alexander T. Stewart and Rowland H. Macy, who had started in the 1840s and 1850s, respectively, built bigger and grander mass-retail stores to accommodate the increase in shoppers and manufactured products. They carried generous selections of clothing, jewelry, linens, and various other product lines intended to lower costs and increase profits. Most dry goods merchants, however, remained small-town tradesmen, as did butchers, bakers, jewelers, and hardware dealers. Stocks and supplies continued to move through distribution channels first established by earlier wholesalers and retailers, only now with greater speed and at longer distances. Between 1815 and 1860, the cost of long-distance travel in the United States declined nearly 95 percent, with goods shipping via rail and steamboat five times faster than by canal boats and

New Hampshire grocer Ernest Cole returns from a buying trip loaded down with supplies. Small dealers like Cole brought the city to the country, carting crates of Ivory Soap and Arm & Hammer Soda from commercial centers to out-of-the-way places. Author's collection.

overland wagons, moving people and goods from interior cities like Cincinnati to the East Coast in less than a week.[27]

Barrels, bottles, and baskets flooded grocers' shops as a result of the growing consumer goods market in mass-produced products. A Tennessee grocer announced in January 1869 the arrival of "300 boxes Spices and Can Goods" in his Memphis store; the following year, a West Virginia man advertised canned foodstuffs for "cheaper than they can be packed." The influx of these latest products prompted new attention to store arrangement and aesthetics. Shelving now had to accomodate canned beans and corned beef tins in addition to flour sacks and lard pails, as retailing practices changed in conjunction with new innovations. Traditional principles still dictated store layouts, though. Former tea man G. F. Kirkman advised *American Grocer* readers in 1870 to spurn "external show and glitter" in favor of fittings that ensured "proper appearance's sake and convenience." They should instead install wide counters with ample drawers, attractive show canisters, and a glass case, which would "make a good impression on entering a store."[28]

These uncomplicated fittings spoke to changes in grocery retailing and merchandising methods and technologies, and in grocers' interest in creating selling environments. Showcases first made their way into grocery shops in the late 1860s to protect baked goods, vegetables, meat, and other food products from dirt, flies, and other unwelcome elements. Grocers' instincts told them that "showing off" wares by highlighting the desirability of their goods with decorative elements and a dash of elegance would tempt customers into buying, an impulse typically attributed to 1890s department stores. Show canisters did more than hold candy or tobacco; they presented products to their best advantage. Light bounced off metal lids and glass bodies, catching customers' eyes while reassuring them that errant hands had not fished their contents. Together, show canisters and cases comprised key elements in grocers' growing arsenal of selling strategies.[29]

The Rochester Show Case Works offered several different models, with countertop cases starting around $15; floor and counter-length varieties cost up to $80, with the most expensive being their circular and round front versions, available in mirror, plain, or "Double Thick French Crystal Glass." Period photographs suggest that most storekeepers favored the affordable countertop models, made from either stained wood or patterned celluloid in eye-catching ebony, tortoise shell, or green agate. Others spared no expense. George Whitlock was lucky to have insured his showcases for $300 before they went up in smoke during an 1875 fire he accidentally started in his Cairo, Illinois, store. The Fort Worth Grocery Company, meanwhile, kept "fine mixed candy and mixed nuts in endless varieties exhibited in large show cases" in its Texas shop, safeguarding the expensive goodies while elevating their delectability.[30]

As interest in selling environments increased, sketches outlining improvements in showcases and other store fixtures flowed into the U.S. Patent Office. Retail grocer and inventor Thomas Parks's 1877 idea for removable showcase tops promised to display "a box of crackers, raisins, or other articles," keeping them free from dust and "also from thieves," distractions the Arkadelphia, Arkansas, storekeeper likely encountered and tried to remedy. Fruit dealer William Lockwood similarly claimed that his 1868 ventilated showcase for "smoked or salted fish, moist fruits, or grocery articles" kept these items "in good condition during several weeks." Dry goods clerk Hans Winder created a grocers' sample case for displaying small product quantities. His 1876 device sought to eliminate "waste of material incident to frequent handling" by exhibiting foodstuffs in a partitioned box under glass covers, keeping bulk cracker and sugar barrels off sales floors and out of customers' reach in days before packaged products were customary. All three men worked to improve retail technologies and methods from behind the counter, tinkering with existing equipment and fashioning inventive solutions to retail problems.[31]

Others tackled new and impending merchandising challenges. An 1875 patent for a "Grocer's Can-Stand" depicted a spindle-legged, round tiered table

Showcases filled with baked goods and cigars lined both sides of this nineteenth-century grocery store, which included a glass-lidded bin allowing customers to judge bulk goods without a clerk's help. Author's collection.

for arranging canned and boxed goods in pyramidal and artistic fashion, the latest packaging innovations creating opportunities for imaginative displays. Lacking a flat back, the can stand was intended to be stationed away from walls in the center of the store where customers could pick from it on their own. It was a far-sighted fixture, to be sure; canned goods in the 1870s lacked the graphic and colorful labels that eventually made them most appealing and decorative, while notions of "self-service" were nearly forty years in the future. A few years later, the Rochester Show Case Works encased a similar table in ebonized walnut and glass, calling it "an entirely new and original style" for selling "fancy" goods, even as they removed its self-service potential. William Volkland's plan for an improved store counter similarly played to ideas about customers helping themselves. His apparatus relieved grocers from showing samples of sugar, coffee, or flour, "as is the usual custom," storing these bulk items in compartments "where the customer, by raising the curved lids" could "examine and compare the several kinds without the attendant." The carpenter turned inventor envisioned his counter "saving time and labor" as well as providing "great economy of space," while freeing storekeepers to tend other customers.[32]

Nobody knows whether Parks's showcase tops or the "Grocer's Can Stand" ever made it into stores. What matters are the men behind the concepts and their ability to foresee revolutionary changes taking place in retailing practices. Most grocery shops never aspired to the grandiose styling of 1880s and 1890s department store shopping emporiums, but the emergence of a consumption-oriented society had no less impact on grocers than on other retailers, even if their attempts seem less obvious. While the nature of perishable items and bulk foodstuffs did not easily lend themselves to elaborate presentations, men like Lockwood nevertheless labored to address these issues. Modifications in display and retailing methods, grocers discovered, could generate financial returns, as might changes that invited women to linger and browse as they did in depart-ment stores. Ohio grocer Ira Clizbe recognized these concerns in 1876, shooing away loafers, smokers, and tobacco chewers who made the atmosphere "impure" for his female shoppers. Clizbe's interest in creating a hospitable business envi-ronment for consumers represented a growing inclination among grocers look-ing for new ways to sell more through changes in selling practices and décor.[33]

This included beautifying store interiors. William Reinhardt, whose German immigrant father operated a grocery business in Owensboro, Kentucky, for many years, envisioned sprucing up the shop after taking over the family operation. Querying *American Grocer* editors in 1876, Reinhardt sought information about where he could purchase "wall paper, such as Chinese figures for decorating walls, for fancy groceries," stores that carried high-end and imported goods typically demanded by wealthier clients. The storekeeper's request reflected both the influence of the recent aesthetic move-ment's "art for art's sake" attitude that favored Chinoiserie and other Asian effects and his awareness of how wallpaper or other decorative enhancements might appeal to status-conscious shoppers, distinguishing his place of busi-ness from others. It was a strategy department store decorators would employ to cultivate a sense of class distinction, delineating rich from poor through high-end design. The editors directed Reinhardt to the New York Tea Caddy Company, one of several houses that carried "fancy wall paper for grocers," implying the popularity of such embellishments among food retailers.[34]

The impulse to decorate extended outward through the large, plate-glass windows fronting stores, transforming what had been a practical way to illumi-nate shops into a selling technology. It was a move predicated in part on grow-ing competition between neighborhood stores and an emerging intensity in retail advertising focused on drawing in customers from new towns and across greater distances with handbills, broadsides, and signage. "Show windows," as they were known, joined these increasingly aggressive advertising forms in the 1870s. Most credit department stores for turning windows' function into form in the 1890s, employing professional "dressers" to create visual drama with manufactured goods. Years earlier, however, Ira Clizbe, the Black brothers in Pennsylvania, and countless other grocers encouraged sidewalk shoppers to sample visually the fruits, candies, and other foods displayed for their benefit in show windows. The enormous scale of plate-glass openings, these merchandising pioneers discovered, had tremendous power to entice consumers. In years before national advertising campaigns, chromolithographed posters and product displays as well as electrical signs became everyday techniques, show windows tempted and informed the public about what lay beyond the glass.[35]

Early efforts at arranging these spaces demonstrate grocers' interest and willingness to play with exhibits to find what worked. Initial attempts routinely emphasized what twenty-first-century admen would call holiday cross-promotional marketing. An 1872 South Carolina article waxed poetic about "valentines displayed in the grocery windows" along Charleston streets, "miscegenating" with "bars of yellow soap, fly-spotted papers of pins, cakes of maple sugar, and all other popular delicacies." Other arrangements had more to do with grabbing shoppers' attention than indicating what they could find inside. The *Frankfort Weekly Roundabout* encouraged readers in 1879 to stop by J. M. Todd's Kentucky grocery store, where "two beautiful antelope heads adorn the show windows." A few tempted passersby with items some found too good to resist. One 1880 summer day Harvey Paulk lost a "large glass jar of preserved pears kept as a show article" when thieves smashed the window of his Sacramento shop, an indication of how the glass barrier distanced the "haves" from the "have nots."[36]

Grocers' windows intentionally traded on notions of abundance, a popular theme producers would emphasize in the 1890s as an example of industrial advancement and material progress. Retailers in the 1870s, however, gave early life to these static motifs. In March 1871, shoppers found the windows of a "New York style" store in Knoxville, Tennessee, "banked up a foot deep with sugars and coffee" and "fuller than the entire stock of some dealers." Symbolic of mass production, these effective but inelegant mounds eventually gave way to more sophisticated visions. Bushrod W. Reed, a longtime resident of Washington, DC, operated a retail business he had opened in 1835; his sons William and Richard joined the firm in 1868. A few years later, in 1875, the men expanded and remodeled their shop, adding "two mammoth plate-glass windows, deep and roomy from the exterior," capable of holding enough "to stock an ordinary grocery store." The Reed brothers, however, understood "the art of displaying their goods to advantage" and took great pains to ensure that their tempting displays were skillfully arranged and not merely piled high and wide. The boys did not miss the chance to use all thirty-three feet of

Cobb and Yerxa, well-known Boston grocers, took advantage of their corner lot and large plate-glass show windows to attract holiday shoppers in 1886 with an elaborate display of goods and paper streamers. Grocers' sophisticated merchandising methods advanced mass-marketing techniques ahead of national trends. Author's collection.

their storefront to demonstrate "the value of advertising," as one store visitor put it. Spectators remarked on the "picture of plenty," a veritable cornucopia of goods, that spilled forth from their windows and doorway.[37]

Out in Utah, managers of Salt Lake City's Zions Cooperative Mercantile Institution, one of the country's earliest department stores, turned to clerk George Manwaring to take charge of their store's grocery windows. In 1879, the twenty-five-year-old English immigrant applied his "artistic work" to the effort, drawing on skills learned while a draper's apprentice back home. He followed up days before Christmas the next year to create the "boss display of groceries in the town," according to a *Salt Lake Herald* reporter. Fruits, canned goods, and "everything that can be described under the heading of groceries," at least "$1,000 worth of goods" filled the space. "The display is simply immense," the awestruck writer remarked. Profusion, however, did not eclipse Manwaring's decorative flair. "George is an artist as a window dresser," the journalist claimed, talents that earned him praise and recognition long before professional window trimmers claimed the vocation. *Window Dressing for Grocers*, published in 1896, put into writing storekeepers' pioneering methods long after Manwaring and others had begun trimming windows and a few years before celebrated window dresser and author of *The Wizard of Oz*, L. Frank Baum, published *The Show Window*, a booklet credited with originating the profession. The grocers' guide encouraged Easter, Washington's Birthday, and July Fourth arrangements, battleships made from canned beans and corn, and horns of plenty overflowing with fruits, vegetables, and packaged teas, ideas pioneered by men like Todd, Paulk, and Manwaring.[38]

By the end of the 1870s, a growing profusion of merchandising and technological innovations available to grocers made it difficult for some to hold back their enthusiasm. In 1879, one eager Michigan grocer ordered fifty "short line telephones for use in his business," a mere three years after Alexander Graham Bell introduced the communications device to the world. The East Saginaw merchant intended to connect his store with fifty of his best customers, a plan some claimed "shows much enterprise." News of the storekeeper's novel idea made it all the way to Pennsylvania, where readers in New Bloomfield marveled at his ambitious scheme. The following year, Elphonzo Youngs, after refitting, repainting, and restocking his Washington, DC, store, informed shoppers about his "telephonic connections," likely used to order from local wholesalers and initiate customer orders, since long-distance connections remained unreliable or nonexistent in most cases. Despite these limitations, storekeepers had little trouble figuring out early how to make the wires work for them.[39]

Grocers who installed telephones, show windows, and glass cases literally were creating new connections between business, mass production, consumption, and technology. More Americans engaged these massive transformations in rural communities and local shops than in big cities and department stores. They came to recognize nationwide changes by what they saw on their grocers' shelves and experienced at the sales counter. Storekeepers augmented their stores' physical structures and arrangements, sales methods, and means of communication in response, altering the commercial landscape and market exchanges with emphasis on both national trends and local concerns. For most, these transformations did not happen overnight or on a grand or elaborate scale, but they happened. In 1896, *New England Grocer* reported on a Maine man who contemplated "connecting the houses of his customers with the store by means of telephone," thinking it would be a "big help" for grocers and customers alike. The Michigan man who nearly twenty years earlier had done the same would have chuckled at the notion.[40]

Accounting for Change

Tucked away in the small town of Freedom, Maine, about twenty miles from the Atlantic coast, Edmund Fuller spent most of his days stocking and dusting shelves, "journalizing & posting up accounts," or "marking goods" in preparation for the next day's trade. In slow times, Fuller documented these daily tasks in a series of eight journals beginning about 1870, when he partnered with Robert Elliot, a local merchant who eventually left the firm, until Fuller's death in 1892. Along the way, he captured in his diary some of the more subtle changes taking place within the trade, especially those pertaining to "keeping the numbers," a task every storekeeper undertook to some degree, even if only to file invoices and collection notices in bins or boxes stashed under store counters.[41]

Grocers' accounting practices, whether sophisticated or rudimentary, documented the transformation of the American economy and marketplace as they moved from neighborhood exchanges to regional and national transactions. Ledger pages brought to light the stream of cash and credit that supported local businessmen and farmers along with urban manufacturers and wholesalers, as bulk goods and branded packages flowed from fields to factories and stores, uniting country and city in an interdependent relationship. Some, like Fuller, were more thoughtful than others in recording these business dealings, carefully noting the names, dates, and dollar amounts of over-the-counter exchanges, capitalism writ small. Their efforts, regardless of how precise or ordered, reveal how rural ventures facilitated commercial developments in tandem with big city enterprises.[42]

Storekeepers and their clerks tracked sales and bills out of both necessity and practicality, using formal and informal accounting methods. Credit dealings made up the bulk of grocers' transactions, requiring regular monitoring to ensure that balances did not go unpaid. Clerks penned information in ledgers or journals, often using single- or double-entry bookkeeping, both methods in use since the eighteenth century. Guidebooks, such as Ira Mayhew's *Practical System of Book-keeping by Single and Double Entry* (1851), offered some assistance, while others learned accounting skills by apprenticeship. A few grocers hired experts like the job-seeking New Yorker who billed himself "a good book-keeper and an experienced grocer" in an 1842 want ad. The many account books, receipts, and dunning letters found in archives attest to retailers' book-keeping strategies. But recollections about storekeepers whose accounting systems consisted of ticks marked on the wall or incoming and outgoing receipts kept in boots make clear that not all early merchants subscribed to such formal measures.[43]

By the time Fuller became sole owner of the Freedom store, he was well versed in the fundamentals of the grocery business and accounting. His diaries abound with talk about the pace of trade, market prices, cash dealings, and orders placed. He spent considerable time pricing stock as it arrived, making certain each item earned a profit. Marking goods involved a cryptic system of letters, numbers, or symbols instituted in the 1830s and 1840s that indicated both the merchant's cost and the customer's price. Although some storekeepers began charging set prices in the 1830s to eliminate haggling, the practice became more commonplace in the 1870s as the wartime speculative boom ended and the 1873 panic geared up, cutting margins on nearly all goods. For Fuller and many others, though, the prices they marked on their goods were still open to negotiation according to whether they were dealing with cash buyers, credit seekers, or those who had a history of nonpayment.[44]

One marking tactic involved assigning each number, one through ten, a letter of the alphabet. This was "the method most frequently taken," as one manual claimed. Some used ten-letter mnemonic words such as "Regulation," having "R" stand for the number one, "e" for the number two, and so on. In this way, a grocer could spell out codes on a package, such as "eui/gan," where "eui" reflected the storekeeper's cost of $2.48, and "gan" represented the selling price of $3.60. Other codes involved a cryptic game of tic-tac-toe, with numbers one through nine placed within the game grid:

1	2	3
4	5	6
7	8	9

Each angle drawn around the number represented a different digit. For example, $1.35 would look something like: ⌐ L □. There were other tactics as well, but all provided ways to establish selling prices. The measures were refined enough to provide useful feedback on purchase costs and selling prices, yet simple enough for any businessman to employ; no special accounting skills were required to implement such a scheme.[45]

As the economic situation tightened in the post–Civil War years, grocers began to take greater interest in the correlation between accurate product pricing and store profits and losses. "Shrinkage in the value of many articles of merchandise has correspondingly cut down the profit on all these articles," *American Grocer* editors explained in 1876. As a result, "it requires economy, and that practiced to a large degree, to secure success." In an 1878 letter to the journal, a Philadelphia grocer listed buying costs and selling prices for dozens of goods and asked readers to judge whether he was "making money or losing." The storekeeper, who identified himself only as "Cash," insisted his profits were greater than his expenses, "as I look to them well." The grocer perhaps was more braggart than supplicant, but his invitation for public inspection followed several others who likewise sought advice and scrutiny about their margins from *American Grocer*'s readers, along with validation that their practices conformed to current conditions. The preliminary steps of "Cash" and his fellow grocers pointed the way toward reducing transaction costs, lowering losses, and increasing profitability through financial accounting.[46]

The sophisticated methods of systematic accounting associated with large corporations and complex institutions were in their infancy during the 1870s when "Cash" and others began analyzing their pricing techniques. Gilded Age railroad corporations, business trusts, and large-scale manufacturing concerns would not implement formal cost accounting, inventory tracking, and credit and financial analyses until the 1880s and 1890s. Small grocers nevertheless had begun adjusting their recordkeeping practices to track incoming and outgoing goods, monies, and credit accounts in ways that helped them learn and understand more about their businesses. "A merchant who 'keeps posted' must know from day to day what proportion his expense account bears to his receipts," *American Grocer* preached in 1876, encouraging storekeepers to manage business accounts on a daily basis instead of waiting until month's end as was customary. Edmund Fuller used his routine of marking goods in conjunction with a variety of ledgers, daybooks, and journals to organize his business. He recorded in his diary that he was constantly "journalizing accounts," "posting books," and "copying bills," administrative functions of a man who kept a close grip on financial matters in his predominantly credit business.[47]

Even in the money-strapped days of the 1870s, most merchants acknowledged cash as the ideal trade medium. It freed retailers from a dependence on wholesalers' credit and consumers from storekeepers' ledgers. Still, most grocers saw few bills or coins pass through their hands. *American Grocer* declared cash trading dead in 1870: "We have long since given up the Utopian dream of a system of business between city and country merchants and consumers based upon absolute cash." A few years earlier, Congress had passed the National Banking Acts of 1863 and 1864, establishing both national banking and a uniform currency, and igniting firestorms about the value of legal tender compared with specie and state-issued currencies. Economic conditions and questions about legal tender's constitutionality combined to hinder expansion of a cash economy. But by the mid-1870s, with a new gold standard in place, a few grocers saw potential in greenbacks. The cash versus credit debate among the nation's retailers was born and would continue well into the 1930s.[48]

William Woolson followed the discussion in *American Grocer* from his Ohio store, pronouncing himself "anxious to catch up any new idea." Although he "adhered as strictly to the cash system as any house I ever knew," Woolson admitted he "sometimes made a financial distinction," extending credit to select customers, which he maintained was the right thing to do. While Woolson waffled between the two schemes, other grocers wanted to make a clean break. "From time to time I see letters in your paper from parties who have adopted the cash system," an alert New Jersey merchant who signed himself "Many Readers" penned in 1876. Two concerns, however, kept him from following suit. The first mirrored Woolson's quandary. "To put up a sign in the store that all goods are sold for cash only, and then allow some of the customers to buy on credit would be to keep a standing lie," one the New Jersey man was unwilling to perpetuate. How could retailers convince customers to open their coin purses? It was a deep-rooted conundrum that reflected both economic necessity and cultural practice, a dilemma *American Grocer* editors admitted they had been unable to solve.[49]

Some tried tackling the issue through innovative (if clumsy) solutions. A grocer in rural Lincolnville, Pennsylvania, issued short-term credit of a week or less only to those "with whom he is well acquainted," placing a "cash slip" on file until the debt was repaid. Down in Cotton Plant, Arkansas, another storekeeper circumnavigated the problem by lending money to "good" customers to make purchases, "so as not to break his rule" about extending credit. *American Grocer* suggested issuing passbooks, a method borrowed from eighteenth-century bankers, where grocers tallied purchases on bound pages customers retained, settling up "once a week or fortnight" instead of monthly. These were workarounds, though, for small-town merchants who knew their customers personally, not permanent solutions for a new commercial climate increasingly filled with strangers.[50]

The New Jersey man's second concern about adopting a cash system was fixated on an apparent lack of trendsetters. "The number is so small," the storekeeper inferred from the dearth of *American Grocer* correspondents promoting their credit-free businesses, "that although many ... would like to take courage from them and follow their example, they think one or two swallows won't make a summer." While many wanted to do away with credit, most could not overcome customer preferences or the paucity of currency. In Hamilton, Ohio, a manufacturing city near Cincinnati, grocer Jacob H. Hoffmann complained in 1875 that while he tried to maintain a strictly cash trade, "Money is very scarce here now." In farming communities, currency continued to ebb and flow with planting and harvest cycles as it had for much of the nation's past. In the course of twenty years, Edmund Fuller mentioned cash transactions on only four occasions, generally when trade was "brisk" or "very brisk" in the rural town. During those times he took in $217 and $73 each day, respectively. A snowstorm in January 1876 brought Fuller the "largest day for cash in a long time." Summing up the situation, Iowa grocer William Home determined that "there are certain localities where the cash system will prove decidedly best," while in other places, "you must credit."[51]

Managing credit dealings sapped storekeepers' time and energy. Nearly every month, Fuller had words with one or more of his customers about their balances. In November 1874, it was Ed White in Halls Mills and John Colby in Montville, whom Fuller visited. White promised to pay $50 by the middle of December, while Colby assured payment of $20 by January first "without fail." When thirty days passed without word or money from White, Fuller contacted him again on December 15, this time receiving White's word that he would pay the $50. On March 1, 1875, Fuller again dropped in on John Colby, who "proposed to pay in some money." The stream of promises almost always outpaced the cash Fuller was able to collect, yet he carried on the routine time and again. When personal calls no longer yielded responses, he sent notices demanding payment on overdue bills. In one instance, the number of petitions had grown so large that he required assistance from his wife Anna, asking her to "write [a] lot of dun[ning] letters." If his notices failed to invoke payment, Fuller pursued legal action as a last resort. Nearly every grocer repeated this pattern of debt accumulation, collection, and legal recourse as part of operating a retail business.[52]

As commerce spread farther and faster, though, grocers bestowed greater significance on these activities by adding new rituals. Jonas Young's bookkeeping methods kept accounts in his Missouri store "footed up and ready to sue on at once, if necessary," a knee-jerk reaction to thousands of nameless homesteaders traveling westward through the state. In the absence of credit agency reports, which judged merchants' creditworthiness with New York wholesalers beginning in the 1840s but did not provide consumer ratings until the twentieth century, retailers needed to determine for themselves the three "Cs" of credit—character, capacity, and capital—for those who came calling. Young knew and trusted regulars in his small town, but he took additional precautions with outsiders. Serving as his own credit agent, he insisted that new customers give "a strict account of their affairs, put it in writing and have them sign it as a basis of credit," just like any businessman who appeared at the Mercantile Agency in New York City.[53]

Others turned to collection agents to find shirkers and dun them for payment. Collection agencies emerged in the mid-nineteenth century at the same time as credit reporting firms—new institutions to address emergent commercial problems. Attorneys, bankers, commercial travelers, and postmasters served as collectors and informants, joining a growing network of men who traded in debt. By the 1870s, organizations like the Gazzam Collection Agency of New York City had woven a nationwide web of "special contracts" with lawyers ready to serve claims for a fee on behalf of stiffed retailers. McKillop, Walker and Company, a credit reporting and collection firm founded in 1842, issued the *Mercantile Register of Reliable Banks and Attorneys* beginning in the early 1880s. It offered merchants a nationwide compendium of "approved" agents who paid the firm one-fourth of all monies collected in return for being labeled "reliable." Fuller and others counted on collection agents to recoup losses from men like Alonzo Bennett, who in August 1874 skipped out on the Maine grocer still owing a $5.50 bill. Three years later, Fuller hired a local man, promising to pay double his fee once he had collected payment from Levi McDonald, who had fled Freedom to take up farming in nearby Monroe.[54]

Guides like McKillop, Walker and Company's directory also briefed store-keepers on ever-evolving state and territorial collection laws, many of which permitted arrest, attachment, and judgments without defense, regulations that helped codify debt. Jonas Young feared being swindled by someone "obtaining goods under false pretenses," a practice that seemed to permeate the nineteenth-century's humbug-filled environment. Missouri's lack of imprisonment or insolvency laws forced Young to protect himself, insisting each customer sign a note for all credit purchases stipulating that if a "suit is brought," the borrower agreed to pay 10 percent of the principal as damages, a legal provision Young could impose if things turned sour. In a market culture filled with strangers, grocers became key figures in capitalism's surveillance networks and legal regulations, participating in the formation of structural solutions for corralling deadbeats and protecting businessmen's interests and assets.[55]

The Big Business of Eggs

The grocery trade's continued dependence on credit left most small dealers short on working capital, forcing many to formulate creative financing strategies to generate cash. For some, this meant engaging in commodities trading, especially for the produce and farm goods they had always handled. Market advantages they enjoyed in the last quarter of the nineteenth century now enabled them to bargain for dollars instead of bartering for goods. Cities' increasing dependence on rural products likewise moved more money from urban to rural areas, creating greater opportunities for storekeepers and produce dealers. *American Grocer* acknowledged the universality of this modern distribution system by quoting daily and weekly prices and market trends for the "country produce" small merchants now shipped instead of personally delivering to commercial centers in New York, Chicago, Boston, and New Orleans. Navigating these commodity markets, grocers engineered improved commercial movements between small businessmen and the geography of capital as it continued to flow from hinterland to cities and back again.[56]

Edmund Fuller's particular trading interests centered on eggs. Production and distribution of eggs shifted in the 1850s from what primarily had been a sideline women and children undertook to subsidize households to a skilled industry operated and sustained by small businessmen and farmers. Observers in *DeBow's Review*, a popular southern business journal, were aghast in 1853 that the 1850 US Census took no account of the egg and poultry business, especially since they considered it "much more important than many other branches of trade that are regularly reported." Others made similarly bold statements about the egg trade's magnitude and scope, with one poultry specialist stating bluntly in 1871 that "eggs form a very important commercial commodity." Although almost every major city traded eggs, the New York market was particularly large, with figures for 1870 claiming that wholesalers sold more than nineteen million dozen (even then the dozen was the standard quantity for selling eggs), a figure that grew to more than thirty-one million in 1873, with a value of nearly $7 million. The data compiler noted that these figures were "exclusive of the immense numbers which find their way to the great metropolis through market-men and small dealers," which in his estimation amounted to an additional 20 percent. By 1879, *Scientific American* claimed that the nation's egg trade generated $180 million every year, making it big business.[57]

Up in Maine, it seemed like everyone in Waldo County dealt in eggs, including Fuller. One 1873 area report boasted, "The egg trade is immense. Thousands of dozens are shipped to Boston every year by every country store." This was especially true during the spring months, when hens laid the majority of their eggs and city demand peaked. Fuller spent one day in January 1874 preparing 789 dozen, punctuating the figure by recalling that he had delivered 4,340 dozen since August 1873, or 52,080 eggs. Boston's market rivaled New York's, recording more than 6.5 million dozen eggs in 1878 alone. Fuller had a small but not unimportant piece of this trade, often making profits in the tens of dollars, just enough to supplement his regular cash takings. He reaped even greater economic rewards, though, from the farmers who sold him eggs and spent some of that money in his shop or used eggs as payment or barter for other goods. Places like Fuller's served as collection points for country produce, where storekeepers warehoused and shipped goods on behalf of farmers who lacked the resources and connections to deal directly with urban markets.[58]

Grocers' ledgers document these commodity flows in detail. When farmers brought eggs to Fuller's store, he logged them in his cash book, noting date, quantity, and the cost he paid, along with the price they achieved once they shipped. These figures not only allowed him to track profits and losses along with cash earnings but also the rise and fall of the Boston egg market. "The price of eggs advanced from 22 to 24 cents with us to day noon," the storekeeper noted in August 1874. When prices dropped the following spring, a frustrated Fuller wrote, "Eggs at 20 cts this morning," the force of his pen dispensing enough ink to bleed through the page.[59]

Fuller's ability to relate the exact time ("to day noon") when prices rose in Boston attests to the increasing alignment between rural and city markets. Although standard time would not be adopted nationwide until November 1883, an event Fuller noted in his diary as "a chang[e] backward here of some 22 minutes from regular sun time or 15 m 44 1/2 sec from Boston time," railroads and the telegraph had already bridged many local and regional markets. Both also made it possible to engage the egg trade from greater distances. In the 1840s, most eggs traveled to New York mainly from nearby towns and down the Erie Canal. By 1874, when railroad shipments had become customary, eggs entered the New York market from states west of the Mississippi River, north from Canada, and south from Georgia and Tennessee. The Detroit firm of McCracken and Company wrote *American Grocer* in 1876 seeking advice on sending eggs to New York City from their Michigan store six hundred miles away. Eager to get the strongest prices, the grocers queried editors if come spring Philadelphia might not "be a better market," likely speculating that the city's upcoming Centennial Exhibition would boost demand.[60]

That same year, merchant Owen Kelly wondered why eggs he sent to New York from his central Ohio farming village of Kirkersville brought "so much less" than New Jersey or Pennsylvania eggs. The town's advantageous location along the Central Ohio line of the Baltimore and Ohio Railroad, which by midcentury extended just west past the rural community to nearby Columbus, connected Kelly with multiple commercial districts. Regional variations in eggs such as size, color, and cleanliness dictated price, even as Kelly insisted that his location should not penalize him. "We take them in fresh," Kelly clarified, "and they are shipped by express, taking but one day in transit." The Ohio dealer likely was feeling the effects of New York's recent efforts to regulate the egg market. Following an 1874 report from the New York Butter and Cheese Exchange, which found "great loss" in eggs shipped "from extreme distances," the city appointed inspectors to examine and grade eggs, sorting them into categories of "Fresh," "Middling Fresh," and "Stale." Once separated, inspectors would then "brand" each package "with the name of the State from whence shipped, grade, date of inspection," and other information. From these data, inspectors and other members of the recently founded Mercantile

Exchange (1874) would then establish market prices. Implementation of such a grading system imposed standards that returned maximum dollars and cents for the best products. *American Grocer* reminded Kelly that "all grocers and retailers of eggs in the city and vicinity will, and are willing to pay a higher price for clean, bright, fresh-laid eggs." Though the Ohio man's eggs were unspoiled, they did not make the grade in other ways.[61]

Grading systems, market regulations, and the aligning of city and country markets were part of an ongoing commercial transformation. Similar processes were under way in the grain and lumber industries, giving rise to new market hubs in Chicago and elsewhere. Venturing away from the burgeoning metropolises and into the small towns and farms that comprised much of the nineteenth-century American landscape, however, it is easier to see how storekeepers like Fuller and Kelly helped organize this revolution from behind their counters. In backwater villages, the tasks of gathering, packing, and distributing the nation's agricultural products took place away from the urban manufacturers and mercantile princes most credited for bridging city and country in the nineteenth century. Undertaking this work, rural merchants expanded the peripheral economy into metropolitan areas, extending capitalism's sphere of influence to encompass both industrial and agricultural markets. Their efforts influenced the development of a sophisticated commercial economy that served the business interests of thousands of farmers and small retailers alike.[62]

Coinciding with this transformation was the imposition of new market standards and expectations of trade knowledge on grocers. Storekeepers orchestrated these latest responsibilities, learning how and when to ship or to hold eggs to their advantage. *American Grocer* offered instructions for packing eggs and encouraged sending them by "fast freight lines at all seasons of the year" to ensure they reached the "market in such order that they can be sold with much less loss" than in years past. Unlike grain and other commodities, nobody speculated in egg futures in the 1870s, making it impossible for egg men to secure prices in advance of shipments. The window for making money was limited, and fresh products paid bigger returns. Some, however, tried to capitalize on the perishability problem by hawking secret formulas designed to preserve eggs for extended periods in the absence of mechanical refrigeration. The appropriately named Archie Cunning promised to help storekeepers "Make Big Money" and manipulate the market. For twenty cents, the Missouri huckster offered a solution for keeping eggs fresh for up to one year, encouraging storekeepers to "Hold your eggs while cheap for higher prices." Not until the 1890s would refrigerated cold storage make it easier (yet no less controversial) to stop time in the interest of bigger profits.[63]

In the meantime, most dealers did not have months to sit on their eggs. If Benjamin Franklin was right that time was money, country produce dealer and "egg packer" Jacob Buckley was willing to prove it in court when he sued the Atlantic and Great Western Railroad for damages because of a bungled egg delivery. In March 1875, Buckley contacted the line asking for "time" on shipping 2,195 dozen eggs to New York City from his store in Springfield, Illinois. "Time" equaled speed in railroad parlance: How fast can you ship? Unlike Brown and Burrows who decades earlier spent weeks shepherding their goods downriver to market, the Illinois man depended on (and was part of) a growing system of middlemen employed to transport and transform his eggs and other products into cash. Atlantic and Great Western assured Buckley that with just one transfer in Cincinnati his shipment would arrive in New York in five days "without a doubt" and promised to keep Buckley abreast of its movement by telegraph. Delays kept the load from arriving as expected; when the eggs went to market a week later than anticipated, prices had dipped twelve cents per dozen, leaving Buckley short more than $260 in anticipated revenue.[64]

Disruptions like the one Buckley experienced were especially detrimental with perishable commodities. Merchants had little control over spoilage, save for icing barrels and implementing customary measures for protecting shells from damage and moisture penetration, which many believed caused decomposition. It was a distribution disadvantage egg men and all produce dealers sought to overcome by coordinating market deliveries. Buckley's "anxiety ... to obtain quick time," the court ruled, "shows that, for some reason" he "regarded 'time' as an important element in the shipments." After all, both parties "undoubtedly knew that in this country the market value of eggs was liable to decline," especially in spring when New York was glutted. Buckley won his case and set a benchmark for distributing perishable commodities, putting the railroad on the hook for damages as determined by the market and not the court. It was just one more way the Illinois egg man synchronized his business dealings with commercial activities in the nation's largest trade center hundreds of miles from his Midwestern store.[65]

What began in the nineteenth century as a central component of regional distribution carried on into the twentieth century, even as newer methods for moving goods evolved. Minnesota grocer Andrew Schoch bought eggs from country storekeepers well into the 1920s. General merchant P. J. Meisch contacted Schoch in March 1923 to sell him five cases and quote him the price of eggs in Hastings and the surrounding area. "I am paying 20¢ to farmers," Meisch informed, "and so are the neighboring towns." The availability of central warehouses and national distribution networks by the 1920s did not negate country storekeepers' roles as principal agents for buying, selling, and distributing farm goods, even if they sold them directly to big city retailers instead of commodities markets. Rather, the persistence of these networks reinforced the essential part small businessmen played in supplying foodstuffs to both rural and urban communities, aligning agricultural and commercial economies. The continuity that linked egg men like Fuller and Buckley with Meisch was neither antiquated nor ineffective but rather fundamental for routing the flow of farm produce and capital between hinterlands and markets.[66]

Setting the Standard

On an early fall day in 1904, Victor Tulane took the podium in Indianapolis at the fifth annual meeting of the National Negro Business League, founded in 1900 by Booker T. Washington to promote the commercial and financial interests of African American businessmen. Tulane recounted for other black merchants the tale of opening his first store in 1891. "My story is indeed very simple," the Alabama grocer began. "It is not the glowing account of one who has climbed to the very summit of glorious success—to the contrary it is but the modest and unvarnished record of one who, by persistent effort, has succeeded in overcoming many adversities." With capital of just $90 and no previous experience, Tulane had purchased a ramshackle store in Montgomery complete with stock and fixtures, which included "a pair of rusty scales, a battered oil tank, two primitive show cases, a few candy jars, a peck measure, one lamp, [and] a broken meat knife." With the addition of a bucket of lard and a dime's worth of salt, he was ready for business.[67]

Tulane's experiences were typical. Over the next several years he did what many other enterprising turn-of-the-century storekeepers did—implemented new methods, updated fixtures, and worked to establish his financial independence. "Knowing full well that a merchant could not succeed without making a profit," he hired a young man with storekeeping experience to show him the ropes, starting with learning how to use his scales. Not long after, he realized he was "crediting more rapidly than collecting," and adjusted his accounting and business techniques accordingly. The purchase of a "Texas pony" and second-hand wagon put Tulane in the ranks of a full-service delivery shop. He eventually erected his own store and house combined, and by the time he spoke in Indianapolis, had plans to build a modern, two-story brick building on a "very desirable cornerlot [sic]." Tulane was just another nineteenth-century corner grocer who aspired to "control a business of my own."[68]

From the start, resourceful men like Tulane saw opportunity in grocery store entrepreneurship and were unafraid to propose and implement new ideas and risk falling flat. Not long after the grocery business began to distinguish itself from its grog shop past, Tulane could look at what once represented cutting-edge retailing tools and see them as "primitive," fundamental fittings that more recent instruments supplanted. Even the prototypical old fogey George Washington Dusenbury acknowledged in 1876 the transformation in merchandising, all the while condemning the "modern" ways of show window pioneers. "We keep our window glass decorated by flies in the highest style of the art," he stated with characteristic sarcasm. Rounding out the display were "old newspapers, wood measures, brooms, pails and a cheesebox full of apple or onions. We keep the other one free for the boys to sit in evenings and gossip." The "go-ahead" storekeepers who subscribed to *American Grocer* could read between the lines of Dusenbury's gripes and recognize the conversion of grocery stores from liquor and food shops into selling environments, formal spaces where social intercourse gave way to mass consumption and modern business operations.

This process would continue throughout the 1880s and 1890s as nationally advertised products further commercialized grocery stores. In 1883, Edmund Fuller heard about "Fleischmann & Co's Compressed yeast," the first industrially produced and packaged product of its kind, introduced to the nation at the 1876 Centennial Exhibition in Philadelphia. Looking to stock his shelves, Fuller sought out a grocer in nearby Searsport, who gave him the name of Fleischmann's representative in Portland. Fuller returned home, wrote up an order, and waited for his yeast to arrive. Five days later, he received by mail one dozen cakes from the Cincinnati, Ohio, manufacturer. It was Fuller's first mention of the branded and packaged foods revolution that by the 1890s would intertwine retailers, wholesalers, and manufacturers into even more complicated alliances centered on distributing groceries in different and potentially more efficient ways.[69]

Meanwhile, *American Grocer* celebrated a decade of publication in 1879 by rereleasing Peter H. Felker's *The Grocers' Manual*, a reprint of a popular volume produced the year before. Felker was an educated man with bachelor of science and master's degrees earned from the Michigan Agricultural College in the early 1870s. From there he embarked on a career editing and publishing scientifically based guides and papers for the grocery trade that instructed storekeepers about the dangers of adulterated goods, a growing problem in the unregulated manufacturing years of the late-nineteenth century. Over the course of three hundred pages, Felker alphabetized and categorized common products and practices found in retail shops across the country. Six pages alone detailed the pork-packing process, with thirteen different terms from "Ordinary Mess Pork" to "Long English" distinguishing the various cuts and products derived from the mass-disassembly process. Descriptions of lard, lead pencils, lemons, and laurel leaves spoke to the broad range of goods many grocery stores continued to carry. At the end of his book, Felker presented informational tables, including US currency values for double eagle, eagle, half eagle, and other types of legal tender; compounded interest by dollar amount and length of time; weights and measures (foreign and domestic), including those of "various articles in different states," alerting grocers that a bushel of buckwheat in New York weighed four pounds less than one from Iowa. It was Felker's way of systematizing nonstandard practices, bringing organization and a sense of control to the trade. While science was not crushing antiquated notions, it certainly was helping grocers modify them to confront new challenges.[70]

The same year Felker's guide returned to bookseller's shelves, a Dayton, Ohio, saloonkeeper and his brother received notification that the US Patent Office had approved their application for an "improvement in cash register and indicator." The newfangled device was intended "for use by store-keepers" as a way to ascertain "at a glance, the total receipts taken in." By the mid-1880s, grocers across the country would discover the innovative machine and find new ways to supplement the hours and days spent recording customer purchases and totaling daily and monthly accounts in ledgers and journals. In time, nearly every retailer would come to regard the cash register's potential for helping them control store receipts as yet another way science was transforming the trade.[71]

2

The Keys to Modernization

In June 1885, John T. Carson thought it was time he knew more about his Nashville, Tennessee, grocery business. Occupying adjacent store fronts on Market Street in the city's downtown area, his shop drew ample trade, enough for the grocer to justify spending $120 on a newfangled device that promised to record retail transactions. Writing to the Dayton, Ohio, firm that manufactured the machine, Carson ordered the company's largest model—a fifty-pound monster, thirty keys wide, in a lacquered cherry-wood cabinet. Shortly after installing the apparatus in his store, he felt obliged to tell the manufacturing company about his satisfaction. "I know it is correct," the merchant confirmed of the machine's ability to record his store's cash dealings, "and I would not do without it for five times what it cost me." Exaggerated or not, his praise eventually turned to prognostication, with the grocer claiming, "In the near future, your machine will be considered a necessity to every well regulated store in the land." Carson was right.[1]

Buying a cash register in the late nineteenth century was one more step Carson and other small grocers took toward controlling and routinizing retail business. Beginning in the 1880s, thousands of cash registers stood sentinel atop counters in grocery stores and other retail shops, with proprietors, clerks, and cashiers figuring out ways to incorporate the latest retail technology into their everyday business practices. Not twenty years later, grocery trade journals truthfully claimed, "You find that most of the stores near you have a cash register." Touted as a better way to track retail transactions, the cash register aimed to "stop leaks" of unaccounted cash moving from the boss's till into employees' pockets by instituting new information and accounting controls, joining previous technologies that altered the retailing landscape and created selling environments.[2]

The cash register was part of a larger "control revolution" in American business and society, a new age in which information was traded like a commodity and flowed like currency between merchants and moguls alike. The device literally tracked the growing profusion of capitalistic activities in Gilded Age society. As paper and coin became standard mediums of exchange, the nature of retail business changed, prompting innovative responses both in technological and methodological terms. Massive bureaucracies and managerial hierarchies integrated production methods and began controlling immense corporations in the 1880s, employing new technologies to collate, store, and disseminate information on a mass scale. Information about business cycles, material supplies, employee productivity, and product output enabled giant firms to systematize and standardize operations in the interest of greater efficiency at every stage. It is big companies, therefore, that historians typically credit for initiating both the control revolution in business and for passing along information technologies to smaller firms.[3]

Grocers' efforts to manage operations with innovative devices reflect a previously unacknowledged history of technology from the bottom up. Small retailers doubtlessly had little need for managerial hierarchies or employee productivity reports in their operations. They nevertheless acknowledged their interest in joining and directing the control revolution first by adjusting their accounting practices, next by retaining collection agents and implementing credit reporting strategies, and then by purchasing cash registers. Those willing to take a risk on the untried machine became the first cash register adopters, making them lead users of the new information technology. Even large department stores of the period initially ignored the apparatus.[4]

The term "information technology" might appear discordant with discussions about the nineteenth century. Most people associate the phrase with electronic tabulation and the origins of the digital age in Herman Hollerith's 1890 US Census punch card system, and later in twentieth-century computing. Yet information processing tools and machines have existed for centuries, from the abacus to the adding machine. These devices and others paved the path to modern information technologies, in the shift from basic recordkeeping to advanced accounting analyses. The cash register was among the first information-processing devices that provided automatically generated feedback based on keyed inputs. Its two primary functions, transaction recording and processing, provided accounting controls, checked cash, and stemmed clerk errors, introducing mechanical oversight to retail environments. The information that cash registers collated gave storekeepers data they could scrutinize in conjunction with ledgers, daybooks, and invoices, allowing them to analyze past practices and future needs. It was, in short, the (proto)computer of its day.[5]

The cash register was one of the few information technologies devised specifically for retailers. It quickly came to symbolize business acumen and "progress," mechanically correlating a user's actions with monetary exchange and enabling grocers to track immediate sales as never before. Small margins and growing competition in the retail grocery business elevated owners' interests in controlling cash flows and eliminating losses. Mass production and consumption also spurred awareness among grocers about moving goods faster and more profitably. Retailers stood on the front lines of this commercial revolution, pioneering objective methods to document and regulate the increasing tide of consumers and cash that flowed into commercial spaces. Machines like the register promised to corral proprietors' pecuniary interests as much as they did clerks' and customers' perceived fallibilities. Storekeepers who kept their money in check guarded both their and their workers' morality, many believed, channeling economic expansion in protected and measured ways that fed industrialization's rationalizing tendencies. Machines helped mediate these new commercial exchanges, supplementing handshakes with keystrokes.[6]

One 1887 advertisement made plain the informational advantages of owning and using the device. In a series of questions, the National Cash Register Company, the industry's foremost manufacturer, apprised merchants of the many ways they could take control of their businesses with the machine:

> Have you received the benefit of all goods sold? Have you not
> often thought that you had paid out something during the day and
> forgotten to charge the party with it? Do you not find more charged
> on the customer's pass-book than is on your ledger? Did you ever
> hasten across the store to ask your clerk if that man had paid for
> those goods? Did your clerk ever say he was just going to charge it?[7]

From cash and credit errors to clerk misdeeds, the cash register became the first technology to address informational disparities that frequently led to market advantages and disadvantages inherent in nineteenth-century retail transactions.

Sales records from the National Cash Register Company (NCR) for nearly three thousand machines sold between January 1885 and July 1887 tell the story of the company's first production years. Bound in one comprehensive ledger, these records concern the first wood-cabinet cash registers built by the firm that eventually dominated the industry. Captured on two hundred pages are particulars about individual purchasers, their places of business, the kinds of registers they purchased, and the terms under which they acquired each machine. Details include customization requests for fancy, hand-carved cabinet decorations and inlays, the type of adding mechanism purchasers requested, and the exact keyboard layouts and functions storekeepers dictated to the company and its sales agents, painting a detailed portrait of technology consumers and users.[8]

These same factors also make it possible to consider the machine's organizational and methodological impact on grocers' routines. Specialized keyboard arrangements in particular suggest how storekeepers thought the machine could fit into their current businesses, making it possible to ask important questions about real purchasers and their adoption and adaptation of retail technology. The one hundred thirty-nine individual grocers (all white males) who purchased 199 registers in NCR's first years outpaced all other tradesmen except saloonkeepers and hotel proprietors, who operated what were regarded primarily as service industries. This makes grocers the largest number of retailers who first put cash registers into stores from New York to Colorado and from the Wyoming Territory to Texas.[9]

While the actual number of grocers who first purchased cash registers was small, their impact as consumers and users of retail technology was significant. As retailers nationwide entered and engaged in the control revolution, grocers and their clerks helped introduce the device to customers and other merchants, acculturating shoppers and businessmen alike to modern retailing. They designed, implemented, and orchestrated the cash register's usage and symbolic association with retail sales. The "ka-ching!" of the bell that signaled every completed sale became synonymous with commercial productivity. As some of the first retailers to put cash registers on their counters, small grocers were the architects of a new methodology focused on rationalizing and controlling the course of modern selling.

When Rhode Island grocer James Eddy started using a register in his shop in 1883 it made front-page news. The *Newport Mercury* reported minute details of how the "enterprising" Eddy worked his machine from the first key stroke to totaling the day's take, noting how the merchant "counted the number of registries [recorded] on the roll and found that change had been made 2142 times during the day." Editorializing, the paper concluded, "one can imagine little loafing time for Mr. Eddy's clerks." This off-the-cuff remark underscored the value of James Eddy's innovativeness: it provided the grocer with greater accounting controls over both his business and his men. Harnessing man's assumed fallibilities—pilfering and laziness—through mechanical means, grocers like James Eddy became leaders in the drive to reconfigure retail methods. By the first years of the twentieth century, trade journals commented that any store without a register looked "like a backwoods one." Grocer John T. Carson's prophecy had been fulfilled.[10]

TABLE 2.1 *Top Twenty-five Trades Represented by NCR Cash Register Purchasers, January 1885–July 1887*[a]

Primary Occupation of Cash Register Purchaser	Number of Unique Purchasers Identified in Ledger	Number of Registers Purchased
NCR agent	32	591
saloon owner/liquor dealer	372	490
hotel proprietor	205	266
grocer	139	199
druggist	98	121
restaurant owner	83	119
cigar dealer	31	36
confectioner	17	32
typewriter dealer	2	29
dry goods merchant	18	26
butcher	23	24
merchant	20	23
hardware dealer	17	19
brewer	7	18
baker	14	16
boot and shoe dealer	11	16
billiards hall owner	8	13
register dealer	4	13
clothing merchant	10	11
farmers' market proprietor	1	11
caterers	1	10
general store merchant	8	9
fruit dealer	7	8
safe dealer	1	8
unknown	478	587

[a]National Cash Register Agent's and Commissions Ledger (1884–1887), serial number 1182-4242, NCR Archive at Dayton History, Dayton, Ohio; US Bureau of the Census, *Tenth Census of the United States, 1880*. Washington, DC: National Archives and Records Administration, 1880; US City Directories on Microfilm collection, Library of Congress, Microfilm Reading Room, Washington, DC.

NCR bookkeepers did not record information regarding purchasers' trades. I cross-referenced names and addresses with census records and city directories published between 1880 and 1885, which provided a representative accounting of register buyers' occupations at the time of purchase.

Inventing and Marketing the Cash Register

The cash register that grocer John Carson bought for his Nashville store had been patented only six years earlier in 1879 by a saloonkeeper in Dayton, Ohio. Inventor James Ritty dubbed his device "The Incorruptible Cashier," a nod to both clerks' assumed shortcomings and the machine's claim to be tamper resistant. The moniker came in part from Ritty's own frustrations with his bartenders, whom he assumed were pocketing change from the till. As the former mechanic watched his thriving liquor operation lose money, he sought to institute better control over his finances and set about building a machine that would allow him to track cash transactions, supplementing individual accountability. The result was a device that many believed could protect a merchant's money.[11]

In the days before cash registers, most storekeepers relied on unsecured drawers mounted under the counter to hold bills and coins, and they depended on clerks' forthrightness to deposit cash sums and record ledger transactions accurately. Less trusting owners purchased tills with alarm bells that warned when anyone opened the drawer. The Miles Alarm Till Manufacturing Company began offering its version of a secured drawer in 1859, claiming it to be an "effectual bar to 'till tapping,' " or robbing the money drawer. The black walnut device contained a "network of protective wires, bolts, [and] locks" designed to thwart would-be burglars and impart "a good deal of confidence" in proprietors and managers, as the *New York Tribune* claimed in 1871 after installing one in its business office. Such contraptions alluded to storeowners' efforts not only to guard their cash from burglars but also to discipline clerks through mechanical means. Devices such as William Seward Burroughs's adding machine, introduced in 1885, meanwhile, offered no cash drawer or visible indicators to alert clerks and customers to sales amounts. Combined, these technologies offered some protections but lacked either theft deterrents or the ability to verify sales data promptly, problems the cash register sought to remedy.[12]

Concern among storekeepers ran high as cautionary tales abounded about employees who lived secret lives on store profits pilfered from unlocked drawers. According to one turn-of-the-century parable, a grocer in New York, "like hundreds of his foolish brethren," placed no safeguards on his cash drawer, only to learn that his counterman "scooped in all money paid." The young man was "of good reputation," and the storekeeper had "trusted the cashier implicitly." Yet after four years of failing to turn a suitable profit, the grocer began to watch the fellow's activities and followed him home one afternoon. There he discovered the clerk "was keeping an expensive family, besides a servant and two horses!" Stories like these multiplied as commerce spread and the familiarity of local exchanges were increasingly entangled in a web of new and unfamilar commercial networks, calling into sharp relief questions about who could and could not be trusted to watch over a merchant's money. Though the alarmed till offered some protection against pilfering, it provided no assistance with bookkeeping or tracking sales, leaving the drawer open to filchers.[13]

The combination of these two concerns—dishonesty and accounting controls—prompted proposals for mechanical solutions that limited human error and rationalized cash transactions. Reporting in 1878, *Scientific American* declared one such device to be "a new machine for making people honest—a consummation to which (if it ever can be attained by machinery) no small amount of inventive genius is just now being brought to bear." James Ritty's prototype register eventually combined the protection of an alarmed till with mechanical accounting controls. His first operational model consisted of two rows of metal keys impressed and painted black with denominations ranging between five cents and $1 along with pop-up indicators that displayed the sale amount to both cashier and customer. Drawing initial inspiration from a ship's propeller rotation counting mechanism, Ritty also installed a "series of co-operating disks marked with numbers on their peripheries," according to the original patent, which rotated with each keystroke, recording total sales. In time, he would add a cash drawer to complete his design. Here was a machine many believed could make people honest.[14]

Coal and retail goods dealer (and future NCR founder) John H. Patterson had doubts about those managing his store when he got wind of Ritty's cash register. Having recently fired employees who he found were giving away merchandise, Patterson wanted some system of oversight on his clerks. Ordering two of the saloonkeeper's machines in May 1882, Patterson put them to work in his store and six months later, he maintained, "our books showed a profit of over five thousand dollars. The registers did it all." Shortly thereafter, Patterson gave up the coal business and purchased a controlling interest in Ritty's former operation. Reorganized in 1884 as the National Cash Register Company, Patterson's new firm began production in a one-room factory in Dayton, Ohio. The coalman turned manufacturer now faced the challenge of convincing others that the device could change retail practices.[15]

Patterson's enthusiasm for the cash register notwithstanding, both he and his company faced an uphill battle in assuring shopkeepers and barmen that the machine was more than "just a contraption for catching light-fingered clerks," as Patterson once put it. The register's design faults and limitations presented their own obstacles. Not every storekeeper who bought a register found it useful for protecting against pilfering clerks, and for good reason. Shortly after the register's introduction, Louis Kork, a San Francisco waiter and recent Los Angeles Business College graduate, wagered his questionable reputation on teaching clerks how to "beat" the device and steal without detection. For $1, interested parties could purchase his pamphlet, "Pointers on How to Do It." Making news nationwide, Kork avowed that his intentions were only to "advise clerks to be honest after selling his circular on thievery," an unlikely aspiration given the $90 that police charged he had stolen from a fellow worker. The machine's fallibilities, however, were widely known in the retail trade, and NCR worked feverishly to provide new and

James Ritty (standing) labored in his Dayton, Ohio, workshop to transform his original dial-faced machine into the "Incorruptible Cashier," a tabulating cash register. John Patterson would make Ritty's device standard technology in nearly every retail store. Courtesy of the Ohio Historical Society.

better protective measures such as locks, tabs, and bells to impede theft and tampering. Virginia grocer John Crilly voiced his suspicions about abandoning trade to the whims of either machines or one's employees: "I don't consider the Register of much use to a man who will leave his business entirely in charge of clerks."[16]

Some counter workers doubtlessly had a vested interest in keeping registers out of shops and easy-to-loot tills in place; NCR claimed that workers blocked store owners from learning about the device by tearing up the company's advertisements or preventing sales agents from entering the building. If clerks sabotaged NCR's efforts to sell cash registers, however, they likely did so not because the device necessarily impelled them to be honest but because it elevated anxieties about key strokes replacing scrivening skills, making the clerks unnecessary. In 1886, John Duerr unwittingly acknowledged clerks' concerns from his Indiana store. Endorsing the cash register, the grocer declared that it "does away with registering sales by pen or pencil." Wisconsin grocer Charley Pardee echoed Duerr, announcing, "I cheerfully recommend it to every business man as being the cheapest cashier they can employ." Increased mechanization in all industries threatened manual laborers including retail workers, with mechanical accounting tools facilitating the replacement of trained bookkeepers with lower-paid clerks. One New Orleans grocery firm made clear that they considered its cash registers to be "perfect accountants."[17]

Those who talked about registers supplanting men spoke to the growing profusion of counter and office workers who quickly were becoming a mainstay in retail enterprises. Clerks and porters who had entered retail in the 1850s continued to help administer industrial expansion, as the accounting, letter writing, and inventory taking tasks associated with organizational bureaucracies became essential tools of commerce. While many small proprietors like Edmund Fuller still toiled over writing dunning letters, marking goods, and packing eggs with the help of family members, others hired specialized trade workers in growing numbers. By 1889, nearly 700,000 retail employees across all trades served as countermen, cashiers, scribes, and deliverymen, a nearly 50 percent increase from the previous decade. The work was especially taxing in grocery stores, which tended to open daily and stay open late hours to accommodate customer needs. In 1893, editors at the *Frankford Roundabout* in Kentucky posted one porter's query as to why grocery clerks "never [have] a day off, not even the 4th of July nor Thanksgiving." Half-kidding, the weary worker faulted himself and others like him, because "the grocery clerk . . . comes so near knowing everything that the town can not spare him for so long a time." Once considered ancillary labor, clerks had become essential retail workers by the end of the century.[18]

Others were less sanguine about the situation. "The life a grocery clerk leads is worse than a horse's," a frustrated toiler wrote in 1894 to the New York *Evening News*, known for voicing the plight of nineteenth-century industrial workers. "Every day in the week he has to get up at 6 o'clock in the morning (most places at 5), and work all day till 9 o'clock at night; on Saturdays till 12 and 1 o'clock, besides Sundays until 11 o'clock," the equivalent of doing "a good nine days' work in a week." Experienced clerks earned approximately $18 a month plus room and board, typically shared with two or three others. It was, in the counterman's estimation, "less than an Italian laborer gets," a position beneath what many deemed to be the lowest paid immigrant worker. Clerks' long hours and mounting responsibilities elevated their accountability as shop owners increasingly depended on salaried employees to help oversee the customers and cash that streamed in and out of their stores. Proprietors' growing dependence on (and potential wariness of) clerks created new conditions and opportunities for innovation. Where family members might be trusted to manage customers and guard store profits, employees, many believed, had to be monitored, a problem some thought could be solved with the cash register.[19]

A Register for Every Store and Size

John Patterson first made quick inroads with his machine into saloons, places where sticky-fingered barmen presumably abounded. The saloon's ubiquity, coupled with its reputation for corrupt activities both behind and in front of the bar, attracted many saloonkeepers to the register's promise. As Patterson understood it, "the only market during those early years was the saloon market." He capitalized on concerns about "light-fingered clerks" by promoting his machines in brewery and saloon trade journals and emphasizing the ways in which his "automatic machinery" would make liquor dealers "free from worry." According to the NCR sales ledger, bar owners ordered almost five hundred registers during the company's first two years. One of NCR's first and most recurrent saloon customers, the company of Hannah and Hogg, purchased twelve registers over the course of two years for their eight Chicago-area locations. The saloon's mahogany machines undoubtedly drew much attention under the "blaze of light" novelist Theodore Dreiser used to describe the firm's opulently illuminated establishments, drawing both drinkers and potential cash register customers to their bars for a closer inspection. Dreiser used both Hannah and Hogg and their registers as inspiration for his *Sister Carrie*, with bar manager George Hurstwood going on the run after pilfering from cash drawers locked in the company's safe.[20]

Patterson, however, saw the limitations in using diatribes about stolen money and other "scare tactics" to market his machine; instead he sought greater sales to retail merchants who could appreciate the machine's accounting controls. Indeed, while NCR offered drawer locks on its earliest models, only a handful (six) of the first registers left the factory with the mechanism installed. Employing an aggressive advertising campaign in tandem with an initially small band of salesmen, Patterson focused on educating retailers about the machine and its uses. Newspaper endorsements and articles commissioned by agents emphasized the register's "best feature," which was to prevent loss not through theft but in "forgetting to make charges of goods sold on credit" and its ability to keep a record of daily sales, encouraging clerks to work "systematically and correctly." By 1887, NCR agents had sold registers to druggists, hardware retailers, confectioners, dry goods merchants, butchers, and fruit dealers from California to New York, in addition to Canada and England, despite competition from other firms selling similar devices. Total sales exploded between 1885 and 1892, from five hundred yearly to more than fifteen thousand, as more merchants recognized the machine as "an immense improvement over the old method of making marks on a paper or merely counting up the cash that happens to be left in the drawer at the close of business," as one Washington, DC, newspaperman claimed in 1885.[21]

New technologies like the cash register renewed both the promise and perils of "progress" in the last decades of the nineteenth century. In 1879, the same year Ritty introduced his device, an *Atlantic Monthly* contributor proclaimed, "In our recent national phenomena there is no other fact so significant, so startling, as the prodigious increase of inventions, both in their number and in their influence over business and daily life." Those who acculturated to the rapidly changing way of things either found recognition for their innovative spirits or disdain from those who questioned such transformations. Critics remarked about the "hurry of life," as did one Rhode Islander in 1882. "The improved facilities of communication and the transmission of news and knowledge have had a contrary effect," the writer judged. As a result, "the pace of life has been increased all around."[22]

Here was a paradox: the same technologies that sped "the pace of life" and business also held the power to restrain it. As the flow of people and information increased, individuals sought to rein in and make sense of once-routine tasks that now seemed to accelerate beyond mere human command. Yet if technology contributed to the problem, it also offered a solution. Typewriters, tabulating machines, mimeographs, and phonographs, used to record memos and letters for later transcription, mechanically helped coordinate information and internal firm operations, especially in the large-scale manufacturing organizations that emerged in the last decades of the nineteenth century. These technologies of written communication also buttressed cost-accounting methods maturing in the 1880s. Cost accounting undergirded new demands on large firms for greater efficiency, speed, regularity, and consistency in bookkeeping to allow for better coordination within firms and across industries. Analyses of overhead, depreciation, interest, and cost flow generated greater feedback on firm operations and commercial organization. These elaborate administrative and bureaucratic networks formed the structural framework on which big business expanded.[23]

Cost accounting originated in large organizations, but it developed simultaneously in retail shops. Grocers and other small merchants faced similar

NCR's Model No. 3, grocers' preferred cash register model. It featured thirty keys, a glass gallery with tab indicators, cash drawer, and the ability to customize the machine's keyboard and decoration, as this grocer did by having the initials "CNR" carved into the machine's case. Author's photographs, courtesy of the NCR Archive at Dayton History.

issues in managing internal and external information and cash flows, if on a more compact scale. Competitive pressures combined with calls for greater efficiency fostered an interest in monitoring expenditures and profits. Although few grocers maintained the kind of complex records developing in big firms, some nevertheless increased oversight of their business activities. The cash register became the first retail machine to address the paradox of speed and control by enabling grocers to oversee accounting on a daily instead of monthly basis, managing customer and clerk transactions, and refining information about day-to-day exchanges. It likewise reduced transaction costs by deskilling the bookkeeping process and facilitating exchanges. The machine, in short, helped grocers begin to systematize and standardize retail transaction processing, providing a quick and accurate accounting of goods and services traded. It was a profound development that ultimately took retail accounting from its origins in nib-and-ink bookkeeping to its maturation in mechanical (and eventually digital) exchanges and analyses.[24]

NCR's standard cash register models and keyboard configurations introduced retailers to mechanized operations. Prices for these basic machines ranged from $70 to $200, with cabinet size, number of keys, and adding mechanism determining functionality and price. Unlike modern registers, which allow cashiers to record prices using a ten-digit keypad, early registers utilized one key for each cash denomination. One customary keyboard provided eleven to thirty keys (depending on the size of the machine) in two parallel rows, numbered from five cents to $10. This arrangement was popular among saloonkeepers who sold mostly nickel drinks and bottles of alcohol, placing a bottom limit on the registered amount (five cents) and reducing the range of keys barmen needed to ring up sales. Another configuration also had eleven to thirty keys, but numbered from one cent to $20. This layout favored confectioners who preferred the eleven-key version for ringing up penny candy, and grocers who favored thirty keys to accommodate their wide variety of priced goods. Nearly 70 percent of grocers represented in the NCR ledger purchased the model No. 3 despite its hefty $200 price ($4,680 in today's dollars), because its expansive keyboard offered greater accounting flexibility.[25]

Recognizing the substantial outlay (and risk) NCR asked retailers to make, the company proposed multiple payment options to ease purchase.

TABLE 2.2 *Number of Grocer-Purchased NCR Cash Registers by Model Number and Size, January 1885 to July 1887*[b] *(Smallest to Largest Sized Machine)*

NCR Model Number	Retail Price	Number Purchased	Percentage
3 key sample	$40	1	<1
No. 1*	$125	3	2
No. 6	$80	13	6
No. 7	$100	15	7
No. 2*	$175	32	16
No. 3*	$200	135	68
Total		199	100

[b]National Cash Register Agent's and Commissions Ledger (1884–1887), serial number 1182–4242, NCR Archive at Dayton History, Dayton, Ohio.
*Totals represent machines sold in full as well as 1/2 sizes, as these machines incorporated the same size keyboards as their full-number counterparts (i.e., No. 3 total includes No. 3 1/2-sized machines). Retail prices reflect typical base price.

Joseph H. Crane, longtime NCR salesman and John H. Patterson's brother-in-law, spelled out the "kinds of terms" available in his 1887 guide, *How I Sell a National Cash Register*. In the first plan, Crane noted, "We ship you a machine, and, five days after shipment, we draw on you at sight the amount less five percent. for cash." The second option allowed a purchaser to take on a note for the full amount of the machine, payable in ninety days. In the final plan, buyers made an initial down payment of cash "at sight," with the balance due in equal payments at intervals of thirty, sixty, and ninety days, extended up to seven months. NCR charged no interest to buyers who chose this option.[26]

Grocers utilized all three payment terms offered by NCR, with 35 percent paying cash for their registers and another 30 percent buying on credit. The remaining purchasers bought their machines using a combination of financing strategies such as consignment, barter, or other repayment arrangements such as extended monthly payments or trade-in allowances for old machines, especially those from other manufacturers in Patterson's vigilant efforts to stamp out competition. Combined, these tactics enabled even the smallest dealers to purchase a cash register for their stores. In 1885, for example, Albert Hussong's grocery business was valued at under $500 and credit agents reported his financial capacity as "limited" when he first set his sights on buying a cash register. The German immigrant had started in Dayton, Ohio, as an upholsterer before opening up both a grocery store and a saloon a few doors away on the downtown's Main Street. It was a move that may have spread Hussong too thin, as reflected in his poor showing with credit agents, who reported in 1888 that while his wife owned the lot and property where he conducted business, he was "wor[th] oof [nothing] the law can reach." In any case, the young merchant did not let his financial situation keep him from installing a register in each of his operations, paying a combined $150, or 30 percent of his shop's value, for both machines.[27]

In hindsight, Hussong's extravagance might seem justified, given what we now recognize about the cash register's information-processing advantages. Yet why would small retailers in the 1880s invest heavily into an unproven technology? After all, the $200 fee for NCR's No. 3 machine was four times the $50 wholesale price of a typical delivery wagon, equipment many grocers deemed essential for business operations. Of the first grocers to buy cash registers, however, several ran businesses with financial capacities R. G. Dun deemed to be $1,000 or less, like Kingman Golledge of Troy, New York. Golledge paid full asking price for his No. 3, despite operating a business valued at less than $500. One explanation for why these men took the risk may be that the register appeared to be a good investment for protecting their limited profits. The cash controls offered by the device probably appealed to men worried about making ends meet, especially if their interests were divided, as Hussong's were. Others perhaps traded "off the books," pocketing their money instead of recording it in ledgers or depositing it in banks. This likely described Luther Cornwall, a Washington, DC, grocer who in 1885 had paid $8,000 for his store, a year before he committed to buying an expensive cash register for a business outsiders valued under $1,000. If so, then the cash register was the ideal technology for a man looking to track money within his store without leaving a paper trail for credit agents to follow. Some, however, may have purchased the device for the sheer novelty of owning and operating the latest technological gadget. The *Newport Mercury*'s announcement about the "enterprising" James Eddy's cash register owed almost as much to the grocer's skill in drawing trade from those curious about the mechanical contraption as it did to his accounting techniques.[28]

Given the cash register's unproven status in the 1880s, purchasing one (let alone two) was a big gamble for any grocer, even those like Frank Hume, partner in the large Washington, DC, wholesale and retail firm of Hume, Cleary and Company. Hume, like Hussong, paid cash for two machines just two years after NCR began selling the device, but he drew on a business capacity of more than $125,000. It is just as easy, perhaps, to see Albert Hussong's and Frank Hume's purchases as foolhardy, flights of fancy for men who dreamed big, sometimes on small resources. This is the likely story of many who were too forward looking to see the potential pitfalls of investing money in novel machines that promised much but potentially delivered little. Both Hussong and Hume easily could have fallen into this category, with the former imperiling more than the latter. Hussong's two small businesses, like so many others, might have failed for lack of capital and trade and for a proprietor who was too ambitious in his plans. As it turns out, the firm of Hume, Cleary and Company appears to have dissolved in 1888, just one year after buying their registers, although both partners carried on independently. Hussong, on the other hand, fared slightly better. He remained in the grocery trade for twenty-plus years, but his saloon shut down shortly after it opened. When Hussong finally closed his store in the 1910s, he went to work for NCR, assembling the same machines he helped bring to the trade.[29]

Grocers' motivations for purchasing cash registers doubtless varied. For every retailer who marveled at the machine's novelty, many others reveled in its capacity to track and analyze information. When Barr and Company, grocers from Washington Court House, Ohio, put a register to work in their store in February 1886, they wrote to NCR, praising the device's accuracy in recording daily transactions. "Yesterday we registered $187.56 and it came out exact. To-day, Saturday, we registered $274.38 in addition to making from the same drawer, over fifty different payments for produce." Money passed in and out of the store under the proprietors' watchful eyes and the register's responsive keys. When Saturday's sales "would not check with the cash by 36 cents," Barr and Company reassured NCR that they "expect, however, to find that error." The cash register alone could not prevent inaccuracy, as the Ohio grocers discovered, but it could alert them to a discrepancy far quicker than did previous methods.[30]

The cash register made immediate what once had been deferred. The time that passed between clerks' recorded ledger transactions and storekeepers' monthly accounting allowed uncertainty, inaccuracy, and forgetfulness to creep into the books. Instead of waiting until month's end, grocers now had the ability to question accounting missteps while the day's transactions were fresh in their minds. While information of this kind was obtainable before the cash register, the quickness with which it could be acquired sped the flow of information necessary for more efficient business control. By the late 1890s, systematic management methods began to make inroads into the retail sector, offering administrative solutions to the problems of information collection and processing. NCR came to capitalize on these new ideas in the 1900s, marketing their machines in conjunction with various "systems" that centered on cost-accounting methods. In the interim, however, their registers lacked the ability to tell grocers at a glance credit sales, accounts receivable, money paid out, individual clerk transactions, or sales made in different product lines— details later cash registers would track. The machine's limited technological capabilities, therefore, forced grocers to improvise.[31]

"Arbiters of Machine Development"

Many small retailers saw ways to put their own fingerprints on the cash register's design, function, and application, making the machine work for them and their businesses. Some used standard machines in innovative fashions, while others asked NCR to change their typical keyboard arrangements and suggested alternative ways to order the keys or vary the denominations and functions of the keys themselves. NCR bookkeepers took careful note of these requests and changes, marking down the exact arrangement of each dollar and cent key demanded by buyers in their sales ledger, along with any additional special requests. Such improvisations reveal much about grocers' influence as design mediators and the ways in which they as users shaped the cash register as a business and information tool. Details grocers wanted and wrested from their machines paralleled larger firms' efforts to create more formal and systematic communications, helping retailers begin to shift away from the ad hoc methods that characterized many small businesses.[32]

Collaboration between technology producers and users was not uncommon in this early period, especially when it came to business machines. Cooperative efforts not only accelerated innovation, producing technologies that addressed immediate information gathering and dissemination issues (some more effectively than others), but they also generated devices that influenced future methods and users. Office machines, often introduced with one function in mind, developed in conjunction with the typists, clerks, bookkeepers, and clerical workers who shaped their use, purpose, and meaning. Typewriters, for example, emerged in the same period as cash registers and developed in tandem with accountants' input, in some cases expanding the machine's abilities to record bookkeeping transactions directly into specially bound ledgers in addition to composing office memos, letters, and invoices. As a result, later devices frequently bore both the original inventor's mark and users' imprint as "learning by selling" spread knowledge among factories, salesmen, and users. In the case of the cash register, this process transformed retail operators into collaborative innovators and altered the register from a rudimentary tabulating device to an information-processing machine.[33]

For NCR, emphasis on the merchant-user as influential innovator was more than just a way to sell more registers. John H. Patterson took a keen interest in gathering and applying feedback from the field to the device's development by encouraging his salesmen to relay users' needs and demands to the Dayton factory. According to one NCR insider, "early developments came about largely through rectifying complaints from users." In an 1889 edition of The N.C.R., Patterson encouraged his agents to document customer gripes, as "These are the Texts from Which the Experimenters Work—By the Complaint Sheet the Register is Bettered—Send Them In." He regularly ran "complaint" columns in the company's in-house publications, claiming, "it is by knowing the faults and weak points of the Register that we are able to correct them and perfect the now almost perfect machine." The large number of criticisms users and salesmen lobbed at the factory suggests that the cash register was anything but "perfect" in these early days. One sales agent became so exasperated with trying to fix his customer's register that he carped, "It has cost more worry, time, and expense than could be told in a hundred-page volume." Another, however, sent encouragement after noticing the 1889 availability of a decimal key, which he believed was "a very good thing." User grievances and customer modifications became opportunities for grocers to alter the machine to extract more information and augment the register's general function along with the nature of retail trade.[34]

Barr and Company's offhand comment about tracking produce purchases was one such improvisation. Their 1886 model had no keys designated for purchases made from different grocery lines, an alteration found on later machines. Instead, they would have assigned an auxiliary key strictly to produce dealings, instructing clerks to strike that button whenever they paid out cash for fruit and vegetable stocks. At the end of the day, the grocers delineated "fifty different payments for produce," information that would have taken them far longer to scribe into their ledgers and tally later on. The desire to obtain details of this kind about specific product lines reflected both the expansion and specialization of mass markets, with retailers seeking to gain greater control over distribution costs as denser commercial networks maintained by a growing army of middlemen supplied a larger volume of goods. Information about customer flow—how many shoppers made purchases—and sales productivity served similar means. Jacob Miller reported to NCR in 1886, "Register received at noon, and it works like a charm. Until evening we recorded 143 sales" in his New Philadelphia, Ohio, grocery shop. The following day, the firm "registered 363 sales."[35]

Connecting clock time with money, Miller and others mechanized and joined together two hallmarks of modern capitalism. Later cash registers literally combined both elements, with NCR equipping its machines with clocks that clerks started when they came to work and stopped during breaks and shift changes. In these early days, however, Miller extemporized to parse information about the pace and volume of trade using the register's basic functions. This potentially enabled the retailer to adjust his operations, scheduling the right number of clerks or delivery boys needed during peak business hours, or ensuring that shipments would arrive before high-volume trading days. The combination of clock time and monetary transactions opened new informational avenues to grocers, creating a more dynamic system where proprietor, clerk, and machine worked in concert.[36]

Grocers' coordination of time with sales depended on the use of one of the two adding mechanisms NCR offered. The self- (or detail) adder comprised a series of counting wheels that tracked the number of times a cashier pressed a particular key. To tally the day's takings, an operator read across the wheels, multiplying the number of key strokes by the denomination of key struck. The paper adder, on the other hand, worked by punching holes in a paper roll with each key struck, not unlike early punch card systems. A cashier counted the number of holes recorded by each key stroke and multiplied that figure by the corresponding key denomination to compute his total sales. Proprietors looking to differentiate periods of customer activity could reset the self-adder's counting wheels following the morning rush and record afternoon sales as an independent figure, or they could advance the paper adder's roll to mark a time break.[37]

NCR salesman Henry E. Blood's 1889 manual noted this practice in relation to one of NCR's paper-adder machines. If, the handbook suggested to storekeepers, "you are leaving the store at 12 o'clock, and desire to ascertain the number of sales made during your absence . . . [b]efore leaving, turn the detail strip wheel . . . and when you return, turn it again, and when the strip is taken off at night, the amounts registered between the blank spaces, will be the amounts registered during your absence." As Blood's sales book indicates and Jacob Miller's and Barr and Company's experiences show, merchants found fresh ways to extract new and different information from their registers that could be used to coordinate and control their operations as never before. The cash register gave structure to the kind of casual observations grocers typically made about customers and sales trends.[38]

Just as nineteenth-century big business benefited and prospered with systematized accounting procedures, so too did small businessmen. Storekeepers began to shift retail enterprise away from observed idiosyncrasy—the "dull" times Maine grocer Edmund Fuller recorded in his diary, for example—toward mechanized rationality. Those who employed cash registers and advanced accounting measures started to differentiate themselves from others who operated on a subsistence or marginal level, covering expenses (or falling short) without gauging overall profitability. Even if not all fully understood or exploited the machine-generated figures and information they now had at their fingertips, rational calculation, as Max Weber explained in his theory of economic organization, nevertheless oriented merchants to think more cogently about prices, competition, and costs, and to expect profits from commercial endeavors, whether large or small. This was the method Andrew Schoch employed to build his St. Paul, Minnesota, grocery business from its 1874 origins in a one-room building to a four-story emporium, utilizing both cash registers and bookkeepers to manage accounts as the firm grew. By 1890, Schoch's registers chronicled customer transactions and his bookkeepers and ledgers tracked accounts in each of his store's multiple departments in addition to capital stock, merchandise, movables and fixtures, insurance, cash, salaries, engine room, freight and cartage, stable [delivery horses], postage, advertising, interest, notes received, notes payable, expenses, discounts, and profits and losses. Fierce competition combined with Schoch's extensive retail and wholesale dealings prompted greater oversight and coordination within his organization in much the same way as the nation's large industrial firms.[39]

The kind of detailed information Schoch and other grocers gathered and recorded oriented their business methods toward profitability and greater

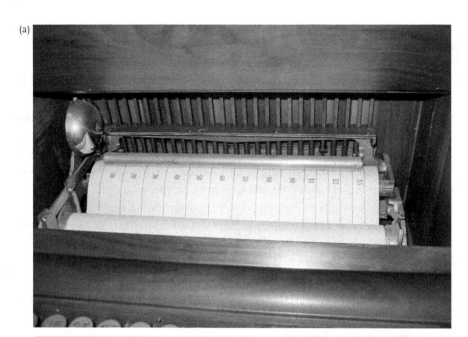

Both the paper adder (top) and self-adder (bottom) enabled grocers to track daily or hourly sales in their shops. The paper adder offered the extra benefit of maintaining a permanent (if rudimentary) record of transactions. Author's photographs, courtesy NCR Archive at Dayton History.

efficiency, instincts historians attribute primarily to the era's industrial manufacturing firms. Yet retailers purposefully tinkered with NCR's standard machines to process more and better information to rationalize their operations, pushing the machine's design functions beyond basic theft and cash controls. NCR salesman Joseph Crane emphasized this innovativeness in his sales pitch. "Now, we have improved this machine from time to time," Crane apprised potential purchasers, "and the suggestions . . . had almost invariably come from parties using the Register." Crediting storekeepers in 1887 for suggesting "improvements that would be advantageous," he specifically plugged the company's self-adder because retailers in fact had helped bring it about. Crane intimated that while the paper-adder's permanent transaction record provided "a splendid check on the business," storekeepers found counting perforations to be laborious and time consuming. Using a register, Crane quoted retail users, "would be much more convenient if . . . counting the holes in the paper be done away with," a problem the self-adder's more efficient mechanical calculations solved.[40]

In a period when independent inventors like Thomas Edison and Alexander Graham Bell thrived and corporations like NCR were just beginning to establish research and development laboratories, technology users comprised an integral part of the invention process. The first grocers to purchase and use cash registers formed a crucial component in NCR's "experimental" model of product development, popular in the absence of more formal engineering and testing procedures. While John Patterson established an in-house "Inventions Department" in 1888, one of the first corporate research facilities he nevertheless encouraged his men to address customer concerns first. The cash register's development mimicked that of the typewriter and tabulating machines, office technologies that benefited from the collaborative process of co-evolution that brought together manufacturers, engineers, and industry users in a reciprocal exchange of ideas. Yet whereas the nineteenth century's biggest insurance firms pushed for changes in punch card systems and tabulating equipment, it was the era's smallest retailers who drove cash register innovation. They communicated their demands to NCR salesmen who visited their shops, to company engineers through letters, and to each other in over-the-counter conversations. "Through [their] needs and suggestions," claimed editor and NCR biographer Isaac F. Marcosson, storekeepers, clerks, and cashiers became "arbiters of machine development."[41]

Nowhere was users' influence more prominent than in the register's keyboard, the primary apparatus for inputting information. Finding that NCR's

standard keyboards did not suit their purposes, many requested modifications. NCR accommodated these changes as part of the invention process and
because they required minor adjustments from a manufacturing standpoint;
the basic function of the machine remained relatively unaffected. Of the 199
cash registers grocers ordered from NCR between 1885 and 1887, sixty-one
(30 percent) included user-requested variations that deviated from the company's basic keyboards, on par with the 32 percent of similarly altered registers
ordered among all trades. The alterations grocers requested indicate that they
were knowledgeable about the fundamentals of information processing and
recognized that the data they extracted from the machine was only as useful
as the information that they and their employees entered.[42]

In 1887, when Carl E. York ordered his cash register, the New Hampshire
grocer was decidedly particular about how he wanted the keyboard configured. York's "well ordered grocery store" featured a range of products,
including the "best brands of flour, sugars, teas, coffees, spices, soap, table
salt, etc., canned goods in great variety, finest creamery and dairy butter,
eggs, and cheese," and featured "all modern conveniences" for butchering
an assortment of meats. Conferring with an NCR agent, York requested
that the upper row of keys on his machine include a few dollar denominations, including a $20, $9, and $3 key, along with others running from
eighty cents to a penny. On the lower row, York demanded additional dollar amounts, such as a $30 and a $2 key, along with some uncommon cent
denominations, including a ninety-cent and two-cent key. The arrangement
was far from typical, with the grocer ordering more dollar keys than most
in addition to forgoing keys that registered in five-cent increments, such as
fifty-five or seventy-five cents, typical on most machines. The changes likely
reflected York's desire to systematize his stocks and pricing, enabling the
grocer to track the sale of specially priced goods as he might have done with
his $7 and $9 keys. In suggesting these fundamental changes, York began
the work of learning more about his business than a standard machine
would have allowed.[43]

The seemingly simple changes York and others requested were small
in nature, but monumental in impact. After all, the innovativeness of these
merchants accelerated the cash register's evolution along with retail information processing, giving small businessmen newfound authority over both the
design and function of a core technology and business method. Not until the
mid-1890s would "sectional adders" or "department cash registers" be able to
total sales for two different categories of goods or operators. Register manufacturers such as the Chicago Cash Register Company and Boston Cash Indicator
and Recorder Company, along with NCR, introduced models used by bankers

and other businesses where coordinating multiple trade lines and money exchanges was desirable. In the ten-year lag between the launch of NCR's earliest machines and these more advanced technologies, retailers had to brainstorm their own solutions.[44]

One variation grocers found particularly useful in this regard was the addition of a "blank" key. This modest alteration gave operators tremendous flexibility in registering transactions by allowing them to record any operation designated by the storekeeper. Ohio grocers Barr and Company, for example, asked NCR to fit their keyboard with a "blank key on end, omitting 55¢ key." This small change enabled the men to differentiate transactions and potentially flag the "fifty different payments for produce" they rang up shortly after receiving their machine. Grocer Lemuel Ergood substituted a blank key for the standard 85¢ key, a denomination the grocer apparently had little use for in his Washington, DC, shop. Ergood may have instructed his clerks to depress it whenever they enacted a credit transaction or possibly sold discounted soap, marking these exchanges for future evaluation. However Ergood used the key, he knew enough about his business to recognize that he had no need to register eighty-five cents and that he could benefit from information supplied by a blank key.

In short order, some user demands became accepted standards. By 1888, retailers along the West Coast and throughout the Southwest adopted one common key substitution. Writing to NCR, one Texas firm directed the company to send them a model No. 3, but requested the "95c tablet [indicator] and key check changed to word 'chg'd'[charged]." As the merchants understood it, this modification would "indicate a credit sale for each time of opening on that key, instead of 95c cash, thereby keeping a record of the number of credit sales made." This change was "known as the 'Pierce System,'" according to the firm's note, named for NCR traveling agent William Pierce, who maintained a cash register store in Oakland, California. The alteration associated with Pierce's name probably originated with the salesman's customers, who wanted a way to track credit sales but found no solution in NCR's typical key configurations or operations. Word about the modification had spread from Pierce's region all the way to Texas, either through the salesman himself or by word of mouth.[45]

Active shapers of retail technology, small retailers also took the lead in rationalizing methods. Indeed, the Texas retailer's order reveals in part the beginning of a collective language built around both the cash register and a simple substitution others found useful. When existing technology failed to address a need (in this case, the inability to tally charges), users suggested a mutually beneficial solution, thus shaping standardization of both the method and the machine. Collaboration between producers and users exemplifies the modernization process, where storekeepers were co-makers of a technologically enhanced and increasingly rationalized business system. It was a development that benefited both producer and user, expanding market acceptance of the cash register by adapting it to fit user-defined needs. In the space between adoption and use, innovation and standardization coexisted and thrived.[46]

The irony of these developments, however, is that while store owners asserted control over the technology, their clerks lost ground as skilled workers. Fine-tuning registers streamlined transaction inputs and accelerated over-the-counter exchanges much as mass production techniques sped manufacturing. Clerks now punched register keys instead of scribing passbooks to tally customer sales, deskilling counterwork and cutting transaction processing costs in the process. As a result, female cashiers (typically young and single) began replacing trained male bookkeepers. This is what happened in one Illinois grocery store, when Miss Emma Waterman was installed as cashier after bookkeeper James Farrell left in October 1887 following two years' employment. Nationwide between 1880 and 1900, the number of female cashiers (retail and otherwise) grew four times faster than did male cashiers, as new technology and sales methods opened doors to women clerical workers, most visibly in the cities' large department stores. The transition to female cashiers, however, limited male clerks' opportunities to rise through the ranks and become partners or proprietors, narrowing the pathway to independence through business ownership. It was a profound transformation experienced by retail enterprises large and small, as machines increasingly mediated clerks' headwork.[47]

Despite these effects, many of the innovative modifications grocers suggested became de rigueur on cash registers and as practice in retail shops. Tracking sales in individual departments, registering credit transactions, and recording hourly receipts developed in tandem with storekeepers' desire to learn more about their stores and their businesses. So too did the 1886 inclusion of easy-to-read indicator tabs that popped up whenever a clerk pressed a register key. A store owner could see from across the sales floor whether a clerk had registered the correct purchase amount by reading the tab. Thus the practice and culture of "keeping tabs" on transactions was born. These modifications elevated grocers' knowledge not only about their own trade but also of how machines could systematize their everyday business routines. From their vantage point as cash register users, storekeepers, in conversation with NCR agents and other register owners, had begun the hard work of sorting out how technological innovations such as the register could enhance long-standing methods and restructure retail trade.[48]

The Pursuit of Retail Technology and Expertise

While word of the cash register's attributes certainly circulated among its users, NCR relied in large part on advertising and its agents to educate consumers about the machine. In time, the firm employed an army of professional salesmen, one of the largest in corporate America. In its first few years, however, only ten men hit the road, supported by a small number of others who set up shops to demonstrate and distribute registers. Together, they offered limited territorial coverage. By 1888, for example, NCR had established agents in only thirty-four cities across the country. Yet the year before, the company had sold registers to merchants in various trades in thirty-seven of the nation's thirty-eight states (along with the majority of recognized territories and several foreign countries). John H. Patterson's print advertising and relentless direct mail campaigns (he claimed to have started by sending advertisements to the same five thousand merchants for eighteen straight days) no doubt addressed gaps in neglected regions, spreading word and information about the cash register. There were many, however, who never received leaflets or calls from NCR salesmen and had to find out about the machine in other ways.[49]

In the absence of a barrage of direct mail or agents, grocers set out on their own to learn what they could about the device. "Some time ago I saw an advertisement in your paper in regard to a cash register," Oliver Collins, a Gloversville, New York, storekeeper wrote to *American Grocer* in 1886. Proprietor of "one of the neatest, best ordered and most popular grocery establishments" in town, Collins's well-appointed store was "tastefully fitted up and admirably kept." Outwardly, he appeared to have things in check; internally, though, Collins struggled. Credit agents noted in 1879 his reputation for slow bill payment and "loose way of d[oin]g business." In 1885, he was (like many) encumbered with debts, having assigned nearly $250 in customer claims to collection agents, factors that may have prompted Collins's interest in instituting mechanical controls over his cash and trade. Keen to add a cash register to his operation, the storekeeper inquired of editors, "If you will please inform me at [sic] the one you think is the best you will greatly oblige." Collins may have remembered an 1884 National Manufacturing Company (predecessor to NCR) advertisement, the first to appear in *American Grocer*. The half-page testimonial espoused the machine's benefits to the trade, drawing on the words of

NATIONAL CASH REGISTER.

A complete line of Registers can be seen at our Show Rooms, 15 Bible House, New York.

REGISTERS SOLD ON TRIAL.

WM. L. JONES, Agt.

NATIONAL MANUFACTURING COMPANY, DAYTON, OHIO.

Price List at Factory, $40.00 to $150.00.

TRY HARVEST HOME BREAD PREPARATION—IT IS GUARANTEED IN EVERY WAY.

This National Manufacturing Company (precursor to NCR) advertisement likely introduced Oliver Collins and countless other grocers to the machine. NCR early on became one of the nation's most prolific advertisers, establishing an in-house printing operation in 1887 to service its direct-mail campaigns. *American Grocer* 31, no. 1 (January 3, 1884), 39.

well-known Cincinnati grocer Joseph R. Peebles, who proclaimed the machine "an assistance to the cashier and [a] great drawback to pilfering." Peebles himself installed several NCR's models in his two stores, making him at the time the Midwest city's largest and most prominent user.[50]

Collins's approach was not unique. More than one quarter of the registers sold to grocers appearing in the NCR ledger traded hands without the assistance of a salesman. The company inadvertently tracked this information, with bookkeepers making note of whether an agent had sold the machine and therefore deserved a commission. They recorded the salesman's name along with his take from the transaction, varying anywhere from 20 to 50 percent of net price, depending on machine, payment type, or negotiations. If no salesman assisted with the sale, bookkeepers documented the agent as "himself" or "themselves," referring to the merchant or partners who placed the order. Of the 199 registers NCR sold to grocers, fifty exchanged hands without benefit of a salesman. Among the first of these buyers was Edward H. Bouton, known later for his involvement with designing Baltimore's Roland Park planned community, among others. In April 1885, though, a twenty-five-year-old Bouton and business partner ran a Kansas City, Missouri, grocery store. The firm ordered its register (requesting custom keyboard configuration) just four months after NCR had started production, placing the grocers among the most dogged technology adopters. It was a pattern Bouton repeated throughout his life, becoming a pioneer in orchestrating several of the nation's streetcar suburbs. In the meantime, he was just one of many small retailers who did not wait for innovation to come calling.[51]

Some who placed their own orders came from locations NCR salesmen rarely (if ever) visited. William V. McQuaid was the first Iowan and only businessman in Creston to purchase a register during NCR's early years, doubtlessly making both him and his machine noteworthy in that small town. McQuaid certainly drew more attention when he installed a second one in his grocery store just a few months after the first. NCR salesmen appear to have bypassed the rural outpost initially, choosing instead to make their way to larger cities such as Des Moines, approximately seventy miles southwest of Creston. McQuaid's small-town ambitions outpaced those of many big-city retailers, prompting him to seek the cash register for his business well before other area merchants. Retail grocers' persistent efforts to employ cash registers account in part for the machine's rapid dissemination and use on local, national, and international levels relatively early in its production.[52]

McQuaid's determination is perhaps even more noteworthy given the general lack of register owners in his region. Many, after all, learned about the machine only after talking with another user or seeing it in a merchant's shop, with business and oral networks helping to sell the device and its benefits. Henry French permitted NCR agent William Pierce to invite potential purchasers to his California shop, undeniably for a price concession. Pierce encouraged interested parties to watch NCR's latest machine "on exhibition" at French's grocery store in downtown San Jose. Such efforts not only helped disseminate knowledge but they also improved sales by bridging advertising's limitations and salesmen's territorial boundaries. In the months following installation of Hannah and Hogg's first register, NCR logged orders from several other area bar owners for machines configured "same as H & Hogg." When word spread about the Chicago saloonkeepers' machine, competing merchants had stopped in to talk with bartenders about its operation and to see the device at work. As a result, Hannah and Hogg's technological know-how quickly became a benchmark for others looking to keep pace with or surpass the city's leading saloonkeepers. Keen competition helped drive diffusion and innovation, as merchants fought for the technological and informational edge.[53]

Experienced users in particular asserted their mastery over the machine by boasting about their conquests. This was the case with Iowa grocer Robert Schroeder, whose Sabula store sat just one block from the Mississippi River. Beginning in 1886, one year after buying his first register, he penned what would become an annual letter to NCR relating his experiences. Schroeder first became aware of the machine through NCR's advertisements, and he "had often thought of inquiring into the merits of the system." In October 1885, "after thinking over the matter carefully," he took the initiative and ordered one for his store without consulting a salesman, hoping it would replace his "old method" of paper checks. Schroeder's initial reports credited his cherry-cabinet Model No. 3 (fitted with a standard keyboard) for conditioning his clerks to feel "anxious that the Cash Register shall come out right" and "ashamed" when they gave incorrect change. The grocer nevertheless claimed, "the clerks feel better over the new system." Proclaiming "all has been changed" since installing the device, Schroeder declared it "perfect in every respect," content to defer to the machine's operations instead of his own acumen.[54]

In short order, however, the storekeeper grew more confident in his technological knowledge. When Schroeder ordered a second machine two years later, he modified the device to fit his practices instead of reforming his clerks to fit the machine. This time he added "as an accommodation" a "No Sale" key for making change, with the understanding that it would count "the number of times change was made during the day." Not long after buying the second register, Schroeder bragged that the 3 percent in net profits he saw in 1884 and 1885 had in 1886 grown to 8 percent on trade he claimed was $45,000 to $60,000 yearly. "Now, while I do not say that the register has directly made me over $2,000 a year," the grocer concluded, "I feel sure that I have saved more than that amount every year by the order and system the register has brought to my store." Five years as a cash register user made Schroeder confident enough to crow in 1890 that he could explain the cash register's operations and benefits "as well as anybody." By 1892, Schroeder informed NCR that he had retired from business, having "set my stake at a certain amount" and "finally arrived there safely." In six short years, the grocer had conquered both the machine and the methods.[55]

Schroeder's path was one of several that cash register users pursued toward becoming experts. Some took a more assertive approach by selling the device on consignment, serving as surrogate salesmen. In the absence of comprehensive sales networks, NCR early on looked to business users to educate and inform others about the machine and how it worked. John Patterson likely drew inspiration for the scheme from his agents, several of whom purchased registers on consignment in addition to selling them on commission. Company bookkeepers distinguished between registers that salesmen bought on consignment for up to a 50-percent discount and those they sold on standard commission. Consignment sales enabled salesmen and business users alike to make up to $100 per machine, if they sold it for full price. In those early days, some nearly five hundred registers shipped on consignment to agents and businesses nationwide. In February 1885, the self-described "enterprising house" of Bovie, Pitrat, and Company bought one register for use in its Gallipolis, Ohio, grocery store, paying nearly full price for the device. One month later, the owners took a second on consignment, paying only $100 of the $200 original cost. These ambitious retailers were not alone; business users from many different trades including saloonkeepers, hardware men, druggists, and dry goods dealers purchased approximately 20 percent of all consignment machines in NCR's first two years. Business owners enthusiastic to sell cash registers enabled the technology (and its corresponding methods) to spread faster and at greater distances than it might have otherwise.[56]

Consignment selling was especially important in the register's first days as Patterson and NCR agents worked to legitimize the machine's use in retail environments. Business users willing to sell other merchants on the machine's benefits advanced this task in ways that salesmen's hotel pitches could not. Grocers and other consignment sellers employed their machines as demonstrative advertisements, exhibiting their function within a working environment where they could talk up the register's advantages and shortcomings with authority. This innovative strategy doubtlessly carried more weight with potential purchasers who sometimes viewed traveling salesmen with skepticism and suspicion, eliminating the kind of practiced arguments NCR agents deployed to counter reticent buyers.[57]

New Jersey grocer Charles F. Eastlack and his family were among the first business users to recognize opportunity in consignment selling. The thirty-nine-year-old Eastlack moved to Camden in the 1870s, where both he and his brother James Rufus Eastlack opened separate retail stores in the city. Locals credited Charles with operating the city's first grocery chain, comprised of three stores by 1887, with credit agents noting he was "continually running it out at low prices" and "does not accumulate old stock." Rufus (as he was known), was no laggard, however. Credit reports cited his "quite large" stock and "good business," which was "conducted on a cash basis." Between 1900 and 1901, Rufus expanded his operation, building what some considered "four of the largest stores in Camden." Innovators in both organizational style and business methods, the Eastlacks early on established themselves as trade leaders with Rufus becoming the state's first cash register owner and user, with his brother following closely behind. In late February 1885, Rufus requisitioned a Model 3 ½ walnut machine, NCR bookkeepers noting, "this for his own use." Over the course of the year, the family placed orders for a combined seventeen cash registers, with Rufus alone purchasing five on consignment. Yet together the brothers owned only four stores in 1885; clearly the twosome (especially Rufus) had something more than just a casual interest in the newfangled machine.[58]

In fact, it seems that the Eastlacks had a penchant for all types of mechanical devices. Charles fancied himself an inventor having earned a patent in 1868 for a platform-triggered pump that delivered water to cattle. In the early 1900s, his son and eventual business partner Oscar became the first person in Camden to own an automobile, a one-cylinder, fire-engine-red vehicle he enjoyed racing across the city's cobblestoned streets. Oscar, like his father, relished tinkering, adding both a rumble seat and homemade steering wheel to his stick-driven Bush motorcar. Rufus perhaps saw in the cash register an occasion to match his relatives' mechanical prowess by becoming both a user and supplier of modern technological devices and knowledge. It was a position credit agents noticed in 1889, reporting that Eastlack possessed $4,500 in fixtures in his two stores, along with fifteen horses and wagons, an elevator, and steam heating. Eastlack's "extensive outlay of cash in improvements" and his enthusiasm for new technologies branded him a "very enterprising" businessman.[59]

Rufus was committed to his new role as the town's cash register expert and salesman. In March 1885, he spent $40 on a three-key sample, a small apparatus NCR agents took door to door demonstrating the cash register's inner workings instead of carting along a full-sized machine. Enclosed in a nondescript leather case (Patterson insisted it have no identifying company marks), the three-key sample's pocket-sized dimensions enabled salesmen to slip past suspicious clerks and store owners who steeled themselves against agents toting massive wood and glass cabinets. In addition to Eastlack, a handful of other non-NCR agents purchased the apparatus; not coincidentally, they too ordered a number of consignment registers. For the New Jersey grocer, though, the three-key sample signaled his role as a surrogate NCR salesman, a small business owner who declared himself an authority on technology. Selling registers from his retail enterprise, Eastlack benefited by dealing with buyers as a kindred business spirit, not as a corporate salesman. Over the course of two years, he moved all five consignment machines. Eastlack's was a limited, but important endeavor that enabled him and other storekeepers to spread modern methods nationwide.[60]

Small operators like Rufus Eastlack, along with others who first used and sold cash registers, were central figures in a business culture that increasingly placed a premium on ingenuity and technological know-how. With inventors being heralded as national heroes, men who held the future in their minds and hands, those who could demonstrate and teach others how to use the latest mechanical devices became local heroes, praiseworthy counterparts to innovators like Edison and Bell. Their early adoption of the cash register and willingness to tinker with the technology, adapting it to existing practices while innovating new and routine methods, paved the way for later systematic management applications that further modernized retail trade in all lines.[61]

Systematizing the Trade

When grocers first began installing cash registers in the 1880s, few sensed that a larger control revolution was under way, save John Carson's prophetic statement. Yet by 1896 the trade journal *New England Grocer* could boast, "Retail merchants will be interested to know that during the past twelve years they have purchased and paid for 109,000 National Cash Registers," a figure that included thousands of small grocers. By 1902, NCR offered a wider range of options on its machines that expanded the register's informational possibilities and assisted merchants in tracking individual transactions, customer counts, detailed sales, and cumulative totals for individual clerks and departments with the push of a button. Writing to NCR that same year, Joseph Campbell, manager for a Logan, Utah, grocery company, noted that the register his firm purchased "helped us to systematize our business," thanks to the six cash drawers (one for each clerk), receipt-printing mechanism, and multiple department keys.[62]

From its initial potential as a way to stop thieving clerks and institute basic accounting controls, the cash register evolved into a machine capable of producing multiple measures of productivity and systemization, reducing transaction costs, and streamlining accounting. The real promise of the machine, then, lay in its ability to transform the ledger-and-daybook method of accounting into a mechanized and standardized system of checks and balances on storekeepers, clerks, and customers. In 1893, when New York grocer Herman Cordts bought his register in the hope of getting "more detail" about his business, systematic management had just begun to make its mark on retail trade. Venturesome grocers, with the aid of their registers, were key factors in aligning the technological facets of systematic management with its informational aspects, laying the foundation for the incorporation of these new methods among all retailers.[63]

In this way, small grocers began standardizing retail trade long before chain stores' vertical integration and cost accounting practices took hold. The men who first purchased cash registers created methods that regularized cash and credit transactions. For every merchant who customized his keyboard or changed the way his register recorded information, countless others benefited by instituting techniques tried and refined by small business users. The democratizing influence of the cash register extended as much to retail transactions as it did the modernization of the grocery trade. Storekeepers making $500 a year had access to and could use the same retail technology as the merchant making $45,000, redrawing the boundaries of who was a "modern" businessman to encompass both small and large retail firms.

The small changes grocers made to both to the machine and their methods were important in challenging prevailing ideas about how capitalism and retailing should proceed. Not all agreed that mechanized transactions would reshape the trade, but many found in the cash register new authority over their businesses and their futures. That future, however, depended not only on regulating accounting transactions but also on interpersonal relationships between proprietor, clerk, and customer. In 1916, when Tennessee grocer Clarence Saunders filed for patent protection on his "self-serving store" design, the innovator and founder of Piggly Wiggly made the cash register an integral part of his plan. All sales, Saunders suggested, would be "recorded on the cash register before the purchaser passes through the exit and ... leaves the store." Emphasizing his point, Saunders made certain to include the device in his application's schematic drawing.[64]

In the nearly forty years between invention of the cash register and Clarence Saunders's patented selling scheme, retailers continued working from inside their stores accumulating, analyzing, and exploiting information to help them transform the trade. Wholesalers, meanwhile, looked outward for better ways to collect intelligence on and coordinate sales between them and the thousands of small grocers scattered far and wide who solicited their credit and goods. Where machines helped retailers control their operations, wholesalers found innovative solutions in old-fashioned manpower. Traveling salesmen became "the line of communication," as a retired roadman put it in 1875, "the telegraph between the manufacturer, importer and wholesale dealer and their customers." Their duty was not only to sell goods "but also to find out the reliability and financial standing of the business men throughout this vast country." They picked up where credit and collection agents left off, digging into back rooms and bank accounts to get the financial scoop on a man, while also seeking his friendship and confidence in the interest of writing an order. What resulted was a modern system that knitted together the web of producers, distributors, and retailers who made up the grocery trade. In the last quarter of the nineteenth century, traveling men and the paths they beat made old lines of business more efficient and new methods more imaginable.[65]

3

Trust Brokers on the Road

In December 1890, when Samuel Iseman stopped in Sumter, South Carolina, he hoped to turn his luck around. The traveling grocery salesman's trip so far had not gone well. Rain had delayed his train by two hours. When Iseman finally arrived, he had time to "drum" up business with only one retailer before drying off and retiring for the evening. The next day was no better; his expense money was dangerously low. He dunned two area merchants for payment on their accounts, eager to refill his coffers, but received only the runaround for his efforts. He checked in on groceryman (and postmaster) Moses W. Harrell in nearby Timmonsville, who made good his account, with one exception. The grocer took issue with a recent delivery of hams that had come from Iseman's Charleston wholesale firm, 120 miles south. Harrell complained to Iseman that the hams were of poor quality and that he had sold only two or three. He asked for a refund. The traveling man felt badly that Harrell had taken the meat because Iseman had talked it up. When the hams failed to satisfy, both the salesman's word and the confidence he had earned were on the line.[1]

Grocery salesmen gathered and processed information and personal knowledge about customers in a time when new information systems, intended to address imperfect markets, created conditions in which some businessmen had greater access than others to financial and trade knowledge used in decision making. One effect was a shifting in the delicate balance between interpersonal and institutionalized mechanisms in judging creditworthiness. Salesmen combined the familiarity of face-to-face meetings with different standards for judging creditworthiness (and other methods of information gathering and reporting) to cultivate commercial intimacy and build networks among strangers. As a result, traveling men expanded the reach of wholesale grocers and the market by drawing on elements of the established order to lay the foundations for a modern grocery distribution network.[2]

As antiquated as men like Samuel Iseman may seem, they were not the peddlers of days past, who drifted from town to town eager to make any and all deals; nor were they the practiced and corporate-trained men who sold office machines in typically one-off transactions. Men who sustained repeat trade had a greater stake in building and maintaining trusted distribution and trade networks than most itinerate grips or manufacturers' agents. Three factors distinguished the fly-by-night from those with regular routes: the middleman functions of grocery wholesalers and their salesmen, the methods by which traveling grocery salesmen built and maintained trade networks, and the grocery trade's training and retention of its commercial travelers.[3]

In some ways, these differences make the grocery trade unique in its composition and operation. By 1900, many consumer goods industries had replaced middlemen and wholesalers' traveling salesmen by incorporating the distribution function in-house through vertical integration, as did the rubber boot and shoes and collars and cuffs trades. The grocery business's decentralized structure, combined with the wide variety of products it handled, dictated a response different from that of many other distribution trades, but it was still comparable to other wholesaler-dependent lines such as pharmaceuticals and hardware. Some large food-processing firms like the National Biscuit Company integrated selling and distribution to address specific product-related problems, but most food manufacturers continued to depend on wholesalers and their salesmen to move and market their goods. As a result, independent grocery wholesalers and their traveling salesmen persisted well into the twentieth century alongside centralized grocery chains. Their interrelationships allowed for economies of scope, maximizing factory output in the absence of scale economies and enabling manufacturers' large product lines to find a broad spectrum of local and regional outlets. Traveling agents' profoundly personal efforts to build sales networks may appear outmoded, but their methods reflected the most efficient way to move groceries in an industry that for much of its history did not support large, centralized operations. Even the Great Atlantic and Pacific Tea Company, the trade's chain store leader, did not vertically integrate until around 1920.[4]

Traveling salesmen worked for wholesale grocers on salary or commission, selling and supplying goods to retail dealers. They spelled out sales terms, fostered collaborative commercial and informational networks, and made promises and guarantees as to the creditworthiness, character, and reliability of both their wholesale house and the retail storekeepers they visited. Some worked solely for food manufacturers, distributing packaged and branded products without going through a middleman wholesaler. Another class of salesmen sold manufacturers' goods on commission directly to consumers. Still others operated as independent agents, brokering deals between importers and distributors for large quantities of manufactured goods stored in dockside warehouses, train depots, or commercial ships. Each performed a particular function and service within the grocery trade. They were, as one contemporary wrote in 1890, "the backbone and sinews of our commercial growth."[5]

The support and muscle grocery wholesalers provided allowed them to manage the many product lines retailers carried in their stores, breaking down manufacturers' large lots into the smaller quantities demanded by individual retailers. One business veteran, looking back in 1903, remarked: "Why, twenty-five or thirty years ago a wholesale grocer didn't handle over 150 or 200 items. We have about 2,000 in our stock book to-day." Most food manufacturers shrank from taking on the labor- and cost-intensive tasks of selling, shipping, billing, and collecting payment for small orders from a fragmented retail sector. The Boston cocoa and chocolate manufacturers Walter Baker and Company and Walter M. Lowney Company claimed well into the 1910s that "the cost of distributing our grocery articles direct to the retail dealer would be very considerable." Wholesalers and their traveling salesmen assumed the overhead costs and time associated with warehousing and distribution, giving retail grocers centralized access to thousands of articles from multiple manufacturing firms. They were the best (and arguably the only) way to surmount the grocery trade's distribution, marketing, and information hurdles and bind together wholesalers, retailers, and traveling salesmen in the making of both the American mass market and a modern industry.[6]

From Street Corners to Regular Routes

In the days when Daniel Brown and John Burrows packed off to New Orleans and others made their way to East Coast commercial centers to replenish supplies, set up future contracts, and arrange shipping terms, major port cities served as distribution hubs, with wholesale and commercial houses dominating wharf districts. These concerns supplied most of the nation's food needs, filling warehouses with domestic and imported goods they sold and delivered to retailers. Once in the city, country merchants typically found themselves surrounded by salesmen who sang out from street corners the praises of their employers' stock and trade. Drummers (so-called because they "drummed up" business) first appeared in the 1830s and 1840s along busy wharf districts. The act of "drumming" linked urban wholesalers specifically to out-of-town merchants. Marked as rubes, rural buyers were assumed to be more easily swayed by the shrewd and savvy pitchmen who fought for their attention.[7]

Drummers used all means possible to draw in new customers, including polished sales pitches, offers of fancy dinners, and cut-rate prices. Once hooked, prospective clients were whisked away to the nearest hotel, where managers rented selling space to wholesalers displaying their wares. Sample rooms, as they were known, served as temporary showrooms where pitchmen demonstrated their products, rehearsed their sales spiels, haggled over prices, and locked up trade. The atmosphere was competitive and chaotic. Drummers eagerly baited dealers away from rival pushers in their efforts to mark an order. Good bargains trumped good manners, and allegedly slick salesmen lured out-of-town merchants with their showmanship as much as with their sales knowledge.[8]

Not surprisingly, such scenes prompted popular and trade press depictions of the street-corner hawker as both a hazard and a nuisance. One mid-nineteenth-century observer declared drumming "neither very modest nor very dignified." Sundry and wholesale merchants shelled out excessive sums of money "paying for wine, oyster-suppers, theatre tickets, and such other means of conciliating the favor of the country merchant." Concerns about such practices prompted editors at *Hunt's Merchants' Magazine* in 1855 to caution readers, "The easiest persons to be drummed are those who have nothing to lose."[9] Clever pitches and false promises could sway only insolvents, sapheads, and other ignorant men, as *Hunt's* saw it. In the telling, a backwater storekeeper on the lookout for a too-good-to-be-true bargain became a huckster's willing victim.[10]

Yet what *Hunt's* and others failed to see was that behind the bedlam and apparent free-for-all of commercial trade centers, urban wholesalers and rural retailers came together, uniting two distinct but interrelated markets. In the crush of wagons, goods, and hawkers, drummers and merchants formed the nascent beginnings of what would become at first a regional and eventually a nationwide distribution and marketing system. These mercantile relationships generated social capital that traveling grocery salesmen would draw on to fashion synthetic networks of unrelated merchants and businessmen with common goals. Economic growth magnified drummers' cries but did not drown out capitalism's pastoral roots in personal connections.[11]

Those early networks grew in the last quarter of the nineteenth century thanks to advancements in transportation and communications technologies. Increased competition arose as midwestern wholesale houses emerged and retailers sprang up in the territory between these and eastern distribution hubs. Trades with product-specific distribution challenges such as unpreserved or heavy goods saw the appearance of wholesalers in frontier cities sooner than in other trades. Retail grocers likewise moved farther inland and away from urban distribution hubs as ice-cooled refrigerated cars—like those Jacob Buckley used to ship his eggs to New York—sent food to and from remote retail outposts. *American Grocer* reported in 1871 that "country merchants throughout the Northwest have not only found out that Chicago is the place to buy, but that they can order goods, and get what they order." The geographic complexities of the expanding grocery trade challenged wholesalers to devise new ways of identifying and judging as creditworthy the far-flung merchants who sought their products.[12]

The traveling grocery salesman was born. Drummers took to the road in growing numbers shortly after the Civil War to pitch wholesalers' goods to merchants who no longer visited commercial centers. Prominent New York City grocery wholesaler Horace K. Thurber was among the first to try this new way of selling in 1870. He employed drummers from his own firm as traveling agents, putting "two practiced and competent salesmen 'on the road.'" That same year, a New Orleans observer noted an influx of "mercantile representatives sent out from the Northern States to exhibit samples and solicit orders in the South," a system the author acknowledged as "long known and universally employed in Europe." Even if the traveling salesman was not a uniquely American creation, his rise to prominence certainly drew attention. An *American Grocer* contributor speculated in the 1870s that New York's burgeoning traveling man population was "said to be 25,000 drummers sent out of this city alone," with "every wholesale house in every city of the country represented by one or more in this great army."[13]

Among those wholesale houses experimenting with this new form of selling was Austin, Nichols, and Company. One of New York's earliest and largest grocery wholesalers, the firm focused its initial efforts on securing rural trade, drawing on relationships it had cultivated since the company's founding in 1855. When the partners shifted from in-house selling efforts and dispatched salesmen sometime in the late 1860s, they hoped to capitalize on these "earlier connections" and "wider acquaintances among country merchants" as a way to "till the old soil and now and then to break new ground." In short order they formed networks with merchants in New England, Pennsylvania, Ohio, and as far away as Michigan and locations in the South. Going after trade, they deemed, was the "only one practical way of getting business." They reinforced their market relationships by having salesmen and company managers make "frequent personal visits . . . in this way cementing by bonds of sentiment that which had been won by industry and merit." Here then were indispensable elements for cultivating commercial intimacy and advancing trade in the nineteenth century.[14]

The business card of Austin, Nichols & Co. traveling salesman Walter M. Smith, about 1890. Smith was one of many intermediaries who brought together rural grocers and city wholesalers in commercial relationships. Author's collection.

The transition from drummers to traveling salesmen, however, was not without its difficulties. Merchants immediately began to question commercial agents' value and methods, with many declaring them insufferable and their approach a burden. In 1871, a series of articles, editorials, and letters in *American Grocer* raised the question, "Does it Pay to Employ 'Drummers?'" Where some thought them indispensable for moving goods, others raised "very serious objections to 'drumming' for trade," as their method of selling "so often gives rise to dissatisfaction on the part of the buyer." The journal accused travelers of "inducing a man against his own judgment to overstock his store . . . ruining the buyer and entailing severe losses upon the seller." The same cautionary tales that warned of rubes swayed by city street-corner drummers were reworked to make shopkeepers victims in their own stores. In the retelling, roadmen now had opportunity to commit more invasive transgressions, crossing the threshold to breach a man's business and his community.[15]

American Grocer alerted proprietors to these over-aggressive salesmen. "We have heard country merchants say that in one day they have been visited by a dozen different 'drummers' and importuned, and begged, and implored to give an order." According to the account, the sales-hungry and desperate agent held merchants captive until they conceded to buy whatever he pushed. Traveling men's assertive sales tactics may have galled grocers and trade journal editors, yet they were not unlike the hard-hitting methods later employed in the office machine, steel, and manufactured food industries, where the science of "salesmanship" thrived in the early twentieth century. What irritated storekeepers was not that salesmen pressed them but that their persuasive pitches had swayed merchants to buy more than they intended. A rural trader duped in the big city elicited sympathy; a businessman blandished in his own shop evoked scorn.[16]

Some called for abolishing drumming in "the best interests of the trade both wholesale and retail." One former Boston traveling man affirmed, "In many stores, over the counting room door, may be seen these words: 'We have no time to devote to 'drummers.'" Even Horace Thurber chose to reduce the number of drummers he put on the road after his brief 1870 experiment with them. By 1871, he opted instead to boost his newspaper advertising. "We employ but one traveling agent," Thurber informed his customers, "and our unparalleled success shows, we think, its correctness."[17]

One of the largest industrial processors and packagers of grocery products in the nineteenth century, the Thurbers distributed and marketed their own brand of goods, enabling this big-city operation to rely on circulars and in-house marketers to do the work of traveling salesmen. "We put ourselves in communication with buyers throughout the country by sending them price-lists and advertising our goods in trade papers," partner Francis B. Thurber emphasized in an 1881 report on US commerce. The New York City company also had the luxury of a large clientele concentrated in a relatively small region, enabling them in 1880 to sell "nearly eighteen million dollars in groceries," as one outsider claimed. Inflated or not, such numbers served only to emphasize the differences between soliciting a ready-made city trade and knitting together country trade. Smaller, lesser-known wholesalers like Charleston grocer Simon Strauss, Samuel Iseman's employer, depended on commercial travelers to canvass small towns for business and to verify retailers' financial abilities. With neither a large, city clientele nor a sales and advertising force, Strauss relied on his traveling agent to push staple goods and unbranded products.[18]

For all the arguments opposing traveling men, most found them necessary for getting trade and staying connected with their customers. One commercial traveler, "having just returned from an extensive trip through the Southern States," in the early 1870s championed their purpose. "It will be found that a great many of the merchants themselves throughout the country prefer to buy from a 'Drummer.' It saves them the expense of a trip to market or the trouble of ordering, and enables them to know definitely the price of the goods they buy." More important for the New Yorker was the certainty that rural grocers "know the 'Drummer,' who is frequently a personal friend, and prefer to give their orders to him." Testifying that traveling grocery salesmen were more than just product pushers and order takers, the agent affirmed they were welcomed sights in many stores and towns.[19]

Nothing backed this claim more than when local newspapers announced commercial travelers' arrivals. "Big Dick Thompson the grocery drummer, was in town yesterday interviewing our merchants," Gentry, Arkansas, reporters informed area merchants. The regularity of their visits made salesmen honorary community members, their stops broadcast in the same affable and familiar terms as townsfolk's comings and goings. Charles Palmer, the "well known grocery drummer from Albany, N.Y.," stopped along his route in North Adams, Massachusetts, to collect a few orders before moving on, while Bob Sommerville "smiled down upon his old friends" during an 1899 sales call to Piqua, Ohio. When James Eagan, a Kansas City salesman became sick with malaria while in the Oklahoma Indian Territory, local papers updated his condition, letting readers know he was "a trifle better." Other grocery travelers were "jolly," "genial," and "popular" among local merchants who saw them frequently. Even the "gray [horse] named Billy" that "well-known grocery drummer" Joseph Stack drove through Boston's snowy streets merited special recognition following an 1892 outing.[20]

These promoters of market confidence worked themselves into business communities by beating the same, defined routes month after month, calling on repeat customers and acquaintances with greater frequency than those in other trades. Groceries necessitated routine calls to retailers' stores to check inventory, restock, and rebate or return items spoiled or damaged during shipping. As the only traveler for a small firm, Samuel Iseman journeyed from

Salesmen armed with sample cases and order books were familiar and welcome sights in many towns. Wholesale and retail grocers depended on these roadmen to convey information about prices, products, and regional market conditions. Author's collection.

Simon Strauss's wholesale house in Charleston, across the eastern seaboard and South Carolina's midsection. Although Iseman had some latitude about where he traveled, he knew that he could not set off haphazardly in search of one-time retail customers; the nature of the grocery trade and its commercial geography defined the limits and scope of his choices, compelling him to delineate a trading network he could service through regular visits. He made biweekly or monthly stops in Camden, Allendale, Barnwell, Florence, Timmonsville, and other small towns, a route that sometimes took him two hundred miles from home.[21]

Iseman and other traveling men established trade routes that predated those coordinated by big-business managers at the turn of the twentieth century. Large wholesale firms with several men on the road divvied up sectors and sections among several agents, each being careful not to overlap or impede upon others' routes. Franklin MacVeagh, a Chicago wholesaler (later treasury secretary under President William Howard Taft) employed ninety-one salesmen by 1899. MacVeagh separated his salesmen into "city" and "country" designations, assigning each distinct sales routes. Fifty-five agents served the out-of-town trade and thirty-six attended to local accounts. MacVeagh managers recommended that metropolitan business be "re-districted and divided up into wards," with a different representative serving each territory. Doing so, the company maintained, would expand salesmen's "calling trade," which they figured had been soliciting only fifteen hundred of Chicago's estimated five thousand retail merchants.[22]

Routine visits generated profits for the thousands who took to the road. Custom in the trade dictated that wholesalers paid their men a commission (although some paid fixed salaries), with the firm covering travel expenses. One estimate suggested that salesmen traveling for New York grocery firms in the early 1870s earned "at least $1,500 each in salary and commission," a figure only "pushers" likely realized given the competitive nature of the business. Years later, several MacVeagh salesmen showed similar potential. The suitably named "Drum" was "starting out fairly well" in 1904, with sales of $4,300 in July, while Johnson had "sold more goods" than his predecessor, even if "his profit percentage was not up to Lindberg's." McDonald, meanwhile, proved "a fair prospect" with the opportunity to succeed in St. Paul and Minneapolis, as long as he "does not go to pieces." Bucking customary practice, a 1901 contract between MacVeagh and his salesmen placed the burden of paying "for all his own traveling and other expenses of every kind" on roadmen. Costs added up quickly once salesmen factored hotel fees, railroad fares, postage, telegrams, and other outlays. One 1880 report estimated a grocery traveler's daily expenses at $9.50, increasing by $1 or $2 "when heavy trunks are carried."[23]

The oversized valises and chests that agents toted held new manufactured and branded products, a marketing method that emerged with industrial capitalism during the 1870s. Food producers were among the first to recognize the challenge of distinguishing their merchandise and convincing retailers and consumers to trust goods made in far-away factories. Industrialists like Henry J. Heinz and Harvey Kellogg, along with the National Biscuit Company (makers of Uneeda Biscuits), pioneered the use of packaging, brands, and trademarks as ways to differentiate their products, safeguard their creations, and enter into larger markets. Wholesale grocers like Franklin MacVeagh manufactured and created their own branded goods to lower costs, earn greater profits, and distinguish themselves in the marketplace. Trademarks substituted for direct relationships between manufacturers and consumers, generating goodwill through recognizable and consistent identifying symbols, reinforced by salesmen's assurances. "Once you decide on a style of label," MacVeagh managers stressed, "never change it again, because a style becomes as familiar to the public as a name." Heinz in particular took pride in using keystone-shaped, clear glass bottles and labels to emphasize his western Pennsylvania roots and to show the purity of his ketchup's ingredients in days before strict food processing regulations.[24]

Quality assurances implied by brand names and emblems, however, did not always guarantee taste or performance (especially with nonprocessed goods). The bulk barrels that gave way to cans, boxes, and wrappers forced buyers to reformulate judgments about freshness and flavor without the benefit of being able to dip a hand in the proverbial cracker bin. Scores of disappointed retailers and consumers often found their storerooms and pantries littered with adulterated, spoiled, or just downright bad-tasking foods. Grocers and customers alike now faced determining product quality and utility only after purchase and through use either in store or at home. Since the proof was in the tasting, so the saying went, sampling became an important element of a salesman's pitch, allowing retailers both to try products before buying and to educate their shoppers. Roadmen's well-worn leather satchels and cases weighed upward of forty-five pounds and were filled with bottles and boxes that illustrated packaging and labeling. Large wholesale firms likewise maintained "sample rooms" where walk-in customers could appraise goods. MacVeagh managers directed "that all lines of samples are kept complete" with "show cases as well as the samples at all times kept clean and in an orderly condition." Sampling proved particularly important in bridging the limits of advertising and trademarking, especially in places where regional preferences, ethnicity, and retailer and consumer demands were potential roadblocks to modern, processed foods. For national brands to take hold, local retailers and shoppers first had to be convinced to buy them.[25]

Michaud Brothers in St. Paul, Minnesota, welcomed retail buyers from around the region to visit their offices and test their products before placing orders. Wholesale grocers' sample rooms often displayed packaged and bottled goods in illuminated showcases in the manner of fine department store wares. Author's collection.

A Network of Confidences

Samuel Iseman was no stranger to the changes industrial capitalism brought to neighborhood businesses. Born in 1868 to a mercantile family, he grew up one of twelve children. The Isemans held the distinction of being one of the founding Jewish families of Marion, South Carolina, a small town that by the 1850s boasted a large Jewish settlement and congregation. Samuel Iseman's father Manuel was a midcentury immigrant from Baden, Germany, who ran a successful dry goods store for many years, amassing personal wealth by 1870 totaling $12,000, a hefty sum for the day. It was said that the merchant's "irreproachable character" and recognition for "honesty and integrity in all his business transactions" tipped the scales in his favor when it came to commercial dealings.[26]

Yet by 1884, Manuel's irreproachable character was unable to save the family business when bad debts forced him to declare bankruptcy. Samuel's uncles, Isaac and Marx, faced their own obstacles. From 1845, the brothers had owned and operated a clothing store in Darlington, South Carolina, until the Civil War put them out of business. Shortly thereafter, Marx opened a bakery in Charleston with the help of his sons and daughters, while Isaac entered the dry goods trade in Darlington and Charleston. In 1872, Isaac had to close his Charleston store due to an outbreak of yellow fever, but he bounced back by opening another shop in Florence that same year.[27]

When Samuel Iseman's cousin Lizzie married Leopold Strauss in 1879, she brought to the Iseman family an enterprising uncle and nephew, opening the door for her younger cousin Samuel's eventual entrance into the grocery business. Leopold Strauss had immigrated to the United States from Germany in 1865, eventually settling in South Carolina. He and his uncle Simon started a dry goods operation in the 1870s, with both men on the road as traveling salesmen much of the time. When the brothers dissolved the partnership in 1882, Leopold briefly opened his own store in Bennettsville, but sold it and eventually took a managerial position in Marx Iseman's bakery. Simon appears to have continued the Bennettsville dry goods business. By 1890, he attempted to branch out into the wholesale grocery trade with a small concern in Charleston, specializing in "meats, lard, butter and cheese." In time, Leopold joined his uncle's grocery venture. Meanwhile, Simon hired Samuel Iseman as the company's sole traveling salesman.[28]

The young man proved to be a good choice for Strauss's budding wholesale enterprise. Iseman had all the makings of a successful traveling man, including but not limited to business sense, tenacity, and perseverance. Best of all for Strauss, he had connections. Born into a family of businessmen, Iseman had a ready network of relationships to call on when he needed advice, information, or recommendations. He likely had hung around his father's dry goods shop, learning the ins and outs of retailing alongside his brothers—one a clerk and the other a bookkeeper. Watching his uncles Marx and Isaac conduct business in the dry goods, clothing, and bakery trades, Samuel no doubt sharpened his retail expertise while also nurturing potential networks for trading goods and knowledge. Through these connections, he not only gained access to information and customers but also the skills needed to sell and market a wide variety of goods, tools essential to any traveling grocery salesman's success.

The networks of confidences Iseman and other traveling grocery salesmen first built with family members were not the byproduct of a competitive commercial economy but rather the foundation for it. Kin and kith networks played a decisive hand in directing the development of capitalistic systems in the eighteenth and early nineteenth centuries. While economic motives lay at the heart of expansion, merchants' business strategies ebbed and flowed with social, cultural, and political factors as much as they did with financial directives. Social and familial ties endured even as the commercial economy expanded. They continued to offer the same fundamental opportunities for accumulating capital, gaining information, and earning entrance and acceptance into trading groups as when used as the basis for older, community-centered business forms.[29]

Before visiting a retailer, Iseman typically checked with family members to see if a stop was worthwhile. In particular, he often consulted his cousin Solomon Iseman for information about potential customers. Sol, as he was better known, began working as a clerk in his father Marx's bakery at the age of fifteen. By 1887, the now twenty-two-year-old had established a wholesale provision trade in Charleston, just a few doors down from Simon Strauss's on East Bay Street, specializing as a commission merchant and produce dealer. Locals knew Sol as one of youngest businessmen in South Carolina, with a reputation for "energy, prompt attention, and honorable dealings" that had earned him a large trade.[30]

Sol initiated Samuel into his network by passing along recommendations for good customers and helping him to get a foot in the door with area storekeepers. Based on "good information" from Sol, Samuel stopped in Blackville in November 1890 to solicit orders from a few local merchants. The salesman pocketed a tidy sum when he sold 150 pounds of sugar-cured hams and some cheese to Bennett and Company, a concern Sol had suggested was "very good." Another referral, however, cost Samuel a bit of money, when he had to sell a grocer some sausage at the "same price as Sol," instead of making a small profit off his cousin's customer. There is both a hint of resignation in the young traveling man's note regarding the sausage sale and a nod to the benefits and opportunities opened up by inclusion into his cousin's network. Whether or not Samuel liked discounting his prices to meet his cousin's, he understood that Sol had forfeited a potential sale in the interest of helping the traveling man gain a foothold in the trade. Such was the way of family networks; they were both steadfast and robust, persistent in their loyalty and constancy.[31]

As a Jewish man who peddled pork products (not uncommon for the period), Samuel Iseman had access to some of the closest-knit merchant networks in nineteenth-century America. Jews throughout the country fashioned successful trade relationships stretching from rural backwaters to commercial centers, creating stable distribution and credit systems that supplied both Jewish and non-Jewish communities. Comprised of wholesalers, retailers, commission merchants, and other middlemen, Jewish networks provided goods and services for a host of merchants and consumers, forming a central component of industrial America's advancement and expansion. The closed nature of their networks, however, often marked Jewish merchants and peddlers as secretive and untrustworthy, stereotypes reinforced by discriminatory attitudes that fluctuated with population growth and movement. By the last quarter of the century, when business and credit reporting increasingly demanded transparency, Jews and their networks at times became suspect for their seeming lack of openness.[32]

While Samuel initially made good use of familial connections, he made no mention of Jews or specific Jewish connections (other than his cousin Sol) in his letters to Simon Strauss, although he probably had other contacts. Born in the United States, Iseman instead moved among both Jewish and non-Jewish networks with fluidity, making connections and customers from among Germans, African Americans, Welshmen, second-generation South Carolinians without identifiable ethnicity, and a host of others. Beyond their shared need for manufactured goods and interest in cured pork, there was little linking these merchants other than the traveling salesman. Iseman's assembled network showed the diminishing importance of ethnic or familial ties in a nation bound by commercial interests. In his role as commercial intermediary, he performed the inherently modern task of knitting a web of strangers into a credit, marketing, and distribution network. His connections were as diffuse and varied as the grocery trade itself, reflecting the complex nature of doing business in a nation of immigrants. Drawing on both family ties and market relations to form new and more diverse associations helped Iseman and other traveling men to facilitate flows of data, goods, and methods between urban wholesalers and rural retailers. Doing so appeared to push the core of trade outward from urban centers and into the hinterlands.[33]

It would be a mistake, however, to think that the countryside waited passively for the city to come calling. The Vincennes, Indiana, merchant who in 1869 advocated specialized trade and centralized warehouses, "to keep pace with the fashion of the times," knew this to be true. When traveling men ventured from their metropolitan commercial houses to distant towns, they encountered market microcosms, places where local and regional governments, banks, retailers, wholesalers, and consumers carried on commercial activities as part of the larger economy, not independent from it. The nature of these markets and their resemblance to how urban commerce functioned (if on a smaller scale) made it possible for Samuel Iseman to make quick and careful work of gathering and parsing information, enumerating orders, and scheduling shipments. By the 1890s, local merchants and tellers did not have to be told why the man with the gripsack was asking questions about storekeepers' pecuniary capacities, even if some failed to grasp exactly how an integrated market economy functioned. In other words, Iseman did not have to explain "big city" ways to small-town businessmen because in most places they were one and the same.[34]

Systemized Selling

Iseman borrowed on the system of numbers and letters New York credit firms used to short-hand conversations about customers' creditworthiness with his contacts. Lewis Tappan's Mercantile Agency (later R. G. Dun and Company), had tracked and cataloged businessmen's financial and character habits since the 1840s. His system worked to close the gap between known and unknown elements inherent in long-distance credit exchanges, much like the collection agencies they spawned. Their agents worked towns and cities with the goal of getting the inside track on area merchants. Subscribers received twice yearly confidential information on tradesmen that included their credit rating (A1 being the best), reputation, personal status, and local conditions, gathered by over ten thousand investigators from sixty-nine branch offices. The purpose of rationalizing and cataloging a man's character was to limit the risks associated with an expanding commercial economy. For many, numbers, codes, and abbreviations substituted for the handshakes and face-to-face appraisals that had always animated confidence. Trust now, according to credit agents' standards, was conveyed in numerical terms, packaged in R. G. Dun's large red ledgers.[35]

Numbers and the stories they told about a man's life, however, never fully captured the complexities of determining worth. While many merchants relied upon agency reports for information on business contacts and customers, not all small-town dealers made their way into a company's ledgers. The expansive web of credit-reporting agents often had trouble keeping up with hordes of rural merchants and hole-in-the-wall storekeepers who opened and closed sometimes within a few months' time. Typical entries in R.G. Dun's ledgers read, "no such man here," or "quit business, no known whereabouts." New York City wholesalers Board and Dean, likely fed up with the lack of information, insisted of its salesmen that "all orders from strangers must be accompanied with a remittance or reference." In 1907, one Boston wholesale firm urged its traveling men: "When you sell to a new customer, please state on the bottom of the order 'This is a new man,' and inform us all you know about him, and oblige." To combat the dearth of verifiable intelligence, credit agencies augmented centralized ledgers by publishing single-industry and local guides. Burnell's Commercial Agency's 1887 index for Buchanan County, Iowa, for example, provided estimated credit ratings for thousands of area merchants. Yet even Burnell's recognized the likelihood that somebody would slip between the cracks and left every other page blank for salesmen and others to note individual assessments and inquiries relevant to a particular dealer. Capitalism's bureaucratizing tendencies could not contain transient proprietors' spontaneity.[36]

Credit agencies like R. G. Dun issued pocket-sized compendiums for salesmen and other subscribers needing quick information about a buyer. The books' numerical credit ratings supplemented traveling men's personal inquiries. Author's collection.

Like all good credit men, travelers made quick friends with local bankers, storekeepers, and other potential sources, returning to them whenever they needed new or updated reports. Spotty reporting or misinformation through a third-party agency was no substitute for hearing it from the horse's mouth or from his neighbors. In this regard, traveling men often were more reliable and went deeper with their assessments than credit agents' reports. Iseman routinely prefaced his calls by conferring with his cousin Sol regarding potential customers' reliability and financial standing. In late November

1890, Samuel checked on William P. Dukes before selling him one hundred pounds of ham. The salesman learned from Sol that Dukes had "the reputation of paying before bills become due," a surefire indicator that Dukes was a safe bet. On another occasion, a grocer referred Iseman to local bankers if he needed more information about the merchant's credit standing. When Iseman visited the depository, he found the doors closed. Iseman took the order, nevertheless, and assured Strauss that the storekeeper had bought from Sol Iseman.[37]

Traveling grocery salesmen's frequent and intimate contact with retailers surpassed credit agents' efforts and positioned them to fill in the missing pages in agency reports. The local trumped the national in these instances, and Samuel Iseman's experiences provide a tantalizing glimpse into a decentralized and oral culture that persisted well into the twentieth century. In the fifty years since the Mercantile Agency had initiated its bureaucratic, centralized system of credit reporting, the personal appraisals of Iseman and other intermediaries remained important not just to the grocery trade but to all business. They were, in fact, the foundation for the very credit reports agencies claimed made market relations more secure and predictable. As late as 1924, wholesalers still held fast to the notion that "by keeping in constant touch with his trade," the traveling salesman "knows the financial standing of his customers and loses little by giving credit." Even as credit reporting and communications technologies matured, nothing exemplified the power grocery men and others vested in personal relationships like a visit from the traveling man. Industrial America thrived on their combination of face-to-face commerce and administrative scrutiny, the local intertwining with the national.[38]

Iseman's characteristic blend of rationalization and geniality enabled him develop a standardized approach for identifying and qualifying creditworthy retailers. Most orders contained a rundown of all he had learned about a storekeeper from neighbors, business partners, or other traveling men. Like most credit reports of the day, Iseman's narratives detailed a man's character, financial status, and personal habits. Morality and business had always been two sides of the same coin, weighted equally when determining a man's capitalistic potential; only now agents compiled both qualities for easier inspection. Iseman noted that Edward Witsell was "well fixed, buys most of his groceries from any of the Savannah houses, and I know him to be O.K." But the traveling man maintained a critical eye. By all appearances Ben Davies was "doing very well," according to Iseman's initial assessment. Along with opening a bar, Davies also did "a large Hotel Business" and had "money in [the] Bank," but the salesman suspected trouble and for good reason. Davies "drinks [ra]ther freely," Iseman later discovered, a habit vilified by credit reporters as the sign of a man whose business and personal life were on the road to ruin. Whether this was fact or rumor, the innkeeper's questionable personal habits and character compelled Iseman to limit Davies's credit and orders.[39]

Iseman's favorite and most reliable informants (beyond family) were local merchants because they followed the comings and goings of area businessmen and were willing to share their appraisals. Frank Simpson was a "responsible colored merchant" with substantial property, recommended to Iseman "by the best merchants in town, [who] said they would sell him any amount." Iseman verified the standing of another customer with Camden grocer William Geisenheimer who "said it was perfectly O.K." to sell him a bill of goods. Geisenheimer also vouched for another dealer, shoring up two sales. Reporting R. D. Kittrell's situation, Iseman noted "party is O.K. buys from [John] Tiedeman[n]," a fellow Charleston wholesale grocer. The salesman also made certain to tell Strauss that "[Kittrell] will remit cash on receipt of goods." Credit appraisals tested a traveling man's abilities to judge business and character and the reliability of his network. Modern enterprise placed greater burdens on an agent's ability to determine who was or was not creditworthy. Slip-ups cost not just the salesman but also his employer and the larger trade, compromising an entire network. The pressures of market prognostication, to predict a merchant's future solvency and business capacity, compelled traveling men to hone their investigative skills and become expert evaluators in the interest of commercial advancement.[40]

Lack of formal sales training or management did not preclude Iseman or others from assuming "professional" methods of selling and orchestrating their own activities. Long before corporate giants like NCR made selling a "science" in the early decades of the twentieth century, the nation's army of roadmen took steps to structure their time and efforts. Iseman's systematic and regular customer evaluations along with the reports he made to Strauss brought order to the regular and repeat transactions he made with country retailers, minimizing wasteful tasks and unnecessary risk. His predictable route and familiarity with local train schedules and ticket prices (knowledge he capitalized on after leaving Strauss) likewise focused his movements, as they did other traders. Responding in 1908 to a salesman frustrated with "the little headway I am making," MacVeagh managers assured him, "We are not looking for the easiest way of doing business, but the most economical and most profitable way, and naturally look to you for assistance." Low sales margins on many groceries and the small nature of most orders necessitated such systematizing steps as ways to lower transaction costs between wholesalers, salesmen, and retailers. In 1890, a Cincinnati wholesaler claimed his margins ranged between 8 percent for coffee to 12 percent for farina cereal in a time when dry goods wholesalers regularly saw 16 percent margins and hardware jobbers realized 19 percent. Warehousing, shipping, and handling costs further compromised gross profits and salesmen's earnings. Traveling agents for Reid, Murdoch, and Company, a Chicago competitor of Franklin MacVeagh, had "no idea as to what percentage of profit [was] figured on different goods." The firm tolerated no "questioning from salesmen on the subject of costs," undoubtedly resigning its agents to economize on travel, hotel, and food expenses to ensure sufficient compensation.[41]

MacVeagh managers, meanwhile, were equally as keen as large manufacturing concerns of the period about systematizing selling and encouraged their roadmen to adopt a more professional sales stance. Every agent, the company underscored in 1900, should be "ready to tell *from memory* the price on every item" in the firm's "Telmo" line of manufactured and branded products, in addition to being "conversant with all the elements that go to make up the superiority of the goods he is selling." These efforts, managers insisted, would make each man "a *salesman* instead of an 'order taker.'" MacVeagh, like Heinz and other big food makers, encouraged agents to build confidence in and promote their products with retailers and consumers. Sales strategies included "helping the merchant display the goods and aiding him in many ways to sell them, in the way of signs, prices, etc.," supplemented by selling lists illustrated with photographs of the company's canned goods and labels. Maintaining uniform prices likewise provided consistency among salesmen. The way MacVeagh's men saw it, "the customer, knowing but one price" would gain "confidence" from the traveling man and "be satisfied that he and his competitors are on equal footing." Just as professional sales methods built trust in brands and products, they also helped alleviate concerns about fly-by-night grips and swindlers. Who but a skilled and practiced man would work so hard to cultivate the sustained loyalty of another?[42]

Brokering Trust

When Samuel Iseman met with Moses Harrell in December 1890 to discuss the grocer's bad hams, he sympathized with the black storekeeper's situation. "The poor fellow could n[o]t sell them," Iseman apprised his employer Strauss, "and as he bought them at my suggestion, [I] thought best to let him return." Caught between preserving his relationship with the grocer and his financial obligations to the wholesaler, Iseman initially fretted about his decision to credit Harrell's account for fear of offending Strauss. "I hope this settlement will be satisfactory to you," the traveling man appealed. In an effort to explain the situation further, Iseman offered his assurances that Harrell was "a good honest Darkey." Granting the refund, Iseman suggested, assured that the grocer would "continue to trade with us when he need[ed] any thing [sic]."[43]

Despite its racial overtones (or perhaps because of them), this exchange indicates the fundamental link between trust and economic relationships, especially in the grocery trade. Charles W. Willis, longtime editor of the *New England Grocer*, summed it up as a matter of keeping promises. "There is nothing classed with malfeasance of duty and of business that is more harmful to the prosperity of the individual or the business man than failing to keep a promise," Willis intoned in a 1910 article. Promise keeping was materialized trust in the marketplace. It was, according to Willis, "the most sacred obligation taken by any human being." He further underscored the importance of moral accountability, placing it above moneymaking. "A man should keep a promise," Willis claimed, "even though he loses money by doing so." Failure to follow through on a pledge not only jeopardized a salesman's immediate transactions but also threatened long-term and repeat commercial relationships, potentially ruining his reputation along with his ability to continue trading. Any short-term loss necessary to keep a promise, Willis believed, would return profits tenfold.[44]

As trust brokers, traveling grocery salesmen anchored relations between wholesalers and retailers by guaranteeing promises (even while making their own). Adam Smith would have concurred with Willis. Smith held fast to the notion that businessmen's desire for commercial advancement and self-interest led them to behave more congenially and cooperatively than they might have otherwise—the *doux commerce* thesis. This was true in the grocery trade where, because of their regular visits, traveling men had to foster reputations for being trustworthy and accommodating, links that bridged capitalism's commercial and moral functions. Smith claimed that a merchant's marketplace fears about preserving both bottom line and reputation voluntarily generated honesty, probity, and civility. In the absence of face-to-face negotiations, some merchants, Smith contended, would turn "a smart trick" because the immediate gain offset "the injury which it does [to] their character." It was a risk inherent in long-distance trade, and one Samuel Iseman struggled to minimize while on the road for his Charleston employer.[45]

Simon Strauss's "smart tricks" plagued Iseman. Time and again, he had to remind the wholesaler of his responsibilities to his rural customers, chiding, "Whatever you do don't disappoint them." The emphatically worded demand for "no stinkers" often accompanied Iseman's long-distance ham orders.

Placing grocer William Sprott's request for sardines and sausage, Iseman directed Strauss, "Please be sure to send the sausage as I promised he would be sure to get them." Pointing out Strauss's sometimes-casual attitude toward his obligations, Iseman instructed him to ship the goods "even if you have to inconvenience yourself a little." Sprott, in the salesman's estimation, was "an A 1 man, and [I] will be able to sell him good many goods in the spring." Iseman may have been Strauss's subordinate but he showed no hesitancy in pointing out the potential costs should the wholesaler fail to meet his responsibilities to both agent and retailer. At the same time, he reminded Strauss that business did not conduct itself; without the traveling man, fewer goods would pass from Charleston to South Carolina's rural towns.[46]

Traveling grocery salesmen thus brokered "strategic trust" with retailers. Iseman tried to leave little to chance when it came to making deals with country merchants. Doing so would have imperiled his reputation, his ability to extend his network, and his financial compensation. The competitive advantages wholesalers and retailers gained through traveling men's inquiries might have appeared to favor the larger, wholesale concern, which often had greater resources through which to gather market information. Yet as traveling salesmen recognized, retailers had the upper hand when it came to knowing their own businesses and covering their debts. No combination of trust, promise keeping, or informants, however, could overcome every obstacle. J. J. Jones, a Bamberg merchant, exasperated both Samuel Iseman and Simon Strauss with his quick talk and empty pledges. Iseman had visited Jones in late November 1890, selling several hundred pounds of ham, along with some butter, cheese, and rice. The agent heard that Jones "is said to be good pay & does a good business," and had references from Sol Iseman and Bollman Brothers, a prominent Charleston wholesaler. One month later, Samuel Iseman again stopped into Jones's shop and sold him a box of meat and a barrel of rice "before asking for money with the hopes that he would pay me."[47]

Neither Iseman's strategy nor his sales methods paid off. Jones gave only assurances that "he would positively be in Charleston on Monday & bal[an]c[e] of the week and would call in & settle." Perhaps questioning his initial judgment of Jones as a good risk, Iseman again inquired about the merchant's standing "and every body reported him in good circumstances doing a good business & making money." Thus, he had "no doubt but that we will get our money out of him." In February 1891, three months after Iseman's initial sale, he was still looking to collect. Iseman sarcastically wrote Leopold Strauss about his latest encounter with Jones. "Called on our friend Mr. Jones," the traveling man reported, "and got nothing but a promise." Clearly fed up with

Jones's shenanigans, Iseman nevertheless held a glimmer of hope that the man would keep his word, telling Strauss, "I think we will yet get our money."[48]

Iseman's frustration with Jones speaks to the moral expectations inherent in nineteenth-century business. One 1895 guide to granting credit reflected, "The majority of men prefer to be, and mean to be, honest, but it is natural to be hopeful and to present the most sanguine view of one's own circumstances and prospects." Jones may have been feeding Iseman and others puffed-up tales of his commercial prowess in an attempt to garner a better reputation and a few goods from the salesman, but only Jones knew whether he was capable of paying for what he ordered. Even if Jones "meant" to be forthright about his financial strength and willingness to pay, Iseman took the merchant's promises to heart, relying on both his sales methods and the trust he had brokered with Jones to predict if the latter was worth his time. Unfortunately, Iseman also likely took the loss when Jones did not pay up. Iseman's local contacts and his ability to foster commercial intimacy with the merchant had failed him. Despite the traveling man's best efforts, Jones ultimately could not be trusted to make good on either his promises or his payments. Fortune and fate, capitalism's antiheroes, combined to keep even the most rational of men from foretelling another's intentions.[49]

While the young salesman had difficulty imagining a business environment where merchants reneged on their words, how did Iseman's customers know they could trust *him*? His interaction with Moses Harrell pointed to the leap of faith retailers took when ordering from a traveler. When Iseman stepped into Harrell's shop, he talked up the superiority and price of the hams he offered. Relying on this pitch ("he bought them at my suggestion"), Harrell expected to receive first-rate goods. Retailers like Harrell could check a wholesale house's references with other merchants or with a credit-reporting agency. That information, however, told them only about the pecuniary standing of a concern and the men who owned and operated it. Credit agents filed no reports on clerks or traveling salesmen. Retailers sometimes inquired with fellow businessmen about a particular traveler's character, hoping someone had dealt successfully (or miserably) with him in past. The most-asked question no doubt went to the trustworthiness of the traveling man's word. Did he keep the promises he made?

American credit agencies managed risk for sellers, not buyers, one of the most significant information disparities in market exchanges. Few rural merchants subscribed to R. G. Dun's services to learn about the financial standing or reliability of the wholesalers with whom they traded. From June 1874 to June 1875, for example, only seven men inquired with Dun about Bollman Brothers, a Charleston wholesale firm serving hundreds of small-town clients. All seven most likely were importers or manufacturers checking Bollman's rating before extending credit to the wholesaler. Agencies like R. G. Dun sought to protect wholesalers from imprudent buyers and unreliable hucksters, but made little provision for the converse—protecting small-town buyers from untrustworthy and manipulative wholesalers. Traveling men addressed these disparities by brokering trust in both directions, guarding sellers as well as buyers.[50]

What happened, then, when a traveling man could not be trusted? W. H. Moseley, one of Iseman's retail customers, penned a letter to Simon Strauss grumbling to the wholesaler that the rice sent to him was not up to the standard "your Mr. Iseman said it should be." The merchant placed the blame squarely on the salesman's shoulders, telling the wholesaler, "I would not have bought of him but he said he would send a good quality." While the burden was Strauss's for shipping substandard goods, Moseley faulted the traveling man for not following through on his promise. "You must make a reduction," Moseley demanded, seeking amends from the wholesaler for the mishandled order. William H. Commander, a Sumter merchant and frequent customer, found himself in June 1891 on the wrong side of a barrel of hams "full of worms." The dealer had "ask[ed] for good hams," a request Iseman had conveyed on Commander's behalf on several other occasions, asking the wholesaler to ship only the "very best select Hams." This time, not only did Strauss ship unacceptable meat, but the grocer also "had the promise of a rebate" from Iseman "and did not get it."[51]

Moseley's and Commander's remonstrations make clear that when a salesman's actions failed to match a customer's expectations, it upset the stability trust brought to business relations. Salesmen conducted personalized trust-building activities for the sake of profit; they were an integral part of capitalism. The cultivation and conservation of mutual trust returned dollars and cents, easily tallied in monthly statements. Moral factors also underlay trading of this kind. Customers of good standing and large trade often asked for and received lower prices, reduced shipping charges, or a higher standard of goods. Such allowances rewarded those "of good character and habits," in credit-reporting parlance, advantaging those who fit popular perceptions of a successful dealer. Men who struggled in trade, who were poor credit risks, or had questionable dispositions could expect to pay higher prices and see fewer benefits. In this way, trust was more than just a mark of reliability; it became the measure of a good businessman. The market rewarded those who kept their obligations, maintained good character, and demonstrated good sense and practices in both pecuniary and noncommercial ways.[52]

Few traveling salesmen easily hoodwinked retailers, though, even when they deliberately set out to do so. The *New England Grocer* warned Waterville, Maine, grocers in 1896 about a "nice-looking young man" who made the rounds to several stores claiming to be an agent for a Portland wholesale firm. His plan was to stir up the local trade by suggesting that their regular sales-man had overcharged them for several different staple items, promising that "he would have to see about those high prices right away." Banking that the grocers would feel "more friendly than ever toward the alleged member of the concern" for pointing out the price discrepancy, the spurious salesman then tried selling molasses and sugar on unusually liberal terms, "by which the fellow expected to gain a few dollars." Wise to the agent's too-good-to-be-true bargains, not one of the Waterville grocers "cared to accept the offer under the circumstances," and the charlatan left town. While such stories suggest that some traveling men managed to cajole unsuspecting merchants into buying cheap goods, the fact that this sharper could not pull one over on Waterville's dealers underscores the trust retailers had in their regular salesmen. None of the rural town's grocers let himself be bamboozled into buying the transient swindler's story or his goods.[53]

The South Carolina men Samuel Iseman dealt with were a lot like Waterville's grocers. Shrewd dealers, they ran "close" businesses, credit agents' favorite descriptor for prudently managed operations. Merchants' careful buy-ing strategies informed Iseman's selling tactics. When the traveling man sized up Columbia dealer Alexander Brooks in December 1890, he found him "per-fectly O.K." after learning that the merchant bought from "Sol [Iseman] and anywhere else he wants to." In fact, the traveling man found Brooks so good that after taking his order for a modest amount of pork, Iseman told Strauss, he "would like to have sold him more as he is good for more than he will buy." Yet Brooks also was a sharp negotiator. He purchased just one barrel of "the very best 1st rejection" hams, but haggled with Iseman to get them at 6¢ per pound, while the traveling man was charging others between 6½¢ and 6¾¢ for the same meat. Iseman made the sale, but Brooks held all the cards. The same was true in February 1891 when the roadman called on W.T. Walker, another close buyer. Iseman wrote an order for just one hundred pounds of lard compound, "all [he] could sell him this trip." Close buyers tested Iseman's salesmanship skills, but not his resolve. The traveling man knew that the reward came not with a merchant's initial purchase but with his repeated sales. Walker, after all, promised to give Iseman "a nice order on my next trip." Men easily swindled into overbuying produced big sales, but offered few prospects for long-term dealing.[54]

Unfortunately for Iseman, his chances of cashing in on Alexander Brooks were dashed with the first order. Dispatching the Columbia man's pork request to Strauss, the salesman warned, "send him goods as near prime as possible," adding the dictum "no stinkers" to emphasize his point. Five days later when Brooks received his hams, however, he found "they are not good at all." The storekeeper wasted no time in letting Strauss know, "[I] will have to ship them back to day, for they are not what I ordered." Brooks's close trade practices left little room for messing about with salesmen and wholesalers who could not be trusted to meet his needs. As a result of the botched order, Iseman lost Brooks's sale and his future business; he never wrote another order for the merchant.[55]

Alexander Brooks's decision to discontinue dealing with Iseman and Strauss demonstrates that merchants held substantial power in forming and preserving the ties that bound wholesalers, traveling men, and retailers. Not dependent on only one wholesaler to supply their needs, grocers could and did shop around for the best deals and goods from a variety of wholesale houses. Joseph St. Louis, a traveling man for wholesaler Franklin MacVeagh, appreciated the authority retailers gained from such competition. When St. Louis failed to turn a profit on nine barrels of flour he sold to a grocer on his central Illinois route, sales supervisors inquired. Aggravated by the managers' insinuation that he had arbitrarily cut his prices, St. Louis responded by instead citing his success in gaining ten cents per barrel over his competitors. "Mr. Boudreau has been buying C[lub] H[ouse] flour of me for 4 years," the agent informed, and "he allowed me 10¢ more . . . when he could have bought Gold Dragon of Deane Bros." With a Nebraska firm ready to undercut St. Louis, the salesman was at the grocer Boudreau's mercy. Powerless, St. Louis let the retailer dictate the sales price and terms, allowing Boudreau to buy for less than the wholesaler's market price. The only thing that saved the deal was the veteran traveler's established relationship with Boudreau, who consented to giving St. Louis a price concession over the other firm.[56]

The close ties St. Louis built with Boudreau superseded the economics of the market. Based on his familiarity with the salesman, the grocer was willing to pay a higher price for a product he easily could have gotten for less from a competitor. For Boudreau, the four-year association he had cultivated with St. Louis had its own market value which he factored into the cost of the flour, allowing St. Louis a small profit over his competition. Monetary factors alone could not prescribe market conditions or relationships. If the cost of doing business meant paying more for trust and the networks it fostered, men like Boudreau and St. Louis were willing to reach deep into their pockets.[57]

Persistence of the Old Order

In the 1890s, when other trades began to centralize and phase out drummers and wholesalers, the diffuse nature of the grocery industry and its countless lines of goods and products made it difficult to follow suit. As a result, traveling grocery salesmen remained the most effective (if not efficient) way to move goods and credit in a complex and decentralized market. It was a structure that endured alongside chains' centralized operations. For even as chains began to dominate, countless small, out-of-the way stores continued to depend on traveling salesmen and wholesalers for credit, goods, and trade. As late as 1949, Maurice Toulme, vice president of the National American Wholesale Grocers' Association, claimed that "some 5,000 wholesale grocery firms" still supplied "nearly 400,000 retail grocery outlets" in the United States. While the number of salesmen declined from those representing the "great army" of the 1870s, traveling men and their methods nevertheless persisted as a function of both the trade's structure and the products it distributed.[58]

In the absence of economies of scale that came with industrialization and mass production, wholesalers and their salesmen offered economies of scope, providing the most efficient methods for moving goods and credit in a largely decentralized trade. Distributing small lots of fresh and semiperishable goods to small retailers clashed with chain store practices, theories, and organizational structures, which emphasized large volume and centralized retail markets. Small-lot jobbing by intermediaries may not have represented optimum efficiency in other lines, but for much of the grocery trade, this strategy kept goods and information flowing between commercial centers and hinterlands through durable networks constructed by traveling salesmen.[59]

Franklin MacVeagh was one of many independent wholesalers who continued to employ roadmen as a necessary part of their marketing and distribution segments. In 1923, at a meeting of the firm's Committee to Reduce the Cost of Doing Business, MacVeagh managers reminded its salesmen about the same fundamental elements of trade Samuel Iseman wrestled with thirty years earlier. "Making guaranteed sales," "giving guarantees of keeping quality on perishable goods," and "salesmen's attention that future orders are taken and given in good faith," remained important components in establishing a grocery salesman's relationship with his customers in the 1920s as they had been in the 1890s. That these same ideals coexisted with the firm's notions of conducting trade efficiently was no accident, a point wholesalers at the turn of the century also made.[60]

Grocery marketing and distribution through traveling salesmen was a profoundly personal, but not old-fashioned, way of doing business. Networks between wholesalers and retailers cultivated by traveling agents bound merchants together in the making of a modern commercial economy. Moving from town to town and store to store, roadmen combined the familiarity of face-to-face meetings with new, rationalized standards of judging creditworthiness to build networks of trust and confidence that crossed local and regional boundaries. Samuel Iseman's efforts to fashion sustainable networks for himself, his employer, and his customers proved potent and lucrative. It was the best—and arguably the only—way to move products and information culled from America's rural retailers to commercial centers and back again. Brokered trust was a multidirectional process; it flowed as much from wholesaler to retailer as it did from retailer to wholesaler. In overcoming both the organizational and geographical hurdles of the trade, wholesalers and their traveling salesmen remained vital intermediaries through whom independent grocers prospered in a multifaceted and sprawling marketplace.

4

Avoiding the Middleman

From a podium in Boston's Parker House hotel, William J. Seaver, vice president of the Boston Wholesale Grocers' Association, pronounced dead the old grocers' maxim that "goods well bought are half sold." That had been the buying credo since the Civil War, but in 1905 it seemed antiquated beside "modern competition," the subject of Seaver's address to the Paint and Oil Club of New England. The grocery wholesaler spoke about the perils of unbridled competition and how it "compels men and corporations to do things against their better judgment." This included trade evils such as cutting prices and underselling wholesale costs, as well as nationwide problems of reducing wages and expenses in order to turn a profit, strategies industrial capitalists such as Andrew Carnegie and John D. Rockefeller had employed to great advantage. Seaver suggested the solution lay in collaboration and cooperation, allowing "agreements between ourselves to correct many of the objectionable, questionable, senseless evils that exist only and because of Competition." The following year, Rockefeller would proclaim in defense of his own collusive efforts in the oil industry, "The day of combination is here to stay."[1]

Seaver spoke from experience. The Boston Wholesale Grocers' Association (BWGA) had long benefited from such an "agreement" between member firms. They believed that it was the best method for controlling competition and maintaining their place in the trade. Beginning in 1875 and continuing for more than thirty years, the BWGA and its affiliates consolidated distribution, fixed prices, and limited access to manufactured goods—actions that not only were antithetical to the spirit of a free market but also undermined retail grocers' abilities to compete with one another and for consumers' business. Not surprisingly, retailers pointed the finger not at unbridled commerce but at wholesalers' collusive agreements as the source of their problems. Their solution was to fight fire with fire. Banding together to form buying syndicates, retail grocers fashioned their own agreements and disrupted the established distribution chain—which moved goods from manufacturers, to wholesalers, and finally consumers—enabling them to purchase products directly from manufacturers and thereby avoiding the middleman wholesaler and his seemingly anti-competitive schemes. In other words, wholesalers and retailers modified the rules to compete in an evolving game.

As part of the late nineteenth-century merger movement, the BWGA's actions and retailers' response typified challenges associated with the emergence of "big business," especially in the BWGA's drive for economic power and market dominance. Competition, the driving force of capitalism and Adam Smith's "invisible hand" of free-market enterprise, now appeared poised to cripple all but the largest firms. A scramble for market share and economic control sent prices spiraling downward, to the detriment of many smaller manufacturers, distributors, and retailers. Overproduction also plagued key industries, limiting entry and growth potential for smaller firms unable to match large-scale competitors' manufacturing technologies and capacities. This mixture of unregulated competition and a quest for more efficient operating methods created conditions in which combination thrived. Between 1865 and 1895, manufacturing industries nationwide from oil, iron, and steel to salt, sugar, and liquor engaged in cartel-like behavior, cooperating to moderate prices, limit production, and centralize control, some more successfully than others. These were the beginnings of large-scale enterprise. Yet if manufacturers used associations and combinations to take the first steps toward growth and expansion though merger, wholesale and retail grocers marched right alongside for a time before diverging down different paths.[2]

Where wholesale grocers saw in combination the same opportunities to temper competition, shore up markets, and stabilize prices as in other industries, retail grocers envisioned an entirely new distribution chain, much like those of the nation's largest centralized firms. Years before chain stores, independent retailers struck first in formulating alternative distribution paths and challenging concentrated enterprise in the grocery industry. Their response to wholesalers' consolidated control over distribution and prices in the 1890s predated by almost twenty years the intense chain store competition of the 1910s and 1920s and the Great Atlantic and Pacific's vertical integration. One 1930 study confirmed that retail buying exchanges "had begun to force readjustments in the wholesale business before the chains had become significant factors." The BWGA made little mention of chains during its meetings, the small numbers of such stores having a negligible effect on the day-to-day dealings of the organization and in trade. In 1890, only six grocery chains operated nationwide. Ten years later, the number stood at twenty-one, and it did not peak until 1927, when 335 chains operated in the marketplace. While national grocery chains were and remain aberrations owing mostly to their specific distribution challenges, local and regional chains also remained relative small in number at the turn of the century. A survey of Boston city directories reveals that in 1900, the city boasted more than 1,650 retail grocery stores but only four local chains operating thirty-three shops. Although the impact of these stores doubtlessly made significant inroads into the area's trade by the mid-1910s, in decades before, most independent retailers resented wholesalers' activities more than they did chain organizations.[3]

That bitterness originated with wholesalers' authority over distribution. As quintessential middlemen, wholesalers controlled the flow of credit and goods between manufacturers and retailers. If wholesalers chose to limit the movement of either, retailers were seemingly at their mercy. The formation of retail buying exchanges laid bare a growing conflict within the trade between wholesalers' long-standing dominance and effectiveness as the primary distributors for manufactured products. At the turn of the twentieth century, retailers now questioned those roles, tapping their collaborative power to change the course of trade. This challenged wholesalers to defend their claims to be the most fitting (and at the time only) grocery distributors. And grocery wholesalers had reason to worry. At the end of the nineteenth century, as manufacturers centralized and consolidated dry goods and other consumer product trades, wholesale grocers had remained confident that their distributive functions were vital for moving groceries. Had retailers now devised a way to eliminate wholesalers?

Price Cutting and the Origins of Wholesalers' Collusion

Wholesalers had started looking for ways to control prices not long after making the shift to the small-lot jobbing that Samuel Iseman and other intermediaries helped orchestrate in the 1870s. Buying smaller lots enabled retailers to "shop around" for the best price on goods instead of making only two or three major purchases per year, adjusting wholesalers' profits and increasing competition. The expansion of wholesale and retail firms in the West likewise chipped away at the long-dominant markets of New York and Boston, circumscribing territories and reducing their reach and business. Looking back, BWGA historian William Bain recalled Boston wholesalers' frustrations at an 1881 meeting, reminding members of a time when "the territory naturally reached by our trade [was] very limited and . . . growing smaller year by year.

Large sections of country outside of New England that we once reached [were] almost entirely closed to us." Prices on some items grew increasingly unstable as more wholesalers took up jobbing and began to undercut one another to earn their share of smaller sales and more customers. Sugar, for example, fluctuated between six and one-half cents per pound in 1879 to seven and one-half cents per pound in New York and other markets in 1880, with greater supplies and availability from eastern and southern ports prompting many to call for price regulation as firms ruthlessly undercut each another.[4]

Competitive price cutting, along with the practices of selling at cost or for a loss, stemmed in large part from shortfalls incurred from the sale of sugar. The profit margin on sugar was so low (often nonexistent) that storekeepers generally expected to lose money on its sale. By the 1870s, sugar had become a "leading article," as one guide suggested, or "loss leader" in modern parlance, its low price intended to draw customers to a wholesale or retail dealer who could then pitch higher-profit items such as tea and coffee to make up the deficit. Selling sugar for a loss was so common it had become trade practice by the 1880s.[5]

Most saw price cutting as a vicious and potentially suicidal business practice, "mercantile harakiri," as one critic described it. Wholesale and retail grocers alike grew concerned that undercutting competition demoralized the trade. Low sugar prices forced both to drive up prices on other goods to offset losses, inflating costs to consumers. "A permanent advance falls of course on the customer," a trade insider advised, "but slight fluctuations are too often borne by the retail dealer who fears that if he advances too quickly, his neighbors will not go with him and his custom will be drawn away." The man who sold at cost or for a loss not only condemned himself and his business, but also the trade, leading both down the road to certain financial and ethical ruin.[6]

Boston wholesalers found their solution to price cutting in limited price plans, a form of cartel. Limited price plans were "gentlemen's agreements" among firms that sought to control destructive competition, as opposed to capital-pooling trusts or combinations that sought to control the market. The Boston Wholesale Grocers' Association devised its limited price plan with the organization's founding in 1875, focusing initially on sugar and seeking to "regul[ate] the sale of merchandise," which would allow members "to realize a sufficient margin of profit to make it possible to protect capital and labor from depreciation and failure." BWGA leaders met daily to set prices at which its members sold sugar to retailers. Those who undersold or cut the price of sugar to gain business were called before a committee, with expulsion from the organization a likely outcome. In this way, the BWGA attempted to regulate sugar sales and prices within Boston and surrounding areas, controlling the trade's most prominent "loss leading" product, and forcing retailers who dealt with BWGA wholesalers to pay their prices.[7]

Cooperation in business abounded at the end of the nineteenth century as concerns brought about by increased rivalries among firms, changes in manufacturing and marketing, and the rise of concentrated capital provoked a variety of responses. Trade associations in particular reflected a modernizing impulse among small and decentralized industries that counted on loose organizations to educate, inform, and compel businessmen to work together, addressing new structural, economic, and political challenges. Europeans (Germans in particular) had long used cooperative capitalism as a form of self-regulation to grow capital-intensive industries—setting rules, prices, policies, and ethical standards—especially in typically unregulated local and regional markets. In the nineteenth-century United States, trade associations were embedded within mainstream capitalism and employed strategies frequently attributed to large-scale enterprise, even if their language and methods appeared to be in opposition to free enterprise's focus on the individual.[8]

While many American industries transitioned to market dominance through mergers, others, including the grocery trade, took more collaborative routes. Unlike manufacturing firms, which evolved from local and regional associations into legalized trusts and then into vertically and horizontally integrated firms, wholesaler-dependent industries such as groceries and hardware continued operating through local, regional, and eventually national channels, using their collective power to work in concert with rather than in opposition to manufacturers. Wholesalers employed this strategy not only to stabilize prices and increase sales margins on manufactured products, but also because they worried that manufacturers' powerful trusts would absorb distributive functions into their operations. For evidence, grocers needed to look no further than their own trade. Firms such as the National Biscuit Company and American Tobacco already had begun moving away from their dependence on wholesalers. In 1898, National Biscuit consolidated three existing firms in the interest of limiting competition and followed the example of Quaker Oats by moving marketing and distribution in-house. That same year, BWGA members noted that some manufacturers had begun selling directly to retailers, with the group carping, "they should not do so." Working with manufacturers and each other, the BWGA believed they could position themselves as producers' allies thereby maintaining their place in the distribution chain.[9]

The BWGA's initial membership included fifty-one wholesalers (growing to sixty-four by the 1880s), concentrated in and around Commercial and State Streets "and all within a radius of half a mile." They represented at various times anywhere between 75 percent and 100 percent of all Boston wholesale grocery firms, a virtual distribution monopoly within the city. The BWGA's influence spread across New England by the 1890s, as wholesale grocers' associations and limited price plans modeled on the BWGA sprang up in Portland, Maine; Providence, Rhode Island; New York; and other places, concentrating sugar distribution in the hands of a small number of firms and organizations. These groups doubtlessly found support from the 1888 founding of the National Wholesale Grocers' Association, which like the BWGA, formed with the goal of regulating the sugar market.[10]

The BWGA based their strategy on an ideal shared by many that manufacturers, wholesalers, and retailers occupied and operated separate trade lines. While most acknowledged that the three branches were inextricably linked, their specialized and particularized functions nevertheless distinguished them in the eyes of their practitioners. "It would be greatly to the advantage of the trade if the three lines were kept clear and distinct," insisted Artemas Ward, longtime manager of Sapolio soap for Enoch Morgan's Sons Company and later trade chronicler. The benefit of maintaining separate lines as many saw it was to reduce friction in a fiercely competitive field. When Thurber, Whyland, and Company, successors to New York wholesalers H. K. and F. B. Thurber, hired a new salesman in 1890, they advised the man "not to seek orders for individual use, as [it] often works detrimentally by becoming a competitor with dealers who naturally should have the benefit of the consumer trade." Some argued that in preserving and respecting distribution boundaries—wholesalers' shorthand for individual enterprise—trade would continue to function and prosper.[11]

The power of cooperation and limited pricing buoyed the BWGA's efforts to protect free enterprise and maintain profitability. The group successfully carried on its collusive work for far longer than most nineteenth-century trade associations, indicating that on some level theirs was an effective and enduring method for conducting business in a traditionally low-profit, cutthroat market. Looking at industrial competitiveness regionally instead of individually, groups like the BWGA used their collective power to stabilize the market while maintaining independent operations. Unlike many manufacturing associations, the BWGA never transitioned into a mammoth, monopolizing firm. Instead, it focused on the advantages of the organization for addressing new industrial problems while preserving individual business ownership. Citing a difference between "an agreement that amounts to a conspiracy, and an agreement between the merchant and manufacturer that will protect the former from unbridled competition," the BWGA drew on the value of coordination and the principles of cooperation to steady the Boston sugar market and mitigate price cutting. As a result, wholesalers across New England grew increasingly powerful as they combined their buying and distribution power to govern a market that had for 150 years remained largely unregulated.[12]

In 1891, the BWGA used the strength of its organization (and possibly the threat of boycott) to cajole the American Sugar Refinery Company, Henry O. Havenmeyer's notorious sugar trust, into a system of price maintenance. At the time, American Sugar controlled approximately 95 percent of the nation's sugar production, quashing competition from independent producers. BWGA members promised to distribute only American's brand of sugar in exchange for price concessions and rebates. "When this Association was formed," one-time BWGA president Hiram Logan recalled in an 1897 speech to members, "it was with reference to sugar almost wholly, and while satisfactory in a measure, became more than satisfactory six years ago, when the refiners espoused the rebate system in response to our urgent request." The rebate system included lucrative kickbacks for BWGA members, a scheme that was not unfamiliar to wholesalers. Manufacturers in many lines, including pharmaceuticals, willingly colluded with wholesalers to sell their goods at fixed or reduced prices in the interest of gaining a monopoly on the promotion and distribution of certain products. Often manufacturers set a minimum price at which their goods could be sold to retailers. At the end of the year, manufacturers compensated wholesalers who promoted their goods over competitors' products and stuck to agreed-upon selling prices.[13]

BWGA members initially earned a seventy-cent reimbursement from American Sugar for every barrel of sugar they sold to retail grocers. Over the course of one six-year period (1891–1897), the BWGA's sixty-four member firms sold 618,000 barrels of American sugar, realizing a rebate from the company totaling $2,596,200, an average of over $40,000 for every BWGA wholesaler. New York wholesalers had a similar agreement with American, earning them just over five cents per pound, "with the understanding that all who did not sell at a less price than this should have a rebate at the end of each three months of 18 3/4 cents on each 100 pounds of sugar purchased." Given such lucrative reimbursements, few could disagree when BWGA member William Wadleigh declared, "The success of our vocation depends upon the right to make trade agreements with manufacturers."[14]

Of course, not everyone agreed with wholesalers' thinking. Collusive efforts were the bane of lawmakers and others who feared that the market was under the influence of a small minority of trusts and combinations. While cartel and trust organizers paradoxically argued that such undertakings enabled fair competition by eliminating hostile undercutting, the federal government sought to regulate the conditions under which collusive groups could operate. Havermeyer's sugar trust, for example, drew fire in

1895 for monopolizing production, prices, and distribution. In *United States v. E.C. Knight*, the federal government tried to force the divestiture of some of the trust's holdings (among them the New Jersey firm of E. C. Knight) but failed. The decision fueled further outrage at the seemingly unstoppable nature of combinations while weakening the power of the recently adopted Sherman Antitrust Act (1890) and state authority over cartels and other collusive associations. Lacking the capital-pooling power of large corporations and trusts, lawmakers initially ignored the BWGA and other trade associations and their actions, even as the organization kept close watch on how antitrust laws might affect their group's future.[15]

In the meantime, the BWGA's iron grip on sugar and its powerful connections prevented competitors from entering the market and quelled legislative forces. In one revealing case, the organization's promise to distribute only American Sugar products forced the Boston branch of Arbuckle Brothers, American's leading competitor, to seek new markets by dealing directly with retailers. In a 1911 series of hearings investigating American Sugar and its practices, William G. Gilmore, a partner in Arbuckle Brothers, testified that sometime around 1900 the firm approached Boston wholesalers about striking a deal. According to Gilmore, the wholesalers "would not take our goods and distribute them" because they were "under the American Sugar Refining Co.'s thumb." When pressed, Gilmore verified that his firm had to go around Boston's wholesaling community to deal directly with retailers after wholesalers "refused the business" in the interest of maintaining their connection to American Sugar. Federal antitrust laws initially had little effect on the BWGA's actions. Although Massachusetts had passed legislation limiting capital stock formation beginning in the 1860s, it took little interest in limited price plans and voluntary organizations until 1903. That year, Massachusetts legislators debated a bill intended to prevent manufacturers from establishing uniform or regulated prices either on their own or in collusion. In a special meeting, the BWGA appointed a committee "to act as they thought best in the matter," while encouraging members to "see the Senators from their district and use their influence toward the defeat of the bill." One month later, the association reported, "the Anti Combine bill before the legislature had been defeated."[16]

Pecuniary interests drove BWGA attempts to halt such legislation. In years following its successful deal with American Sugar, the BWGA made additional reimbursement arrangements with a number of manufacturers, including the Akron, Ohio-based American Cereal Company, makers of Quaker Oats, and Cambridge, Massachusetts, soap makers Curtis Davis & Company. Through the Curtis deal, BWGA firms, along with members of the New England Wholesale Grocers' Association, agreed to carry the manufacturer's Welcome branded products in exchange for a rebate of thirty cents per case. The first quarterly check from the concern totaled more than $10,000. To earn that money, BWGA members vowed "not to keep the products of the Lever Bros. Co," Curtis Davis's rival manufacturer. The BWGA made similar deals with the Walter Baker Company for distribution of its chocolate products, Procter and Gamble for the sale of Ivory soap, and the N. K. Fairbanks Company for distribution of its lard substitute, Cottolene. Working in concert with producers, the BWGA and other wholesalers' organizations minimized losses incurred in buying and selling low-margin products thanks to manufacturers' lucrative agreements, and also dominated distribution of several high-demand consumer goods, handcuffing retail grocers and forcing them to deal with BWGA members at their prices.[17]

Combating Collusion: Retailers and Cooperative Innovation

The BWGA's control over wholesaling rankled retailers. The collective force of the organization's influence over the price and availability of certain products brought new pressures to bear on area storekeepers. Initially, though, retailers did not balk. One sympathetic journal condoned selling sugar at "a regular price" as a way to guarantee a "moderate but fixed profit" from retail grocers' investment of "paper, string, and the turn of the scale" in preparing it for sale. The uniform prices wholesalers' negotiated with manufacturers, the BWGA and other trade groups argued, allowed both wholesaler and retailer a profit where traditionally there had been none. As beneficiaries, retailers at first had little need or incentive to question wholesale trade organizations.[18]

Yet by the late 1890s, as wholesalers expanded their influence and control, retailers increasingly felt squeezed by middlemen. In response, retailers innovated by establishing their own collective organizations in the form of buying syndicates (or exchanges) to bypass wholesalers and deal directly with manufacturers. John Nickerson, a well-known Boston wholesaler and onetime leader of the BWGA, remarked on this trend at the group's 1898 annual meeting. "To-day syndicates are being formed all over the City. One I know of composed six retailer grocers. They buy the same as we do; get all the discounts, and divide them up." A few years after Nickerson sounded the alarm, Edric Eldridge amplified the situation by informing his fellow BWGA members, "Retail dealers are combining and calling themselves wholesale grocers for the purpose of purchasing goods direct of the manufacturer at the manufacturer's price." Retail grocers, it seemed, had found a way to beat the BWGA at its own game, acting as wholesalers to forge their own deals with manufacturers for lower prices and discounts. Eldridge's message, however, made clear the real fear wholesalers felt from retail syndicates: they held the potential to assume wholesalers' functions and restructure the distribution chain.[19]

Retailers' sharp and inventive departure from the long-established structure of the grocery industry tests commonly held notions that chain stores alone blazed paths toward vertical integration in retailing. Faced with the same economic conditions that compelled manufacturing firms to integrate horizontally, but circumscribed by their geographically scattered stores and perishable goods, retail grocers responded by integrating outside the boundaries of the firm. As late as 1916, observers paired buying exchanges and chain stores as "new factors in the distribution of food" deserving of "prompt attention and careful consideration." Southern merchants in 1909 likewise asked, "Has the present system of distribution served its purpose? Is it antedated and antiquated and worn out? Is there a better way?" Through their flexible agreements and organizational structures, retailers revealed the trade's capacity to centralize on a regional level and reap the benefits that followed. For more than twenty years, exchanges moved toward fresh and potentially more efficient distribution methods, well before chains eventually diverged to pursue vertical integration. In the meantime, both the course of trade and its final destination remained undetermined.[20]

Buying syndicates differed in subtle but important ways from their better-known counterparts, retail selling cooperatives. Buying syndicates' primary goal was to circumnavigate wholesalers' organizations and buy goods directly from manufacturers. Most selling cooperatives, on the other hand, focused their energies on trading goods to consumers at uniform prices through collective pricing campaigns. Unlike buying syndicates, selling cooperatives formed almost wholly in response to chain store competition. The best-known selling cooperative, the Independent Grocers Alliance (IGA), did not organize until 1926, when chain stores posed a significant threat to the independent retail trade. Initially composed of one hundred stores, the IGA brought together wholesalers and retailers in a voluntary organization with corporate headquarters regulating buying, advertising, and prices, along with the manufacturing of IGA-branded foods, eventually gaining a national presence by the 1930s. Thirty years before chain store competition prompted selling cooperatives, however, retail grocers' buying exchanges fought the initial battle over wholesalers' ostensible distribution domination.[21]

One of the earliest (and largest) documented retail buying syndicates formed in 1893 in Philadelphia with twelve member firms. Shortly after its founding, the Frankford Grocers' Exchange merged with the Frankford Grocers' Association, eventually incorporating and collectively organizing the Frankford Grocery Company as a wholesaling operation for members only. The syndicate operated its own warehouse—billed as one of the largest in the city, a "thoroly [sic] modern, concrete building, with direct railroad connection." Retailers wishing to join were required to invest in the company's stock or to maintain sufficient cash deposits in either the organization's vacation or savings funds. A designated "buyer" conducted negotiations with manufacturers and made purchases on behalf of the entire group, paying cash for all transactions. Members placed orders for a week's supply at a time, with payment in full due on the Monday following receipt of goods. By 1920, the Frankford Grocery Company and its partner the Frankford Grocers' Association counted nearly eight hundred Philadelphia retailers among its members.[22]

The Philadelphia syndicate was just one of many urban buying groups that emerged in the 1890s. City retailers' proximity to manufacturers and each other made it easier than it did for country retailers to coordinate buying and distribution among member firms. Syndicates appeared in San Francisco,

Philadelphia dealers organized the Frankford Grocery Company, one of the first retail buyers' syndicates. Their central warehouse (photographed around 1934) served as a collection point for distributing members' orders around the city. Author's collection.

New York City, and Chicago, along with a host of other metropolises. Rural syndicates also emerged, only in smaller numbers. A correspondent for the trade journal *Grocery World* believed that buying exchanges could work in nearly any rural location. Dividing up a district into cooperative groups, country merchants could "employ a buyer to go to the city and make the purchase and have them delivered in a lump quantity to some one located near the railway station." The journalist believed "the possibilities of this system are limitless." Merchants in one Illinois region organized a buying exchange in 1900 to gain an advantage over mail-order houses, another form of competition retailers worked to combat. The group's organization consisted of 452 "shareholders" who contributed initial capital of $100,000 with purchasing points in two nearby cities, able to order "anything their customers may want, whether it is in their own line or not." Dubbed the "Co-operating Merchants Company," the exchange paid 8 percent of its dividends to capital stock, with remaining monies distributed among its participants "in proportion as they have helped create the profit by their purchases."[23]

There is no telling exactly how many grocers formed retail syndicates. *Thomas' Register of the Grocery and Kindred Trades* (grocers' unofficial credit and business directory) listed only thirteen "recognized" exchanges in the United States as of 1910, a number that grew to twenty-eight by 1915. The majority of even urban syndicates, however, tended to be informal agreements, lacking the structured rules and regulations of larger organizations like the Philadelphia or Illinois groups. Of the dozen syndicates claimed to operate in New York City at the turn of the century, most were simply friendly agreements between neighborhood dealers to pool money for bulk purchases. One San Francisco group operated for several years as a cooperative buying club without ever establishing a centralized warehouse or organization like the Philadelphia exchange. Smaller syndicates often found little need for formalized policies, procedures, and facilities that defined the large exchanges and instead carried out their buying and selling on a familiar basis through weekly meetings and collaborative ordering.[24]

The informality of most buying syndicates accounts for the paucity of details regarding their form and function. As a result, much of what we know about these alliances comes from wholesalers' reactions. This makes for complex and complicated storytelling, as most particulars about retail exchanges emerge through the lens of wholesalers' frustrations, anxieties, and fears over their own position in the trade. The BWGA met often about the "problem" of buying exchanges, airing their grievances and devising strategies to overcome syndicates' growing power. Their meeting minutes ring with angry and confused voices as the wholesalers struggled to understand changes that had come to their trade and to learn more about retail syndicates' intentions and operations. Although many of retail grocers' collaborative dealings were not committed to paper, they were no less methodical or effective in achieving their goals.

Buying syndicates' lack of formalized organization nevertheless made the groups a popular way for retailers to contend with wholesalers' limited price plans. By 1904, the buying exchange trend in Boston had spread beyond the city, with BWGA leaders expressing concern that "new syndicates are continually forming in our neighboring towns." Five years later, the Boston Retail Grocers' Association, counterpart to the BWGA, cheered the enterprising storekeepers. President Archibald L. Stark affirmed in 1909 that retail syndicates had begun "not from choice, but [were] forced by existing conditions to enter the wholesale field or buy direct from the manufacturers in order to compete with other wholesale[rs]." Without mentioning the BWGA, Stark acknowledged that Boston wholesalers' stronghold on prices and distribution had pushed retailers to rethink their reliance on middlemen and seek innovative ways to become more self-sufficient.[25]

Manufacturers' growing willingness to deal directly with retailers spurred on their cooperative energies. In 1869, for example, manufacturers sold 44 percent of all factory-made food products to wholesalers for distribution to independent grocers; that same year, producers sent only 7 percent of their goods directly to retailers. Thirty years later, the picture looked somewhat different. The internalization of marketing and distribution by some concerns like National Biscuit contributed to this shift, while other firms did what Arbuckle Brothers had done and purposefully sought retailers' business, avoiding groups like the BWGA and their restrictive practices. Chain stores, on the other hand, played a relatively minor part in these early years. In 1899, only 4 percent of manufacturers' goods shipped directly to grocery chains. That same year, 29 percent of manufactured food products shipped to wholesalers for distribution, while 13 percent went directly to retailers, nearly doubling manufacturers' direct sales to storekeepers in thirty years.[26]

In real and profound ways, retailers' buying syndicates altered grocery distribution by demonstrating how to excise wholesalers from the distribution chain. Such endeavors naturally threatened BWGA wholesalers who resolved that "our strength should be used to prevail upon the manufacturers not to sell the Retailer," with many deeming the problem "the most important matter in connection with the future of the business." This issue headlined the organization's annual meeting in 1904. "The selling by manufacturers direct to retailers or retail syndicates," President William Wadleigh informed his fellow members, "began in a small way, but has grown so fast that no doubt every one of the larger dealers among you has lost tens of thousands of dollars worth of business." Wadleigh further lamented, "While there are exceptions, there is hardly a manufacturer or manufacturer's agent or broker, but will sell to them, and as cheaply or nearly so, as to you."[27]

Boston's wholesalers commiserated with other middlemen. Jobbers in New York in 1905 made the "well-worn claim" that producers had "no ethical right to ignore the jobber, because it has always been understood that the manufacturer sold the wholesaler, and the wholesaler the retailer." Some manufacturers sided with wholesalers' plight. Speaking to the Kentucky Retail Grocers' Association, Ellis Howland, trade relations spokesman for Kellogg's, affirmed, "we believe that the wholesaler, who on the average costs the manufacturer approximately 10 percent, is entitled to at least that reward for the services he performs." Most manufacturers, however, had little sympathy. "We have not the slightest intention, under any circumstances or in the face of any demands, of placing the distribution of our products entirely in the hands of the wholesalers," a New York producer asserted anonymously, cautious of how his statement might affect business. Some manufacturers blamed wholesalers for creating their own troubles, citing the tendency of larger wholesale concerns like Chicago's Franklin MacVeagh to manufacture and distribute their own branded goods, undercutting manufacturers' prices in favor of wholesalers' own products. The same nameless producer issued a succinct warning: "The jobber must remember that he is between the upper and nether millstones, and unless he is exceedingly careful he may be ground to a powder."[28]

Blurring Distribution's Boundaries

The manufacturer's metaphor was apt but inaccurate. The distribution chain at the turn of the twentieth century was neither as fixed nor as defined as many claimed. No one form or method dominated. In addition to disruptions brought about by retailers' buying exchanges, some wholesalers sold directly to consumers, bypassing retailers altogether, and mail-order houses and department stores added food to their litany of merchandise. These developments, like buying syndicates, upset conventional distribution paths and provoked many to question wholesalers' claims that they were the best and only way to move groceries from manufacturers to retailers and consumers.

As early as the 1870s, wholesalers in various lines began vending goods to shoppers, not unlike department store moguls Alexander T. Stewart and Marshall Field, who eliminated links in the distribution chain by opening ancillary retail enterprises for their bulk wares. One Indiana tea jobber in 1874, for example, unabashedly proclaimed on his billhead that he sold "direct to the consumers." He justified his actions as a solution to distribution inefficiencies. "NO MIDDLE MEN," he avowed, "shall eat the profits between them [consumers] and us." *American Grocer* blamed the situation in 1875 on "the dullness in business" and customers' desire to save "for themselves the profits of from one to three middlemen through whose hands the goods they buy would have to pass in the natural course of trade." That same year retailer Benjamin Hildreth complained about the "injustice" such wholesalers levied on "legitimate trade," letting others know that "not only are the retailers in New York suffering," but "other towns around us in Ohio are also suffering from the same cause," brought about by "wholesale merchants ... scattered all over our land." By the 1880s, trade observers noted the continued "desirability of checking retail sales on the part of Jobbers." While many like the BWGA argued that the distribution chain was fixed, the fluidity of distribution paths belied those claims, oftentimes blurring the boundaries between wholesaler and retailer.[29]

In the 1890s, farmers joined the initiative, blaming wholesalers and other intermediaries for low prices and declining profits on their crops and products and creating measures to reduce distribution inefficiencies. Across the Midwest, suggestions for eliminating commercial middlemen from all trades echoed similar demands made in the 1870s by Grangers, a coalition of Midwest farmers who fought against railroads' monopolistic shipping practices by supporting initiatives such as consumers' cooperatives and rural free delivery. When Grangers proposed to infringe on merchants' territory to "set up supply stores for general merchandise," grocers balked. The editors of *American Grocer* expressed their concerns. "Grangers are doing a good and useful work by their organization so long as they confine themselves to legitimate purposes, they have no right morally to injure any other class in the community." Twenty years later under the banner of Populism, farmers again came together to challenge middlemen. In Texas, the Farmers' Alliance blamed both wholesalers for using deceitful practices to drive down the price of cotton and retailers who used similar tactics to control the market, denying farmers fair money for their goods. Farmers contended that doing away with all middlemen would enable them to control the distribution and selling of their own products, raising profits and lowering costs to consumers.[30]

Grangers and Populists, like retail grocers, were not immune to economies of scale and their power to wrest greater profits from smaller margins. Populists in particular used their agriculturally based membership to gain political momentum in the 1890s by calling for economic and business reform, and the regulation of banks, corporations, and transportation to protect farmers from big business. Farmers' adoption of cooperative methods

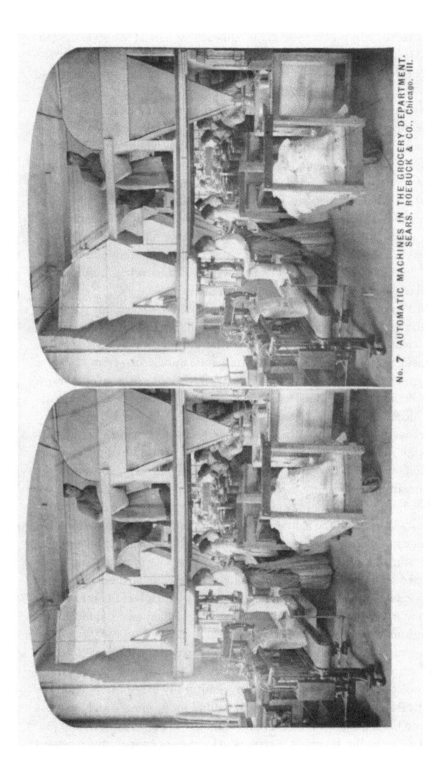

No. 7 AUTOMATIC MACHINES IN THE GROCERY DEPARTMENT.
SEARS, ROEBUCK & CO., Chicago, Ill.

Sears, Roebuck and Company's ability to mass produce grocery staples, as depicted in this 1900s stereoview, and distribute them direct to consumers through mail-order catalogs disrupted and threatened wholesale and retail grocers' established distribution channels. Stereoscopic images allowed the public to see how machines and automated processes were altering food production. Author's collection.

(along with transportation and communications advantages businessmen shared) placed them squarely within the realm of modern industrialism. Using capitalism's tools, farmers and grocers alike crafted organizations that allowed them to compete within regional markets, even if storekeepers worried that Granger outlets invaded their particular selling sphere. Both experimented with bulk buying groups, cooperatively owned warehouses, and consumer price controls. Their common goal—challenging concentrated capital—generated a language of modernity that spoke to ideas about efficiency and competition that were just as relevant to farming and store-keeping as they were to big businesses. Directly challenging the emerging corporate capitalism (while also part of it), both constructed visions of regionally and locally based enterprises attuned to collective needs as much as individual interests. Indeed, farmers and small retailers shared far more than they might have admitted in the 1890s, especially as new distribution and selling methods continued to put all on guard against any changes that might cull them from the market.[31]

Discontent with distribution inefficiencies ranged as far and wide as the solutions that were proposed. Some enterprising merchants saw the answer in mail-order catalog sales, which threatened not just grocers but retailers in other lines as well. Started by the likes of Montgomery Ward and Sears, Roebuck and Company, catalog grocery sales proposed to reduce much of the handling and distribution costs associated with manufactured goods. Ward himself had been an ardent Granger and later became a Populist, seeing in mail order and free delivery opportunities to monopolize distribution to farmers, elevating both their living standards and access to his products. He initially steered clear of food marketing, however, especially "heavy groceries" such as sugar, rice, and coffee, explaining in his 1875 catalog that "they add to the cost of transportation to an alarming degree." The advent of rural free delivery in 1896 and parcel post in the 1910s cleared the way for both Ward and Sears, Roebuck to expand into making and packaging their own brand-named grocery products, including chocolates, flour, and smoked herring. Each maintained enormous distribution facilities and realized significant economies of scale by eliminating markups paid to middlemen. As a result, consumers benefited from lower costs, while some retailers watched their businesses decline. One insider estimated that the average retail grocer sold coffee to only 50 percent of his customers, with the other half ordering from mail-order catalogs or purchasing it in alternative venues.[32]

Additional pressure came from companies like Larkin, a Buffalo, New York, soap manufacturer, which sold through the mail and door-to-door.

A 1909 New York meeting of grocery manufacturers, jobbers, and retailers, mulled over Larkin's "factory-to-family" plan. This economic theory and method suggested that by making manufacturers sole distributors to consumers, both wholesalers and retailers could be eliminated, reducing prices to consumers and increasing efficiency. The grocerymen who attended the meeting labeled both theory and practice a "fallacy" and urged members to educate the public to its dangers. They insisted that "factory-to-family" did not represent real savings and instead argued that "the regular channel of distribution is from the retailer to the consumer, and the same is the most economical means of delivering." Larkin, however, posed an added threat to retailers by encouraging women to form their own cooperatives, solicit orders from neighbors, and buy in bulk directly from the company. In time, home economists and others would tout consumer cooperatives as the best way for families to achieve lower foods costs, so long as "the machinery of distribution was in the hands of the so-called middlemen." Such methods had a chilling effect on both wholesalers and retailers as each fretted about losing out to concentrated enterprise.[33]

It was department stores, however, that struck closest to home, especially among urban grocery retailers. These large emporiums encroached on grocers' business by offering a range of staple and fancy goods. A number of New York and Chicago department stores, for example, boasted large selections of refrigerated meats, cheeses, and fresh vegetables, along with a variety of canned goods, liquors, coffees, and teas. "An hour in our Grocery department," Macy's bragged to its shoppers, "is a revelation." Abundant goods stacked in decorative displays represented "real economy" for those looking for savings. As department stores gained footholds in major cities, retail grocers like those in Brooklyn, New York, gathered to voice their protestations "against the business departure" of department stores that sold groceries. Ironically, the problem, as many saw it, was that Macy's and other emporiums used "deceptive" practices such as selling goods below cost to lure shoppers to other departments where markups and profits were greater.[34]

The volume discounts that department stores received (along with the kickbacks wholesalers' organizations negotiated) from manufacturers triggered much of the hostility grocers maintained toward corporate enterprise. Chain stores like A&P used the same tactics, inveigling producers to give them special consideration because of their size, whereas most buying exchanges managed to match wholesalers' prices only when dealing with producers. Manufacturers, however, encouraged volume buying because it guaranteed sales of large quantities and the economies associated with mass production and distribution. Volume discounts, however, challenged individual retail and wholesale grocers' ability to compete, provoking them to fight against the advantages enjoyed by large firms, often to no avail. In 1894, when Macy's decided to sell pickles made by Crosse & Blackwell (a prominent European brand), New York jobbers successfully blocked their attempt by refusing to supply the delicacy. Macy's owner Isidor Straus instead simply cabled the company the same day for one hundred barrels of the pickles, a transaction that cost him less money than he would have paid local agents.[35]

Straus's actions struck at the core of grocers' anxieties. Concentrating greater economic power into fewer hands had allowed one man to circumvent an entire cadre of businessmen. Individual enterprise and independence seemed to evaporate with one telegram. Department stores and their unmitigated success at converging wholesaling and retailing stood for grocers as large and visible symbols of the dangers of unbridled competition and the need for collusion among small retailers. Where concentration in manufacturing affected a few key products that wholesalers distributed, department stores were poised to imperil the entire industry by adapting the form to selling nearly all goods. Their economies of scale and the direct relationship they had with consumers suggested to wholesale and retail grocers a future bound not in sole proprietorships but in concentrated capital. In 1906, BWGA members, meeting to discuss antitrust laws and their potential impact on collusive trade agreements such as those the BWGA made with Quaker Oats, made clear the dangers they saw in consolidated firms, with Secretary William Seaver stating bluntly, "They immediately form a huge corporation, which secures to them all of the benefits of such agreements. They have killed the individual in business and annihilated competition."[36]

Following Straus's successful circumvention, New York grocers met to discuss the situation. In addition to their gripes about the ways in which "inside rebates" disadvantaged retailers, they accused department stores of selling cut-rate goods and mislabeled products along with luring women into buying whiskey in corset-wrapped bottles. All were tricks, they believed, designed to draw customers away from grocers' shops. "Pretty soon these dry goods stores will be advertising coffins free in order to induce people to buy flour. They'll be offering inducements to people to die," Manhattan wholesaler Herman Rohrs chided. G. Waldo Smith, president of the New York Wholesale Grocers' Association, pitched what amounted to the BWGA's original solution to the problem: a limited price scheme. Retailers blasted the plan. "The limited price and rebate system is the detriment of the retail grocers," one storekeeper contended, because it advantaged volume buyers over smaller firms. Another stated simply that limited pricing "is not in the interest of the retail grocers." Artemas Ward provided both reassurance and cause for concern when he announced that his firm had negotiated a contract with wholesalers for shipping Sapolio soap, "which forbids them to sell to dry goods stores."[37]

The very thing retailers protested, both Ward and Smith endorsed. Yet where wholesalers and manufacturers found salvation in limited pricing and volume discounts, New York retailers saw only the undermining of their trade as "fair competition" gave way to the "advantageous position" claimed by large-scale enterprise. For the first time, small businessmen came face-to-face with giant firms at the crossroads of commerce and chose to take free enterprise's moral high road to defend their position. They expressed their concerns about those who blurred the boundaries of distribution by suggesting that such actions were "degrading" and "a trade demoralizer." Such talk clearly referred to the loss of business and the decline of financial gains that surely would accompany the elimination of either retailers or wholesalers from the distribution chain. Severing an artery of the grocery trade would hemorrhage profits, wages, and labor from the economy, creating a maelstrom of effects on local and national levels. Their language also spoke to concerns about the decline of business ethics and the discomfiture some felt when their competitors tried to "steal" business from others. Wholesaler Thomas C. Jenkins made this point on every billhead, declaring in bold lettering that he had "no retail store or any connection with any retail house in any shape or form" and refused to sell goods directly to consumers. With obvious finger pointing, Jenkins poked at fellow wholesalers who encroached on retailers' territory.[38]

Whatever retail grocers thought of department stores, mail-order houses, and rebellious wholesalers, none had managed to displace fully the entrenched distribution chain that continued to move the majority of the nation's food. Department stores and mail-order houses in particular failed to provide all the products consumers demanded and typical wholesale and retail grocers offered. While some catalogs and department emporiums offered lower prices than retailers thanks to their volume discounts, they did so with only a small number of packaged articles. Most did not supply the fresh fruits, meats, cheeses, butter, eggs, or countless other items grocers carried. Mail-order distributors likewise could not guarantee the delivery time of their merchandise. It took a savvy homemaker to plan all her meals and budget around the delivery of groceries from hundreds of miles and days away, especially when home (and shipping) refrigeration still was rudimentary at best. While mail-order houses and department stores threatened independent grocers early on, firms such as Sears, Roebuck eventually quit their mail-order grocery operations in the 1920s when consumers expressed their preference for the convenience of shopping in neighborhood stores (which offered similar savings) over waiting for postal deliveries.[39]

The Retail Buying Syndicate Menace

Retail buying exchanges, however, continued to pose a real threat to wholesalers. This point became clear to the BWGA in October 1905 when it faced a fundamental crisis. Leaders called a special meeting "for the purpose of considering the subject of maintaining prices in the face of existing competition." Members debated the feasibility of its fixed pricing scheme, and by extension the BWGA, in "the day of Department Stores [and] Retail buying syndicates." Just two years earlier, BWGA member William Wadleigh had forewarned that "existing conditions, occasioned by the innovation of new methods, have led some to feel that the usefulness of our Association was about over." Boston wholesaler Edric Eldridge later confirmed that retail exchanges "had become a power. They could buy goods as cheaply as the Wholesaler and sell without restriction."[40]

Those assembled confronted the issue of whether wholesalers' fixed pricing and control over distribution still had the influence to govern the market and fight the growth of retail syndicates. Where collusion once protected wholesalers from destructive price wars, it now seemed to offer little shelter from retailers who negotiated their own prices with manufacturers. Competition from retail syndicates had opened fissures in the limited price plan as early as 1902, when BWGA members met to reaffirm their beliefs "that a continuance of the Rebate and Limited Price System on the sale of Standard and Proprietary Goods is necessary to the success of the Wholesale Grocery Business." Wholesalers increasingly faced the dual challenges of supporting both the collusive foundations of their organization and the basic belief that theirs was the best method for distributing groceries. The middleman, once considered the distribution chain's strongest link, now appeared to be weakening.[41]

The anxiety the BWGA felt in 1905 over the possible collapse of its limited price plan escalated in response to sugar refiners' announcement earlier in the year that they would discontinue offering price guarantees to wholesale grocers. This meant that wholesalers no longer would enjoy volume discounts, lower costs, and selling at higher prices. "The jobber will buy sugar at his own risk, and his own judgment will be his only protection," refiners warned. Once sheltered by their limited price plan and substantial reimbursements, the BWGA and other wholesalers now were exposed to the vagaries of the sugar market. Would more manufacturers follow suit?[42]

Fortunately for the BWGA and other wholesalers, several key producers were unwilling to deal with retail buying syndicates. Procter and Gamble, the Diamond Match Company, and the Toasted Corn Flake Company, for example, yielded to wholesalers' pressures in the early 1900s and did not sell directly to Philadelphia's powerful buying exchange. The reality that both manufacturers and retailers continued to depend on wholesalers for distribution placed groups like the BWGA in a strong position. A manufacturer's representative emphasized this point, noting, "There were so many lines and kinds of proprietary goods now in the retail grocery trade that it was impossible for any retail grocer to do his business and buy ALL he had to have from a manufacturer." This gap between what buying exchanges could purchase and what retailers needed to stock their stores exposed a weakness in the power of cooperative retail buying and also provided a foothold for wholesalers in the battle to control the distribution chain.[43]

Much of the BWGA's chatter regarding retail syndicates centered on convincing manufacturers that retailers had little to offer in terms of distributing, promoting, and selling their goods. Most agreed that the best tactic was "to stop the Manufacturers from selling [to] the Retail Trade and have trade

Like many manufacturers, the makers of Hart's Yeast resisted blurring distribution lines in the 1890s. The firm's proclamation and preference in dealing with wholesale jobbers heralded their support of independent enterprise. Author's collection.

flow through legitimate channels." BWGA member John Nickerson proposed sending an ultimatum to manufacturers: "Will you select us to sell your product, or do you prefer to take the retailer, if so we will not handle your goods." This tough talk exposed wholesalers' frustrations with manufacturers and retailers alike, as each found innovative ways to work around middlemen. Edric Eldridge had once insisted at a 1901 BWGA meeting, "As wholesale dealers we should firmly maintain our rights and oppose this with all the strength that we possess." Urging members to throw their collective weight into the matter, Eldridge advised, "We should give [sic] the broker to understand that they cannot hope to sell [to] the retail dealer and at the same time retain the patronage of the wholesale merchants." Committed to a long-standing trade structure that once (and in many ways still) required a wide range of intermediaries to move goods, Eldridge and the BWGA failed to see that some manufacturers and retailers no longer needed their business or their services.[44]

The group nevertheless hoped that by implementing strong-arm tactics they could force manufacturers into selling exclusively to them, thereby accomplishing three important goals: preservation of the BWGA; destruction of retail syndicates; and reaffirmation of wholesalers as sole grocery distributors. A 1905 BWGA committee appointed to investigate the matter determined that the best course was to strike back by "consolidating our purchasing power," thereby establishing "loyalty on our part to the manufacturer." This in turn, BWGA officials predicted, would promote the selling of manufacturers' goods "through one main channel only, namely, ourselves." Taking their cue from retailers, the BWGA proposed uniting with fellow New England wholesalers to create buying power greater than that of the syndicates. In this way, the BWGA intended to use both its cooperative muscle and collusive sway to convince manufacturers once and for all that wholesalers' centralized control of the distribution chain was indeed the best and most effective method. Bigness, wholesalers now believed, could save independent businessmen instead of destroying them.[45]

Yet when wholesale grocers in other parts of the country tried similar tactics, pressuring manufacturers to keep them from selling directly to retailers, they incurred lawmakers' wrath. In 1910, the US Department of Justice charged the Southern Wholesale Grocers' Association (SWGA) with violating the Sherman Antitrust Act. Organized in 1891 along the same lines as the BWGA, the SWGA initially comprised over 150 southern wholesalers who supported the principle that "trade should pass through regular channels." Prosecutors, however, alleged that the SWGA through coercion was "preventing manufacturers from selling the actual necessities of life direct to the retail dealer or consumer." The Department of Justice likewise targeted the SWGA for fixing limited selling prices and receiving substantial rebates for maintaining those prices on a number of items. In June 1910, the organization made front-page news when Oliver D. Street, US attorney for the Northern District of Alabama, filed a petition on behalf of the Department of Justice seeking (and eventually winning) an injunction against the SWGA for being "an illegal combination in restraint of trade."[46]

What distinguished the SWGA from the BWGA was the scale and depth of the SWGA's collusion. Where the BWGA controlled the wholesale trade in Boston, the SWGA coordinated wholesaling across much of the South, including the District of Columbia, making it a much larger and more visible target for antitrust discipline. It was the degree to which the SWGA coerced manufacturers into respecting traditional trade boundaries, however, that lay at the heart of the charges. The SWGA maintained a "Green Book," a pamphlet listing the names of its members. Alone, the book did not pose a problem. What made it a deadly weapon was its dissemination to manufacturers with the implicit understanding that if producers sold their products to non-SWGA members or retailers they faced boycott from the nearly one thousand wholesalers and trade associates listed. That damning testimony came from Hinton G. Clabaugh, a Birmingham, Alabama, independent wholesaler later turned special agent for the Department of Justice. Early in 1910, Clabaugh had won a $30,000 judgment against the SWGA for forcing him out of business because he tried undercutting the group's prices and selling by catalog to retail grocers. Letters from several manufacturers rejecting Clabaugh's orders because he was not a member of the SWGA proved the most damning evidence against the organization's methods.[47]

Join or die: that was the message groups like the SWGA and BWGA sent wholesalers. For men like Clabaugh, it undoubtedly sounded much like the signal John D. Rockefeller had once imparted to oil refiners through his Southern Improvement Company (SIC). Orchestrated in 1872 as a secret alliance between Rockefeller and Pennsylvania Railroad president Tom Scott, the SIC united large oil refiners with railroads in an attempt to halt destructive price-cutting in both industries and control transportation rates, thus ensuring profitable margins and lucrative rebates for all involved. Rockefeller used the threat of his coalition's bigness to buy out smaller refiners (although he denied taking such measures), consolidating more than twenty firms in what became known as the "Cleveland Massacre." In the aftermath, independent holdouts who refused to join Rockefeller's budding trust faced higher prices for shipping their oil, among other competitive disadvantages. Many small refiners faced two choices: sell out or be crushed, a likely reality given Standard's overwhelming power. Non-membership had its price. Surveying the scene in 1910, independent grocery wholesalers might have taken comfort in knowing that the SWGA's anti-competitive schemes had been found out, but worried that imitators lay ahead. Could grocery trade organizations follow suit and evolve into single-firm trusts?[48]

As far as the BWGA was concerned, this was never a possibility. The group's members always envisioned their cartel and agreements as necessary for protecting independent enterprise, not for monopolizing the industry through corporate merger. "We are pleading for the life of the individual in business," William Wadleigh insisted in 1906 while arguing for antitrust law reforms, and "we cannot and would not destroy competition." Wanting to continue their cooperative alliances with manufacturers and each other, the BWGA blamed the Sherman Act's potential to "drive out *individuals* in trade, when individual effort is the proper thing to encourage,—the *best* thing for communities and the country at large." In light of the SWGA decision and no forthcoming Sherman amendments that would allow the kinds of trade agreements the organization claimed necessary to protect their interests, the BWGA ceased limiting sugar prices in February 1911. Organization leaders later conceded that such practices "would be a clear case of violation of the law and might lead to imprisonment." Wholesalers' associations in general operated under heightened scrutiny in the wake of the SWGA affair. During an October 1910 meeting, BWGA president George B. Wason rallied members to take a greater interest in politics especially "when the Department of Justice is following us so closely for getting together and getting a living profit."[49]

Agitation over the increased cost of living that swept the nation beginning in the 1910s likewise put wholesalers, including the BWGA, on even higher alert. Concerns that politicians would "try to make [middlemen] the Goat" for increasing costs associated with buying and selling groceries rattled not just the BWGA but all wholesalers. The 10 percent to 20 percent each intermediary added to the cost of handling goods, many observers believed, bore directly on the inflated prices consumers found in their local stores. For some, retailers' battle to eliminate middlemen through cooperative buying offered a solution for economy in the grocery trade even as wholesalers protested their "right" to distribute manufacturers' products. The collusive and sometimes coercive practices wholesalers' associations used to "get a living profit" increasingly became circumspect, especially as retail syndicates continued to point the finger at wholesalers and their "old methods" for keeping prices high. Legislative action combined with economic pressures and retailers' buying syndicates placed wholesalers on the brink of being eliminated from the trade.[50]

The Limitations of Trade Cooperation

Retailers' dependence on middlemen's traditional functions ultimately prevented buying syndicates from permanently redrawing the path of distribution. Between 1908 and 1927, nearly 90 of 170 retail grocery exchanges disbanded owing to a number of complaints from exchange members about organizational deficiencies. A survey of the situation in 1930 noted that while "buying associations have existed in the United States for over 40 years," more recent failures reflected long-standing problems with syndicates. Retailers cited "inadequate stock of merchandise" as the primary reason they did not buy all their merchandise from exchanges, with respondents remarking, "No one organization has a full line." When asked why he did not trade with a syndicate, one retailer replied succinctly, "The wholesalers do more for you. They'll deliver the goods when you want them, send salesmen around after your orders, and help you over tight places." Other rationales for not using exchanges concerned getting "lower prices from other sources," including manufacturers and salesmen who offered special deals, and inadequate service, defined by some as extending more credit to some grocers than others.[51]

Generous credit lines were, in part, a tool wholesalers used to smooth distribution and generate greater stock turnover. They functioned as a rational response to a market deficiency—the lack of adequate working capital among small retailers. Wholesale houses remedied those shortfalls by readily financing storekeepers' purchases, enabling products to flow more rapidly through distribution channels. While fruits, vegetables, and staples would have made their way to the market without intermediary financiers, they would not have done so as quickly or in as great a quantity. "It is not possible to do a wholesale business upon a strictly cash basis," *American Grocer* contended as early as the 1870s, "nor is it desirable that it should be done." When it came to the wholesale trade, editors estimated that "If all business operations were reduced to a system of absolute and inexorable cash, it would diminish the amount of commerce and exchange, by at least one-half if not two thirds." Whether this estimate was accurate, most grocers acknowledged without reservation that more than thirty years later, wholesalers' credit still funded the continuous stream of goods that flowed across the country.[52]

Retail buying exchanges challenged this custom with limited success. The structure and operation of retail buying exchanges varied in certain degrees, but most shared one characteristic: cash trading only. This way of doing business was relatively new for most retailers, who had regularly turned to wholesalers' long and lenient credit-buying terms to help them weather turbulent times. Unlike banks that granted secured cash loans, wholesalers advanced goods and services on a contractual and unsecured basis. Retail dealers seeking mercantile credit promised to settle their accounts within a predetermined time, typically from one to six months, although wholesalers sometimes carried accounts for well over a year. Interest on accounts not paid in full by six months ranged between 6 percent and 10 percent. Cash buyers often negotiated cheaper prices and better terms, with many wholesale houses offering a one to one-half percent discount for full cash payment. While some retailers asked for and maintained a line of credit with only one or two wholesale dealers, the majority held accounts with a number of different houses.[53]

Buying syndicates' cash policies motivated wholesalers to reason that if retailers willingly paid cash to purchase goods directly from manufacturers who refused to extend credit, they could pay cash more frequently to wholesalers. In Philadelphia, the formation of the Frankford Grocers' Exchange and other area syndicates prompted wholesalers to begin restricting credit extensions and require prompter payments. Many wholesalers reduced the time they carried retailers' accounts from a customary six months to thirty days with a one percent deduction if paid within ten days. "That pressure," admitted an industry commentator, came largely "from the influence of the co-operative associations." In 1901, the BWGA codified these shorter terms as the "conditions of sale of merchandise," with an agreement "not to allow our customers to abuse this privilege."[54]

Wholesalers, however, remained unconvinced that they should do away with credit entirely. The small profit margin afforded by groceries pressured wholesalers to compensate by boosting stock turnover—grocerymen's equivalent of manufacturers' throughput. A 1916 study by the Harvard Bureau of Business Research reported that grocery wholesalers turned their stock on average once every two months, with some larger firms claiming stock turns of over nine times every year. Those who managed faster turnover enjoyed "a substantial reduction in their ratio of total expense to net sales," according to a later report. In other words, grocers who moved large amounts of goods more frequently (and generally through credit channels) realized greater economies than those who moved fewer goods. Wholesalers whose sales exceeded their accounts receivable (those who sold more for cash than they credited out) recognized savings of only "four-tenths of one percent of net sales," according to Harvard's 1919 follow-up survey. This was a figure experts tried to puff as "a difference that is by no means negligible in a trade that operates on so narrow a margin as the wholesale grocery business." The advantages to cash dealing in the early decades of the twentieth century, therefore, appeared marginal compared to the benefits of maintaining crediting practices and ties.[55]

Some nevertheless saw buying syndicates' cash-only policies as a sign of "more efficient and economical business methods." Wholesalers' increasingly stringent credit requirements coupled with buying exchanges' strict cash rules promised to raise entry barriers in the retail grocery trade, reducing the number of storekeepers reliant on wholesale credit for starting and staying in business. Cash dealing could potentially weed out retailers who had insufficient funds to trade without credit, thereby "restricting the retail grocery business to those who have some responsibility." Others nevertheless continued to complain that the overpopulation of undercapitalized retail stores created a drain on wholesalers' credit and services.[56]

Despite critics' high hopes, buying exchanges did not stop "irresponsible" storekeepers from entering the trade nor did they eliminate such grocers' dependence on wholesale credit. A 1920s survey of conditions in Louisville, Kentucky, revealed that of the twenty-four retail grocers who failed in one year, all did so "with considerable loss to creditors." Many "simply walked out of [their] store[s] leaving no assets, except a few dozen articles of canned goods, some fixtures, the title to which was in an installment house, and some uncollectible accounts receivable." The situation in Buffalo, New York, was similar. Between 1918 and 1927, approximately 5,700 new independent grocers entered trade, with 83 percent closing their doors by 1928, "most of the capital" having been "furnished by wholesalers." Some refused to blame buying syndicates for failing to grant credit and alleviate retailers' dependence on wholesalers, while others chalked up the inability of the exchanges to remake crediting practices to "the continuation of the old methods of the wholesalers."[57]

Although buying exchanges failed to purge so-called old methods, wholesalers no longer could claim sole control over distribution. Instead, they reveled in their endurance. In 1921, the National Wholesale Grocers' Association boasted, "Of all the ingenious systems that have been devised, not one has eliminated the middleman's costs and services." Wholesalers remained an essential part of the grocery trade, especially for independent retailers. At the same time chain stores began integrating intermediary functions into their organizations, wholesalers continued providing goods to those who operated outside the chain structure. In 1935, for example, wholesalers still supplied 57.8 percent of the trade, while manufacturers shipped 37.9 percent of their products directly to retail stores. The wholesaling trade itself, however, did not remain static. New methods, including "cash-and-carry" and "self-service" wholesaling, combined with customary full-service wholesaling "further lowered operating overhead in the never-ending competitive struggle in the food field." The middleman endured.[58]

What's Old Is New Again

Between 1890 and 1915, retail syndicates jabbed at wholesale grocers. By the end of the 1910s, however, a rapid influx of chain stores into the market took the spotlight away from retail buying syndicates. In Boston alone, A&P opened ninety-five of its cash-and-carry economy stores in one six-month period during 1915. New York looked the same. According to one estimate, the city's independent retail grocery stores increased just 54 percent between 1903 and 1914, while chain stores grew 360 percent. Buying syndicates, once wholesalers' greatest threat, now took a back seat to the potential menace chain stores posed. Middlemen, however, continued to profess that they were the "logical medium of distribution between the manufacturer and the retailer." A 1928 Department of Commerce study focusing on wholesale grocers' problems reconfirmed that in the past "a pronounced effect on distribution methods ... tended to upset channels of movement which were deemed fixed and unalterable." Nevertheless, the study concluded, "because of his past record," the wholesaler had "good reason to suppose that his services are still required in the same degree as formerly."[59]

Well into the twentieth century, wholesalers convincingly argued that the old order was, for a large component of the trade, the most efficient order. It was, by standards most often evoked by contemporary business critics and economists, outmoded, expensive, and wasteful. The small lots of perishable goods retail grocers ordered to please their customers' many tastes were incompatible with theories of economy idealized and practiced by other industries because they required quick delivery and frequent turnover. As wholesalers worked to move stocks of an increasing number and variety from a greater range of manufacturers, they still relied on long-established distribution channels and methods of financing. While their insistence on having distribution "rights" rang antiquated and hypocritical in the ears of many, most wholesale grocers found that by preserving the old order through trade agreements and collusion, they could address problems brought on by mass production and the influx of chain store competition. Summing up, the Department of Commerce reasoned, "The activities may be transferred into other hands, but the assembling and warehousing at convenient points must be continued, and the cost of doing it remains." In the long run, there was no avoiding the middleman.[60]

In many ways, buying syndicates and wholesalers' trade associations were both the road taken and not taken. In the interwar years, retail exchanges increased in number owing in part to competition from chains and the economic difficulties of the Great Depression, which spurred greater cooperation between retailers. In 1935, for example, 1.9 percent of wholesale grocery sales originated from retail syndicate warehouses. Four years later, that number had grown to 2.5 percent, a small, but important indicator of retail syndicates' potential. Most important, though, was that retailers' fresh ideas had forever put wholesalers on guard against interlopers by showing both them and chains the feasibility of shortening the distribution path for groceries. Retailers' syndicates and wholesalers' associations also demonstrated the benefits of centralizing the geographically and organizationally diffuse trade outside the firm, bringing together a large number of independent grocers to take advantage of distribution economies, coordinated markets, and manufacturers' volume discounts. Redrawing the boundaries of distribution, local grocers pointed toward methods that ultimately defined the modern grocery trade. The irony, however, is that chains used the same tools retailers and wholesalers created to overtake the trade. In many ways, then, independent grocers' innovativeness became their downfall.[61]

5

Making Small Business Big

Frederick E. Croxton, a young statistician and economics instructor at Ohio State University and later administrator with the Great Depression–era Reconstruction Finance Corporation, charged his students in 1924 with the task of ascertaining "the approximate importance of the various types of food retailers" among Columbus-area homemakers. The survey asked consumers to rank by store type the places where they purchased four categories of food-stuffs. Croxton hoped to address several questions regarding women's buying habits but primarily sought to determine the importance of neighborhood groceries versus chain stores. Foremost on the statistician's mind was whether "the enormous buying power of the chain organization" and its ability to sell at cheaper prices drew more housewives than did independent stores, despite the fact that neighborhood shops "usually grant credit, make deliveries, and generally feature the appeal of service." Croxton's timely survey struck at the heart of the grocery trade's prevailing anxiety: Would corporate chains eliminate independent grocers?[1]

The answer seems preordained, given the advantage of hindsight. In the 1920s and 1930s, however, nobody knew with any certainty what the outcome might be. By 1931, chains accounted for nearly 45 percent of sales in the grocery trade, with A&P selling $1 billion in goods in 1929 through its nearly 16,000 outlets, the first retailer to achieve that mark. Despite the seemingly meteoric rise and prominence of chain stores in the early twentieth century, their future as the dominant business model was not assured. The same year A&P out-stripped all grocers, chain stores accounted for only 50,000 of the more than 300,000 grocery stores nationwide, with the number of chains dipping during the Great Depression. Chains' larger market share with fewer stores signaled their economic benefits to many, while others felt optimistic that small, local grocers held important advantages over anonymous chain corporations. Frederick Croxton, for example, discovered in his survey that many consumers still overwhelmingly preferred neighborhood grocery stores for the vast majority of their food purchases. They gave "first choice to the unit [independent] store as compared with the chain store" in all four grocery-buying categories, leading Croxton to conclude that the local grocer "was the more important" for consumers. Many surveyed, though, "did not know whether the store in question was a chain store or a so-called unit store," suggesting how the two organizational styles and methods blurred lines in consumers' minds as well as in practice.[2]

At stake in the battle between chain and independent grocers was both the definition and future of small business in America. Independent grocers' notions of personal independence enabled them to build both businesses and status in their local communities, serving the needs of neighbors and friends as well as towns and villages. For much of the nation's history, they were the model for American enterprise, the first (and often the only) rung on the ladder to business and personal success, elements fitting of the "American dream" popularized by historian James Truslow Adams in 1931. Chains threatened to remake that vision as their own, blocking the pathway to independence through small business ownership by raising the trade's historically low entry barriers. Few alone could afford Clarence Saunders's $10,000 franchise fee for his Piggly Wiggly system's plans and fixtures. Enterprising spirit, knowledge of local markets, and commitment to service had made small grocers exemplars of nineteenth-century business; chain corporations' large-scale productivity and operations threatened to become the new twentieth-century criteria by which all retail businesses would be defined and judged.[3]

Throughout the 1920s and 1930s, independents and chains battled both for market supremacy and to determine whether the archetypal independent merchant or the national chain organizer was the better commercial and social model for American enterprise. When independent grocers and small businessmen found support from Congress in the New Deal era, the fight took on new significance and meaning as local, state, and national lawmakers debated the potential value and hazards of large-scale operations. Dissenting from a 1933 Supreme Court decision regarding chain growth and regulation, Justice Louis D. Brandeis questioned the belief that "the privilege of doing business in corporate form [was] inherent in the citizen." Recalling more than two hundred years of small business domination, Brandeis lectured, "Throughout the greater part of our history a different view prevailed" whereby "incorporation for business was commonly denied . . . because of fear. Fear of encroachment upon the liberties and opportunities of the individual."[4]

Raymond Moley, a onetime member of the New Deal "Brain Trust" turned conservative critic, denounced Brandeis's opinions. He suggested that the longtime justice had placed his faith in the notion that "America once more could become a nation of small proprietors, of corner grocers and smithies under spreading chestnut trees." Chain store corporations lobbed these same accusations at independent merchants, suggesting that they were trying to preserve some long-forgotten past. What Moley and chain corporations failed to recognize in their nostalgic characterizations—and what Brandeis and others clearly understood—was that the foundations of American business created by "corner grocers and smithies" ran as deep and as strong as the roots of the spreading chestnut trees under which they conducted trade, and neither would be easily felled.[5]

Self-Service vs. Personalized Retailing

Clarence Saunders, a drummer turned grocer, filed his "self-serving" store patent in October 1916, seeking to protect his ideas and plans for the store equipment "by which the customer will be enabled to serve himself." His strategy was to do away with "a large proportion of the usual incidental expenses, or overhead charges," by directing customers to pick and choose items on their own. As part of his application, Saunders included a floor plan featuring a "circuitous path" that forced customers to pass every shelf and item as they navigated the store, stopping only to check out at the cash register. This method, the grocer believed, allowed a customer to "either buy or not buy, according to his own desire and means." Eliminating costly services such as multiple clerks, home delivery, and telephone ordering, Saunders hoped to make what he dubbed his Piggly Wiggly system "a part of the economic life of the entire nation." Two years after patenting his idea, Saunders saw self-service and Piggly Wiggly become nationwide trends, with stores opening in forty cities around the country.[6]

Piggly Wiggly spoke to what many in the industry came to see along with volume discounts as key differences between chain stores and independents, especially before vertically integrated firms emerged in the 1920s. Whereas independent storekeepers tended to favor full-service methods, offering their customers credit, delivery, and clerks to assist with shopping, many chain stores initially operated under the principles of self-service, or "cash-and-carry," which did away with credit and most other personal services in the interest of efficiency. Even if the lines were not always distinct, especially in the minds of shoppers, the two styles nevertheless spoke to issues of convenience, economy,

Clarence Saunders's patented self-service system and fixtures forced customers to enter and exit his Piggly-Wiggly store through turnstiles, protecting grocers from light-fingered patrons seeking to take advantage of the new way to shop. Saunders's methods signaled key changes that became industry standard by the 1930s. Author's collection.

familiarity, novelty, and the ways in which retailers understood their customers and their buying habits. The debate between independent and chain grocers in part became a battleground for the right to define modern retailing along the lines of either personalized service or systematized self-service. It was a microcosm of the larger question: Would individuals or corporations come to define American enterprise? What many businessmen, politicians, and consumers discovered, though, was that the line between independent stores and chain firms was neither fixed nor clear-cut.[7]

The increased presence of self-service stores in the 1910s and 1920s marked an important departure. In cities across the country, self-service chains such as the Atlanta-based Nifty Jiffy and Chicago-area Jewel stores initially captured shoppers as much with their novelty as with their low prices. "You are your own clerk," an Ohio self-service grocer puffed to shoppers in 1918; "you simply wait on yourself." Independent grocers long had fostered a sense of community through their services and individualized attention—finding profits in being neighborly—even as twentieth-century business and commerce increasingly became standardized. An expert on food, business, and local conditions, the neighborhood grocer was a community authority, a man who knew both his trade and his customers and introduced rational methods into small retail shops. As the twentieth century progressed, chain stores and self-service threatened to disrupt this relationship by depersonalizing what had never before been an impersonal experience.[8]

While many people credit Clarence Saunders as the originator of self-service, the practice already was in use in other contexts well before the grocer opened his model store. Self-service originated in cafeteria-style restaurants around 1900, where proprietors urged patrons to help themselves to food instead of depending on wait staff. One such eatery in Syracuse, New York, attributed the popularity of its "good home cooking at low prices" to its novel operation. Business had grown so large by 1908 that the owners claimed "in the early autumn days the waiting line extended far out into the street." The notion soon caught on in other lines, such as clothing retailers and manufacturers. One appliance maker proclaimed that the best feature of its electric toaster was "the 'self-service' it permits," instructing purchasers in 1914 to "let each person make his own toast." An enterprising Ohio storekeeper already was conducting a "self service grocery," months before Saunders opened his first Memphis store in September 1916. Saunders himself was said to have been influenced by a Montana grocer who employed the style as early as 1914. Initiated by independent retailers, the concept eventually became industry standard.[9]

Even if self-service was not an entirely fresh idea in the 1910s, the notion that some grocers would no longer call customers for their orders, deliver their goods (often several times a day), or assist them with their purchases was jarring to some shoppers and also disrupting to fixed concepts of mass marketing on the local level. Manufacturers who sold goods directly to retailers leaned on grocers and clerks as powerful allies to pitch their products and influence customer purchases. Companies like Heinz and Morton Salt cultivated relationships with retailers much like wholesalers' traveling salesmen did, passing along information, selling tips, and small tokens like pencil clips or free samples to curry grocers' favor. National brands and their ubiquity in women's magazines and local newspapers may have bolstered the standardization of self-service, but advertising campaigns still encouraged shoppers to "Ask your Grocer" for name-brand products. Neighborhood dealers also depended on knowing their customers and catering to their particular needs as ways to build and keep business, concepts that clashed with self-service principles and many chain store methods.[10]

Ideas for curbing customer services and reducing overhead came from both self-service grocers and methods A&P originated. In 1912, A&P opened the first of its "economy stores," a smaller version of its typical shops but with-out the delivery, telephone service, and premium giveaways found in its other retail outlets. "The way we were set up," recalled New Jersey A&P supervisor O. C. Adams, "it was come and get it!" Cutting delivery alone saved the company nearly 20 percent in overhead and expenses, another A&P manager estimated. Carting groceries to shoppers' doorsteps routinely cost St. Paul independent grocer Andrew Schoch upward of $13,000 per year for rent, insurance, feed, and shoeing for his fleet of twenty-two horses and wagons. Piggly Wiggly–style methods combined with A&P's economy stores created a new focus on the financial benefits of limiting services as ways to tackle the mounting cost of living and food prices in the 1910s, which rose 35 percent between 1900 and 1912. Many attributed these changes to a multitude of factors including tar-iffs, the gold standard, urbanization, cold storage, and excessive middlemen. Grocers and their services stood at the front of a long line of businessmen and politicians that consumers and others put under the microscope in the 1910s.[11]

Retailers' full-service offerings drew further scrutiny during World War I, when neighborhood merchants were encouraged to reduce their spending in support of military efforts. The Commercial Economy Board of the Council of National Defense, formed in 1917 to "investigate and advise in regard to the

Andrew Schoch's horse-drawn delivery wagons were a common sight in St. Paul, Minnesota, neighborhoods in the years before World War I. In the 1920s, Schoch transitioned to delivering groceries with a fleet of twenty motorized trucks, as wartime ridicule about home delivery being unpatriotic dissipated. Author's collection.

economic distribution of commodities," urged grocery and other retail traders to moderate services to "conserve both capital and personnel for the national defense." The board recommended cutting regular deliveries to "one per day over each route," ending "special deliveries," and forming "cooperative delivery systems in all small and medium-sized towns." Combining manpower and delivery costs with other retail merchants, the board maintained, would cut expenses and free up workers for wartime jobs where "there is greater need." Grocers in Richmond, Virginia, responded by collectively agreeing to "limit deliveries to two a day, and not to send any purchase amounting to less than 50 cents," a resolution aimed at "economizing horses, men and feed, as well as automobiles and gasoline."[12]

Self-service grocers used the Commercial Economy Board's recommendations to boost their status not only as economical retailers but also as nationalistic enterprises. John Scovel, a Humeston, Iowa, dealer, pushed consumers to "Be Patriotic!" by shopping at his store. "The government is asking every one to do their bit by paying cash and carrying every thing possible," he advised; "we appeal to your patriotic nature to trade with us." Scovel's policies of "No Free Delivery" and "No Credit" spoke to the board's recommendations while promoting the grocer's belief that cash-and-carry (cousin to self-service) served the interests of the country over his community. "A package under the arm was a mark of patriotism," board members maintained. In this way, government and business urged shoppers to give up their local allegiances to neighborhood grocers' services in support of their nation. Carrying a "market basket," like those found at the entrance to Piggly Wiggly and other self-service shops, claimed one Syracuse, New York, newspaper, "is the new slogan of patriotic women, the badge of honor." One trade journal maintained in 1919, "It cannot be denied that during the period of our late war, the so-called 'Cash and Carry Plan,' in the retail grocery business, made some slight headway."[13]

Wartime emphasis on economizing likewise brought about a larger cultural transformation. For much of the nineteenth and early twentieth centuries, the notion of paying for groceries on credit was commonplace, especially among the middle and wealthier classes. Few paid cash for all their food needs. By the close of the war, however, grocery shopping on credit began to carry with it a stigma. The majority of women polled in Frederick Croxton's postwar survey, when questioned about their preferred payment method, claimed they "took pride in the fact that they paid cash thinking that to buy on credit was a reflection upon them." Students conducting the investigation believed, though, that the number of credit shoppers was "underestimated." Croxton questioned women's self-conscious attitudes toward buying on the books, "since credit is usually extended only to responsible persons and should be regarded as a compliment to their financial integrity." Other factors contributed to consumers' change in mindset, including concerns over escalating food prices and the development of home economics, which infused industrial management and production methods into the domestic sphere. During the war, both government officials and home economists called on women to be sensible with their dollars by paying cash for household expenses. "Like everything else," *Ladies Home Journal* chided readers in a 1917 article, "personal buying convenience must yield whenever to war needs."[14]

This shift in postwar attitudes, however, is paradoxical given the increased availability and acceptability of consumer credit in the 1920s and 1930s. As shoppers' ability to buy household goods such as washing machines, vacuum cleaners, and radios on the installment plan rose, the convention of buying food on credit declined. While many continued to rely on credit for groceries, increased emphasis on cash trading had begun to change what it meant to buy on account, making women feel anxious about not being "economical" and prudent with their purchases. A&P's "economy" stores inadvertently played into and provided a market for these new concerns. The impression that grocery shopping on credit was no longer acceptable further extended to manufacturers, who in a 1926 poll concurred that the practice was reckless. By 1929, the US Census of Distribution revealed that of 170,595 grocery stores surveyed, more than 93,000 (approximately 55 percent) operated on an all-cash basis, with remaining stores granting between 10 percent and more than 80 percent credit. Chains' preferences for and their widespread success in cash selling had begun to redefine grocery retailing as a cash-only experience for many shoppers.[15]

While chains that ran on a cash basis doubtlessly benefited from the wartime talk about economy, consumers supported their policies by and large because of the savings they realized in their food bills. Price comparisons between credit and cash dealers confirmed that as a rule, cash-only stores offered goods at cheaper prices, making them an attractive option for those on a budget. The economies of scale that chains achieved through vertical integration, generally by manufacturing and producing their own branded goods—as did A&P with its Eight O'Clock coffee, baked goods, and other products—enabled many to claim that their business methods offered benefits independent grocers could not match. One 1930s study of New York retail grocery prices revealed that the savings chains offered were "significant," with goods sold at nearly 13 percent less than at independent grocers. A&P, for example, saw prices in its stores drop 10 percent between 1925 and 1929 while the average store volume doubled between 1925 and 1928. Investigations in other towns found prices closer on average, but the majority concluded that consumers could expect to find lower prices on almost all items at chain stores.[16]

Yet despite chains' apparent advantages, many remained unconvinced that they represented the best way to buy and sell groceries. "I see you have a notice 'We Aim to Please,'" one popular witticism poked at a chain store slogan, with a dissatisfied customer providing the punch line: "You ought to take a little time off for target practice." Even home economics matron Christine Frederick, a staunch supporter of self-service and frequent contributor to *Chain Store Age*, a leading trade journal, confessed in 1925 that she shopped one particular chain store only because the manager "does a dozen other things which are positively not typical chain store services." Frederick acknowledged, "He remembers details of my needs," delivered on request, and cashed her checks, all "things which have been regarded as *the independent* retailer's special province." The message to chains was clear: self-service and lower prices were not enough to sway a nation of shoppers accustomed to individualized treatment from neighborhood businessmen.[17]

Many chain grocers realized that cash-and-carry would work long term only if brought into alignment with consumers' expectations of both service and the role of small business within a community. A survey of Chicago women in the 1930s revealed that of those who preferred self-service to full-service stores, the vast majority indicated "a lack of trust in the clerk" as the reason they shopped self-service chains. Yet when asked why they did not patronize the only self-service chain in Chicago (Jewel stores), the same group of women held steadfast in their support for full-service shopping, noting their reasons as "independent gives credit," "independent delivers free," and "can give independent phone order." The most telling (and most frequent) response came from women who preferred independent stores because they offered "a more pleasing personal relationship." Despite the initial novelty and popularity of self-service, consumers and grocers alike struggled to trade personal service and attention for cheaper prices. As a result, some chains began to integrate local grocers' amenities with their self-service practices to create stores that addressed both the economics of large-scale retailing with the culture of local consumption. According to a Federal Trade Commission (FTC) report, by 1934, 43 percent of grocery chains offered delivery service to their customers. It was, as one insider suggested, "an essential or desirable part of efficient operation," muddying notions of what constituted "efficiency."[18]

Both the Chicago survey and the FTC's summary underscored big business's organizational and methodological shortcomings when it came to local-level retailing. The future of chain stores would depend heavily on adopting small businessmen's emphasis on the individual customer, which included personalizing shoppers' experiences in their stores and with their employees. Ernest R. Ham, advertising manager for Twentieth Century Stores, an Oregon and Washington grocery chain, recognized this disparity between chains' relative facelessness and consumers' familiarity with small business proprietors. Ham suggested that "something ought to be done to bring the public and our stores closer together." In 1925, he steered Twentieth Century Stores' advertising campaign to get "a little closer to our customers" through a regular circular conveying "ideas of personality, friendship, courtesy and service." The aptly named Ham believed the publication would help "cement consumer good will" by introducing store managers on the front page of handbills "circulating in his neighborhood." National Tea, a Chicago-based grocery firm with over seven hundred outlets by 1925, likewise encouraged customers to chat up their store managers at regular "Get Acquainted" sales in its neighborhood shops. Constructing local identities for corporate men, marketers personalized the managerial hierarchies that buttressed large-scale operations, bringing chains into closer alignment with independent grocers and their methods. It was one of many calculated maneuvers that made it increasingly difficult to distinguish big business from small enterprise.[19]

Ham's approach also exposed nationwide concerns about who was controlling community-based businesses. The growing presence of chain managers in neighborhood shops signaled a fundamental shift in business operations. For much of the country's business past, proprietors who had a vested stake in local affairs manned retail counters. Now it appeared that anonymous chain store operators and out-of-state firms with no connection to a particular "place" stood ready to strip communities of their heterogeneous commerce and character and deprive small businessmen of their ability to foster local economic development. Debates over the issue led to a crisis of authority both within the grocery trade and among townsfolk. When the "Life Study Club" of Warren, Pennsylvania, invited independent and chain merchants to its March 1928 meeting, the topic of whether chain stores were "desirable enterprises in this community" provoked such conflict, club leader John Siggins announced that "newspapers had agreed not to publish names of speakers, in order to stimulate discussion." As the club debated the value of small businesses, one outspoken member stressed that the local dealer was "more than a merchant to his customers. He is a friend of the community. He is glad to help community enterprises, no less than individuals." James Truslow Adams, himself a businessman turned historian, asked on the eve of the Great Depression, "What stockbroker, manufacturing company, railway or electric light corporation with all their talk about service would ever consider running their business at a voluntary loss in order to . . . tide the public over a crisis?" Deriding large firms' lack of "community spirit," another Life Study Club speaker added, "Who ever heard of a chain store paying their help when they were sick, or paying anything toward the Community Chest?"[20]

Others insisted, however, that chains made important contributions. In 1925, not long before the Warren Life Study Club met, Virginia real estate agent Henry Raab offered a defense of big organizations (published in *Chain Store Age*) by composing a list of five things chain stores do for a community. In addition to the typical economic advantages often claimed by such stores, including their ability to "reduce expenses and pass this saving to the buying public," Raab (not surprisingly) highlighted chains' tendency toward real estate development as well as sprucing up Main Street with new storefronts and signage. He further suggested that chain stores had become community leaders on the basis of their "immense capital and purchasing powers." It was a statement that undoubtedly riled small retailers annoyed with the idea that economic might trumped local knowledge when it came to judging community leadership. After all, small-town merchants had led neighborhood economic development for decades, endorsing transportation, communication, and government improvements in the name of progress. Their protestations centered not on a reluctance to move forward—especially since they had been doing so for over a hundred years—but on which kind of businessman was better equipped to serve community needs in the present and in years to come.[21]

Maryland high schooler Eloise Schaffer touched on these points in her 1930 prizewinning essay about "community builders" for a *Cumberland Evening Times* contest. Schaffer tied the "progress of a small town" to "its Independent Merchants," noting that store owners helped turn "our commonplace village into a city beautiful." It was a sentimental argument for certain, but one that linked both the foundations of American enterprise and the potential for future growth to small business proprietors. Although only a handful of independent proprietors in any town ever rose to become community leaders, what they and their stores represented was of far greater importance for those who would grow up to become core customers and residents. Schaffer predicted that the loss of independent businessmen would not only spell economic disaster but also would find chains and their managers relocating "to another town where business is good," leaving behind empty buildings and unemployed neighbors. Members of the Warren Life Study Club agreed: "You never see chain stores go into a dead community in an attempt to build business."[22]

Most disconcerting, perhaps, was the potential conversion of independent businessmen to dependent employees. Sounding a premature death knell for neighborhood merchants, Raab suggested independent proprietors could "earn a larger income as an employee of a progressive chain store organization than they have been drawing as net profits from their store." Unceremoniously stripping small business owners of their authority while demoting them to workers, Raab touched on an essential concern embedded within the chain store question. Nineteenth-century ideals about a nation of autonomous strivers may have appeared anachronistic by the 1920s, when the majority of Americans labored for others, but thousands continued pushing for personal independence by opening their own small businesses, despite the financial unpredictability of this decision. Chains, however, challenged deep-seated notions about individuality of thought and action inherent in small business ownership in exchange for a regular paycheck to their managers and employees. "From the nature of the business," a longtime hardware dealer observed, "a chain organization cannot afford to allow its branch managers to be individualists or to act according to their own inclinations." Chains instead traded individuality for the "machinelike atmosphere" of efficiency.[23]

Few welcomed the ways in which systematic productivity seemed to displace individualism. For laborers in a variety of industries, though, it was a familiar story. For small-business owners, the thought of corporate chains diminishing them to mere employees was jarring. Certainly, the economic stability that chains claimed to offer their clerks and cashiers countered the vagaries of proprietorship and the uncertainty of free market enterprise. Yet there was no getting around the pervasive philosophy of American self-reliance and what individuals sacrificed to become dependent on another for their livelihood. Labor strikes and unionism in the 1930s would highlight these costs, as a nation of workers fought for better pay, improved work conditions, and a unified voice. For enterprising types, a 1945 guide bluntly titled *A Small Store and Independence* reminded returning servicemen that working for oneself "epitomizes the yearning for security, for economic freedom, for independence."[24]

Chains countered the "absolute irresistible urge to own and operate" a business by pointing to the railroad, automobile, and steel industries, among others. "Consider the folly of the man who would condemn [working for] these enterprises because there is little chance of owning, by himself, a railroad, a bank, a shipping line or a telephone system," one chain supporter blasted at anti-chain proponents. Others argued that chains provided schooling for a budding storekeeper, allowing him to "train under big business for a time and then paddle his own canoe." For small businessmen who recognized in themselves a nascent Vanderbilt, Morgan, or Bell, the proposition of giving up individual opportunity in the name of corporate productivity was a difficult pill to swallow and one they resisted taking.[25]

Redefining Small Business through Regulation

The alarming growth of chain stores provoked many to seek relief and protection to rebalance the market through legislative efforts. Five of the leading grocery chains expanded from nearly 7,800 to more than 30,000 stores between 1920 and 1930, an imposing prospect for local dealers. As the Great Depression and its economic effects loomed large and threatening to small business owners, many questioned whether government could stem the chain store tide. Commenting on the situation, US Senator Royal S. Copeland (Democrat-New York) declared that if chains continued to grow and dominate, they would "undermine the foundations of the country." Here then was the real fear behind the "chain store question" for small grocers and some lawmakers: left unchecked, chains would not only destroy local communities and independent merchants but also the underpinnings of American business and the country. Independent men had help make small business ownership a viable avenue to achieving the "American dream." If chain corporations blocked that path, redefining retail enterprise solely in terms of "bigness" and "efficiency," how many Americans would then have access to that dream?[26]

Organized antagonism toward chain stores had first developed in the 1910s and 1920s as independent retailers, wholesalers, and manufacturers fought their encroachment into all branches of the trade. As early as 1914, the cereal manufacturer Kellogg's advised retailers about "the menace of the chain store" and its threat to small merchants. Comparing the hazard to the mobilization of military forces in World War I, Kellogg's warned against chains' "vast aggregations of capital [that] move faster than any army." Kellogg's was not alone in its unease. Local radio stations, newspapers, and community organizations similarly raised the alert, asking lawmakers "what could be done to keep chain numbers from growing."[27]

By the 1920s, these initial concerns had become reality. According to a 1927 study by advertising firm J. Walter Thompson, grocery store chains had assumed "probably very close to half of the grocery business in the cities of over 100,000" with the large-scale enterprises conducting "approximately one-third" of trade in cities with populations over 25,000. Thompson claimed that 800 chains operating 57,000 stores in 1927 did business equivalent to 150,000 retailers, compared with the 500 chains and 8,000 stores that controlled approximately 5 percent of the US retail grocery business in 1914. Despite these imposing figures, Thompson cautioned, "The future of the grocery chain store is not altogether clear," as "the road over which it has traveled during the past few years has not been entirely smooth."[28]

Chain stores' rough road through the grocery trade in 1922 led to the National Association of Retail Grocers convention in Los Angeles. There, trade leaders proposed limiting the number of chains operating in any one community. Those in attendance discussed two possible methods for achieving such a goal. The first included imposing a state licensing tax harsh enough to cripple store profits and chains' desire and ability for further expansion. Missouri was among the first states to introduce such a measure, suggesting a $50 tax on a chain's third store, doubling with every successive store so that a chain with five shops in one community would be taxed $750 per year. Although the Missouri bill did not pass, other states had greater success. Between 1923 and 1933, state legislatures introduced 689 anti-chain tax bills, with twenty-eight entering into law in Indiana, Georgia, Minnesota, Wisconsin, and elsewhere. Local ordinances also passed in several midwestern cities such as Cleveland, Columbus, and Youngstown, Ohio, bolstering community coffers (if only marginally).[29]

Chain store taxes became a popular and punitive way to tackle the chain store "problem," bolstered by a 1931 Supreme Court decision affirming the constitutionality of Indiana's newly enacted tax. Chain stores, the Court asserted, enjoyed competitive advantages independents did not and thus could be considered a distinct business type for taxation purposes. A flood of new chain taxes followed. In Wisconsin, lawmakers passed an initial measure in 1932 based on stores' gross incomes before the state Supreme Court ruled it unconstitutional the following year. Legislators replaced it with a graduated license tax requiring owner-operators of between two and five stores to pay an annual tax of $25. Chains operating over twenty stores faced penalties of $200 per store.[30]

Other states were more aggressive. Louisiana governor Huey Long and radio personality W. K. Henderson's army of Merchant's Minute Men (whose donations financed the broadcast of anti-chain speakers at Henderson's KWKH radio station) were particularly vociferous anti-chain crusaders in the South. Louisiana's graduated yet severe penalties fined chains with five hundred or more stores $550 per unit, with fifteen chains paying over $120,000 in taxes in 1934 alone, most of it likely coming from A&P, which was one of the few grocery chains that met the tax's highest threshold. Nationwide, state chain taxes generated more than $2 million in 1933, with several municipalities joining the taxation bandwagon as a way to alleviate financial shortfalls brought about by the Depression while attempting to temper chain growth.[31]

Despite a rocky start, Wisconsin's tax proved particularly resilient owing primarily to staunch political support. Governor Philip LaFollette, who with his brother Robert M. LaFollette Jr. founded the Wisconsin Progressive Party, made the chain problem a centerpiece of his 1930 gubernatorial campaign. Together they lent support to small businesses under the guise that taxation should be used to direct social policy, an idea their father, Robert M. LaFollette Sr., introduced in the 1910s as a presidential candidate. A 1931 survey initiated by Philip LaFollette concluded that, based on book value of goods, independent merchants were taxed at a higher rate than chains. He believed that small retailers were entitled to maintain their substantial equity by preventing "monopoly methods, unfair practices and evasion of the tax burden." He made clear, however, that "the independent business interests of this state have never asked, do not expect, and are not entitled to have their competitors legislated out of business." Wisconsin's chain tax, as LaFollette intended it, neither generated substantial revenue for the state nor destroyed chains but rather sought to rebalance the tax burden. The seemingly equitable nature of Wisconsin's tax, further, did not distinguish between out-of-town corporate chains or local, independently owned ones. Retail firms operating more than one outlet (with a few exceptions) were subject to the same graduated license tax as larger, multi-unit organizations. Tax commissioners estimated that in 1933, the licensing law applied to five or six thousand retail outlets, including large department store firms such as Marshall Field, which operated several branches, along with smaller grocery retailers like the Markesan Quality Grocery.[32]

The democratic nature of the tax led to some confusion about how commissioners defined a "chain." In 1937, the Markesan store's owners wrote seeking clarity on the issue, asking whether "an independent grocer is obliged to pay a chain store tax," because they planned to open a second store in nearby Princeton. The tax commission's narrow definition (two or more outlets operating under the same ownership) obligated the owners to pay up once they expanded their operation. This pigeonholed small businesses into the restrictive classification of single-store enterprises, as both national chains and local retailers now fell under the same descriptive parameters of a "chain," regardless of organization or operation. It was a decision that both perplexed and piqued many small grocers who wondered what purpose the tax actually held. Though LaFollette had been upfront about the law's intention, it was clear that proprietors did not see things the same way.[33]

The commission's characterization of small business should not have surprised retailers. Limiting local operators to a one-store, one-owner model was the second strategy merchants had discussed at the 1922 meeting of the National Association of Retail Grocers. Wisconsin's chain store tax merely codified this earlier vision. Yet while many independents fell within these parameters, those who did not faced scrutiny from agents seeking to understand the differences between local and large-scale businesses. Grocer Artie Severson's initial inquiry to tax commissioners asked for clarification about whether he too would fall under the category of a "chain" by opening another shop. When agents followed up to see if he had indeed enlarged his operation, Severson "refused to make a [tax] return" and "refused to answer" the commission's letters. Rather than let the matter lie, the state pursed him doggedly, demanding that supervisor of assessments Ethan A. Cleasby visit Severson personally to ascertain "whether or not he comes within the scope of the law." When Cleasby finally caught up with Severson, he learned that the once-enterprising grocer had fled to take a grocery job in Pasadena, California, a state without a chain store tax.[34]

The Wisconsin Tax Commission's unrelenting pursuit of independent merchants provoked ire among small grocers who, like many, believed that chain store taxes were intended to target big corporations, not local business-men. Milwaukee grocer Carl Kaiser faced the commission's wrath in 1936, when the agency found three "places of business" operating under the name Kaiser's Food Shop in local listings. Officials threatened the grocer with "heavy penalties" of $25 to $100 per day "for the illegal operation of each sales outlet subject to the law." In a handwritten letter, Kaiser informed agents that he operated only one of the listed businesses, drawing attention to the com-mission's failure to note "the listing of the [other] two stores is in the plural whereas my store is listed in the singular form." Kaiser further chided tax agents for their source of details about local businesses. "It is quite evident that you have again resorted to the telephone directory for information," he com-plained. Kaiser's frustrations are understandable; administrators had raised the same question the year prior. "I thought my explanation sent in last year was clear enough for you to understand," Kaiser reproached. In a final effort to satisfy the commission, the grocer submitted an application for a 1936 chain store license with the declaration "I don't operate a chain store," in place of list-ing each of his presumed outlets.[35]

The tax commission's dealings with Kaiser illuminated a major fault within chain tax laws: the commission had little understanding of (or sympathy for) the ways in which locally owned businesses operated. In 1936, Rose Lernor and her family's concern came to the attention of tax agents when they discovered two stores operating in Wauwatosa under the name "Forman's Food Market." When contacted, Lernor informed the agency that her father Ben Forman ran one shop, while her husband, "Mr. Forman's son-in-law" Leo Lernor, owned and operated the other. Asked if Leo Lernor had any business interest in Ben Forman's store, Rose responded, "Mr. Forman is allowing us to run this store under his name because it is well established in this city." Lernor's explana-tion drew on long-established concepts of goodwill to distinguish her family's business from a corporate chain. Well into the twentieth century, local retailers understood that reputation and community standing were commercial elements of a neighborhood culture cultivated over time, something chain store managers struggled to generate through print advertising and other means. The commission's demand for clarification, though, suggested that family businesses and their complexities challenged evolving notions of what constituted small business. If the Lernors could not run two stores without tax agents labeling them a chain, what did that mean for countless other family-run operations?[36]

Independent grocers' annoyance with the Wisconsin Tax Commission reflected the contradictions between what legislators claimed regulation would do for small businessmen and how it actually affected them. Lawmakers held fast to the notion that chain store taxes would protect independent enterprise from competition while at the same time vigorously pursuing anyone who appeared to fall outside the state's purview. When Milwaukee grocer Grover Gould learned in 1934 that tax commissioners wanted an explanation as to why he had not paid tax on his two-store Daisy Market "chain," Gould informed agents that he had closed one shop in 1933 and no longer was "in the chain store business." Two years later, when another embittered merchant hounded by tax authorities learned that the nation's largest grocery chain might attempt to dodge their heavy tax burden by leasing stores to clerks, he rebuked commissioners to "spend some time investigating the 'A and P Stores'" rather than harassing small dealers.[37]

True or not, independent grocers had good reason to direct tax agents to look more closely at national chains' maneuverings. A&P, along with Kroger, Safeway, and other grocery firms operating in Wisconsin, had combined to fight passage of the state's 1935 chain store tax, employing both Progressive- and Democratic-leaning attorneys to represent their interests in Madison. The state's department and drug store chain corporations likewise organized a powerful lobby known as the Wisconsin Progressive Distributors, its ambiguous name drew cachet from the governor's Progressive stance while hiding its deep-pocketed financiers. The party, comprising the Walgreen, J. C. Penney, S. S. Kresge, and F. W. Woolworth corporations, spent nearly $3,500 in 1933 to lobby the state's influential lawmakers, more than any other interest group save steam railroads. Member firms paid attorneys' assessments of $5 for each store they operated in the state, with J. C. Penney contributing the most at $235 for its forty-seven outlets. Such well-financed and coordinated efforts, however, failed to block passage of a new chain store tax in 1935, and commissioners continued for the next four years to "ferret out" giant grocery chains.[38]

Tax commissioners' zealous attitude toward defeating chains, however, did little to bolster independents' confidence in their business style, as the agency continued to persuade conformity to state regulations. What tax agents failed to acknowledge, though, was that local retailers who anticipated protection from and investigation of chain methods instead found their small enterprises placed under the microscope. Compliance with state parameters forced some to provide affidavits attesting that their firms met the state's criteria. Sam Shniderman, another Wauwatosa grocer, hired a lawyer and submitted a notarized statement in March 1934 vowing that he operated only one store "under the firm name of 'Schneider's Grocer.'" Shniderman assured agents that he had no connection "either direct or indirect" with another Schneider's Grocery listed in the telephone directory, which commissioners found to be a convenient if flawed aid for tracking down potential scofflaws. The agency explained the need for legal affirmation claiming, "The law establishes a presumption that operation under a common name is, unless shown to the contrary, deemed to constitute operation under the same general management, supervision or ownership." While the logic may have appeared sound to agents given how difficult it was becoming to discern large-scale chains from other types of business organizations, such assumptions only made it harder for independent grocers to conduct trade beyond the one-store, one-owner model the state established through its regulatory measures.[39]

Looking for new ways to expand their businesses without tax penalties and to compete with big firms, independent retailers muddied the definitional waters even more by acting like corporate chains. Wisconsin's tax laws encouraged small retailers to combine under the guise of a voluntary chain, an organizational model that had roots in turn-of-the-century retail buying syndicates. Voluntary chains borrowed from syndicates by pooling independents' buying power but also integrated national chain methods for coordinating selling, advertising, branding, and store appearance. According to Wisconsin tax agents, if a local merchant owned his shop and purchased goods from a wholesale organization operating under a "trade name," as did voluntary chains like the Independent Grocers Alliance (IGA) and Red and White Stores, then the law "cannot include them" as a taxable entity, since "the arrangement there is substantially the same as before. The local grocers are in reality independent merchants." In 1933, more than 1,800 Wisconsin retailers belonged to voluntary chains, a number that rose slightly, to nearly 2,000, three years later. Shielded from the burden of chain store taxes, voluntary chains became the only way Wisconsin grocers could expand the scope of their businesses and take advantage of chains' economies of scale while staying within the parameters of taxation laws. They joined a host of small retailers nationwide who realized that one way to meet big business competition while maintaining their place in the trade was to ban together and behave like chain organizations.[40]

Volunteering to Be a Chain

One of the earliest voluntary chains, Red and White Stores organized around 1922 in Buffalo, New York. Its purpose was "to give the independent retail grocer the advantages enjoyed by his corporate chain competitor," according to Red and White's general manager Asa Strause, who detailed the system's methods for Wisconsin tax commission agents. Red and White storefronts appeared nationwide, recruiting members from small towns to major cities. The group's plan, as Red and White's one-time president and later wholesale grocery mogul Smith Flickinger described it, was "a merger of purchasing power without any merger of capital structure." Affiliates agreed to buy merchandise (including Red and White Brand Products) from a central warehouse, remodel their stores to meet the group's standards, and take part in regional advertising campaigns. From outward appearances, Red and White looked like one of any number of corporate chains, but its internal structure made it unique in the world of food distribution and retailing.[41]

Emphasizing independent store ownership, the voluntary chain reassured local customers that when they patronized Red and White stores they would find "the same proprietors and, in many cases, the same clerks, who have been serving them for years." Advertising campaigns stressed the individuality and personal services of local retailers in addition to the uniformity of store appearances and prices. Members further pointed out that while their stores offered "every advantage of a great corporation-owned organization," they did so "without the disadvantages such as impersonal service, refusal of credit and absence of delivery." Voluntary chains' economically advantageous structure enabled small retailers to retain their independent status while distinguishing themselves from corporate chains, many of which had taken to opening stores next door to local grocers as a way to draw off area shoppers.[42]

Not far from Red and White's Buffalo headquarters in Poughkeepsie, New York, J. Frank Grimes, an outspoken opponent of corporate chains, organized the Independent Grocers Alliance. Grimes's plan required all IGA retail members to purchase goods from a central wholesaler, which controlled distribution of proprietary goods within a designated region. Wholesalers recruited independent dealers from within their territories, explained the system, and signed interested parties to a three-year contract. Retail members

Minneapolis grocer Arthur R. Johnson joined Red and White in the 1920s. His store's uniform color scheme, layout, and signage imitated chain store appearances, but the cooperative's slogan, "Every store a unit, not a link," made clear its foundation in independent ownership. Courtesy of the Minnesota Historical Society.

paid territorial wholesalers $3.50 per week for their buying and distribution services, receiving IGA advertising posters, placards, broadsides, and national sales campaign bulletins in return. Contract terms bound retailers to use "in good faith" the service, signs, and emblems of the organization; operate strictly on cash; paint storefronts and keep shops clean and orderly; and rearrange and redecorate in accordance with IGA plans and colors. To observers, the cooperative, much like Red and White, resembled other chain corporations. IGA's tidy stores, uniform stocks and appearances, and lower prices appealed to economically minded shoppers while telephone ordering, home delivery, and credit spoke to independent grocers' long-standing individualized services. It was, by some appearances, the best of both worlds.[43]

Countless other retailers agreed. By 1931, the US Department of Commerce estimated that 19,000 grocery cooperatives operated in the United States, with a Michigan marketing scholar forecasting "a considerable increase of cooperative activity" in the near future. One contemporary proclaimed in 1936 that IGA maintained "more retailers' outlets than the Great Atlantic and Pacific Tea Co." That same year, IGA numbered 6,775 member stores nationwide with Red and White stores totaling 6,326. Combined, these largest of the voluntary chains came close to matching A&P's 14,000-plus outlets, their numbers having declined in recent years owing to reorganization and a focus on consolidating smaller stores into larger markets. Nationally, however, more than 25,000 independent grocers belonged to eleven different voluntary chains, outpacing A&P in their store numbers and presence in every state.[44]

Wholesalers in particular favored voluntary chains for their large, centralized orders. The benefit of such arrangements for wholesalers was to secure their place in the trade as grocery distributors, a fight they had carried on since the late nineteenth century. By the early decades of the twentieth century, conditions for wholesalers were even more troubling, as chains were better poised to do what buying syndicates had not, eliminate them from the trade. For many middlemen, cooperative associations proved a way to remain viable. Not long after Wisconsin wholesaler Edwin R. Godfrey founded his organization in 1911, the company discovered "they were 'pikers' in the wholesale grocery business," small gamblers in a changing trade. By the 1920s, they had signed a distribution deal with IGA while also assisting Milwaukee retailers in converting their businesses from credit to cash and making their stores "as efficient and profitable as possible." Where independent wholesalers and retailers once battled each other for their place in the trade, they now worked together to fend off a common foe.[45]

Yet not all independent grocers had access to the nation's largest voluntary chains. While membership criteria fluctuated across organizations, most enforced general restrictions, including location, creditworthiness, sales capacity, and race. Some upheld strict rules, limiting the number of independent retailers within a city or town to those separated by two blocks, to keep stores from competing. Moreover, retailers with annual sales volume of $40,000 and superior credit ratings took preference over smaller proprietors purchasing less than $300 in goods per week, thus slanting membership toward higher-performing businesses. Race likewise factored into membership considerations; one association claimed that it did not accept foreign-born grocers, using this as a way to exclude those operating "parlor" businesses, small shops typically run out of family homes. Other cooperatives likewise dissuaded Jewish grocers from joining, limiting participation by setting quotas, admitting them as non-voting members, or requiring large cash deposits. Rather than face discriminatory policies, some, such as the largely Jewish-owned District Grocery Stores in Washington, DC, started their own regional cooperatives.[46]

African American merchants, however, typically found the road through white-run cooperatives closed. Financial qualifications excluded the vast majority of black grocers, most of whom operated on a very small scale and faced discriminatory crediting policies and characterizations. It was a situation that National Negro Business League (NNBL) leaders indirectly recognized in their groundbreaking 1928 study of black business ownership. Of the 526 grocery businesses surveyed, only 2 percent reported gross annual volume of over $50,000. A 1930 study of voluntary chains likewise revealed that some cooperatives complained that selling to black retailers was "a problem," likely from their lack of capital and access to credit. The NNBL showed that over 40 percent of retailers in all lines bought goods with cash, versus 16 percent of credit users. A larger number of black grocers similarly purchased goods from wholesalers using cash or a combination of cash and credit, rather than credit alone.[47]

Though grocery stores were among the most popular black enterprises in the 1920s, undoubtedly for what at the time were its low entry barriers, the NNBL pointed out that chains had disadvantaged African American proprietors in particular. One survey concluded that black merchants suffered from a general lack of knowledge about "efficiency, economic principles, and service." The recommended solution was twofold: "further development of more scientific and active methods of individual store-keeping" and "group buying in the form of buying associations or even of chain store operations." Addressing the NNBL's 1929 annual meeting, association president and Tuskegee Institute principal Robert R. Moton concurred. "The day of the small dependent merchant has passed. The hope of the future for the Negro business man . . . is to become identified with these vast organizations and to go along with the tide of progress."[48]

In Alabama, the drive to organize black grocers had already begun by the time Moton took the podium. The year before, a group of enterprising men from Montgomery met to establish a cooperative they named the Colored Merchants Association (CMA). The group functioned much like other voluntary chains, meeting weekly to pool orders, solicit wholesalers' best prices, and distribute bulk discounted purchases, along with sharing advertising costs and promotional literature. Word about the arrangement reached the NNBL in short order, and association secretary Albon L. Holsey traveled south to learn more. Holsey, director of the 1928 survey, liked what he saw and moved to make the CMA a national movement with the NNBL and Moton's support. He chose the Winston-Salem area of North Carolina to expand his ideas, remodeling one black proprietor's shop along the lines of *Progressive Grocer* editor Carl Dipman's model grocery store. It was the first of many times Holsey would borrow from and call on white businessmen to aid in moving the CMA forward. By 1929, he had mapped out plans to bring existing grocers into the fold and open the doors for others desiring to become businessmen. Holsey intended to "fight the devil on his own ground with his own weapon," by building a national voluntary chain.[49]

Holsey recognized in the CMA an occasion not just to meet chain competition but also to create business opportunities for African Americans. While most white voluntary cooperatives formed simply to maintain independent trade, the CMA represented new pathways for blacks both as business owners and as employees. Efforts to establish a separate black economy, a strategy promoted by Booker T. Washington and the NNBL, rested on the idea of African American consumers supporting black commerce instead of bolstering ethnic grocers and white chains. Writing to Moton in 1929, Atlanta Brown-Lipscomb, a New Jersey homemaker, detailed the retailing landscape in Montclair, which looked similar to that of many American towns in the 1920s. The observant woman counted several Jewish and Italian stores, along with three chain stores dependent on black consumers' patronage. The problem as she saw it was the absence not just of a black-run grocery store (two previous efforts had failed owing to a lack of "business training") but the near-absence of African American workers. "Only two or three of the Jew stores and one of the A&P stores employ any colored help," the New Jersey woman grumbled, "and that only in the capacity of delivery boys."[50]

These conditions radiated beyond the eastern seaboard and throughout the country, where African Americans found few advancement opportunities in white-run businesses. Movements such as the "Don't Buy Where You Can't Work" campaign of the 1930s targeted retail venues as sites where black consumer spending outpaced African American employment in white-collar jobs. Pickets and boycotts reminded black shoppers to patronize "race enterprises" in support of generating economic advancement within the community. Centered in Harlem, where a diverse black population pushed for reform through a range of groups and leaders, the "Don't Buy" movement—along with programs such as the "New Economic Program" sponsored by the National Association for the Advancement of Colored People (NAACP)—negotiated with white retailers to hire black clerks and generate greater economic opportunities and advancement for African Americans. For Holsey and others, these efforts meant creating jobs both in retail and along new commercial lines. Assuring that future plans for the CMA included educating blacks to become "expert Negro buyers" for local cooperatives, Holsey emphasized that his organization was "opening an entirely new field for the young men of our race." If successful, the CMA in Holsey's estimation would bring about "a reorientation of the grocery business . . . that would at once inure to the benefit of the colored citizens of this country as well as to the leaders of the enterprise."[51]

By 1930, the CMA had located its national headquarters in Harlem, and Holsey announced the organization's incorporation, along with its board of directors composed of black leaders and several "successful white friends." Seeking financial support through capital stock offerings, Holsey hired a salesman to solicit nationwide for stockholders, garnering nearly $16,000 in subscriptions by November 1931. In addition to working with independent grocers on opening several model shops in and around Harlem, Holsey had also contracted with wholesale houses for distribution, eventually opening a CMA warehouse in the area. Like IGA and Red and White, the CMA next turned to manufacturing and distributing its own branded products, both to recognize substantial cost savings and to spread awareness of the group. It also built on the black consuming public's preference for standardized and branded goods, a trend Holsey acknowledged. Products included coffee, tobacco, condiments, spices, and pickles among others. "The colored people will buy the C.M.A. groceries much faster than they will buy the C.M.A. stock," Holsey suggested in a 1931 letter to Moton. "I am, therefore, endeavoring to build the permanent organization on that basis." Holsey anticipated moving $100,000 worth of goods monthly, not only to grocery stores but also through institutional contracts he had established with schools, hospitals, and other outlets, putting the organization "upon a self-sustaining and profit-making basis."[52]

Yet the CMA would fall short of its lofty goals. By 1933, the group suffered from a lack of operating capital and support from the public. Just two years earlier, Moton had predicted such an outcome, telling Holsey, "I don't believe you can succeed in selling sufficient stock to Negroes to justify an organization of the kind that is being set up." As far as Moton was concerned, Holsey had tried building too large an association, suggesting that the CMA should instead remain "a rather close corporation." While he applauded Holsey's ambitions on behalf of blacks, Moton believed he was "wasting good energy, time and money." In fact, Holsey had succeeded in convincing the public to pledge $100,000 in stock options, but by December 1932, less than $60,000 had materialized. A few months later, statements showed a $22,000 deficit, with newspaperman and CMA treasurer Fred R. Moore accusing Holsey of selling stock to cover salaries, "a clear violation of the law" according to Moore. Without additional capital, Holsey warned, the group could not expand its efforts geographically nor could it "develop the gross volume" of CMA products necessary to stay ahead financially. Holsey's plan to apply "the principles of big business" made clear the limitations of voluntary cooperation as a race movement. Holsey responded, "A voluntary grocery chain among the whites

343 DISCRIMINATING COFFEE DRINKERS SELECTED THIS BLEND

YOU remember the nation-wide contest conducted by the C.M.A. Stores and the National Negro Business League last year to secure the best blend of coffee for the C.M.A. Stores. An overwhelming majority of them selected the blend now bearing the trademark "C.M.A. Coffee."

There's a good reason, therefore, why C.M.A. COFFEE is such a favorite. The reason is simple.

C.M.A. COFFEE is specially and expertly blended—coffee that brews a rich, delicious beverage. And as for flavor—well just try it yourself and *taste* the difference.

Once you try C.M.A. COFFEE, you will always drink it.

It's a sign of the times—and a healthy sign— that these discriminating coffee drinkers selected the C.M.A. Brand.

It's excellent, delicious, refreshing coffee. That's the story in the can. That's why these people selected it.

Your C.M.A. Grocer has this best-liked brand of coffee. Visit him today and take home a can.

GROCERS
If you do not now carry C.M.A. Coffee in stock, communicate with us immediately. Your customers will be demanding this brand.

NATIONAL C. M. A. STORES, INC.
145 West 41st Street, New York

A voluntary chain of grocery stores owned and operated by Negroes

Identified only as Mrs. Jenkins, the African American woman posing for this 1931 advertisement represented the Colored Merchants Association's manufactured and branded products, including coffee. The voluntary cooperative sought to educate black entrepreneurs and consumers about new products, methods of buying and selling, and business opportunities. Courtesy Moton Family Papers, Manuscript Division, Library of Congress.

does not encounter the same type of problems in merchandise distribution as a similar organization among Negroes.... We have had to follow many 'untrodden paths,' as well as to find new ones."[53]

Ultimately, Holsey blamed both black consumers for failing to buy CMA products and black grocers for their lack of enthusiasm. Admonishing store owners, Holsey complained that in one eight-month period in 1932 they had sold only $5,000 in CMA-manufactured goods. *"In that period our people could easily have purchased ten times that amount,"* he blasted. Part of the problem, Holsey admitted, was "due to Negro indifference." Shoppers faulted CMA stores for their prices, which many claimed were higher than A&P and other white chains, an allegation Holsey fought in the press by inviting consumers to visit CMA shops to see that "prices are practically the same." Prices alone, however, could not draw black consumers away from white chains, many of whom favored well-known national brands over untried CMA products and the no-haggle environment of cash-and-carry shops. *Pittsburgh Courier* editors reproached black patrons who preferred being "flattered by having a white clerk serve them" instead of visiting CMA stores. External factors also overwhelmed efforts to advance black business in the 1930s, as racism, the Depression, and white-centered economic development took precedence. Although the CMA could adopt the operating principles and façade of a corporate organization, it could not convince the buying public that its stores offered advantages over white chains.[54]

It was grocers' disengagement, though, that frustrated Holsey most. Black retailers' lack of business experience was one factor the CMA sought to overcome by offering training in "modern business principles and practices," including standardized record-keeping methods, inventory controls, and marketing. Despite the group's offers to provide these services, few independent grocers seemed eager to accept the help. "The peculiar thing in connection with the C.M.A. program," Holsey noted early in 1931, "is that both white and colored people have responded with far more enthusiasm than the grocers themselves." It was, he proclaimed, "one of the most puzzling experiences that I have ever had." A year later, Holsey quietly confessed his annoyance with the "ungrateful grocers with whom we have been dealing," suggesting that his energies would have been better spent developing institutional partnerships such as schools for distributing CMA goods. In 1933, after nearly four years of laboring to educate black retailers on modern business methods, Holsey still characterized many of the now 270 grocers who belonged to the organization as being "ill prepared for the work they had selected."[55]

Part of the problem stemmed from a lack of understanding about the principles of voluntary cooperation. One enthusiastic Georgia grocer had scheduled a meeting of eleven black storekeepers to discuss forming a local CMA branch, where "the plans were carefully read and every detail explained." In the next week, when the group intended to formalize their arrangement, only two grocers showed up. "We need some one to lecture to the grocers," the deflated businessman declared; "they just can't understand organizing." The

Pittsburgh Courier agreed, blaming grocers for being "so shortsighted as not to see the absolute necessity of buying their goods through the central buying organization." Black grocers' lack of business experience coupled with concerns about giving up autonomy likely undergirded their reluctance to work together. Though the CMA never asked retailers to relinquish ownership of their stores, they took a heavy-handed approach to overseeing operations. The group required all stores to have "uniform storefronts, fixtures, cash registers, scales, shelving, counters, and other accessories," demanding substantial capital expenditures and the loss of personalization and independence. Further requirements included weekly $2 fees (payable in advance), a $3 charge for a "Certificate of Franchise," and an obligation to purchase and pay cash "promptly" for all CMA products. Grocers also had to agree to let field representatives audit their books "from time to time" to ensure they profited from the "large-scale purchasing, merchandizing, and selling methods under the supervision of expert executives." For inexperienced black grocers seeking to become self-sufficient, the CMA's financial obligations and regulations must have seemed excessive and controlling.[56]

Voluntary cooperation may have preserved the paper definition of independent proprietorship in sole ownership, but in practice it demanded that black and white grocers relinquish autonomy in the interest of trying to match chains' efficiency and lower prices. Standardized storefronts, stocks, and record-keeping further divorced individualism from independent retailing in what some saw as the "tendency to buy ready-made thoughts and ideas." This was how one storekeeper distinguished between local and national businesses, where ingenuity gave way to homogeneity, especially in "stereotyped advertisements," which carried "nothing of the merchant's personality" and conveyed "no idea of the atmosphere of his store." J. George Frederick, promoter of scientific management and husband of home economist Christine Frederick, insisted that the benefits of standardization and cooperation outweighed the sovereignty of small-scale enterprise. "To deplore this as a threat to the happy independence of the small man," Frederick continued, "is to ignore the fact that the small man's lot was never very happy . . . no matter how individualistic he may be."[57]

Although voluntary chains assured that they preserved independent business ownership, their efforts to adopt corporate chain methods made it increasingly difficult both to distinguish between the two business forms and to defend the place of local small business in the American economy. Moreover, while voluntary chains realized price advantages over single-store independent grocers, they remained "far from meeting chain store competition," according to a 1935 study of New York grocers. Cooperatives' continued focus on quantity buying instead of vertical integration blinded them to the real reason corporate chains outsold them on the basis of price. Both independent grocers and voluntary chains nevertheless doggedly pursued large-scale purchasing discounts enjoyed by companies like A&P as their competitive strategy. Doing so, however, demanded federal-level intervention and regulation of chain corporations' buying practices.[58]

Regulation's Unintended Consequences

Independent businessmen historically had strong allies in Washington, including Louis D. Brandeis, who scorned monopolies and trusts in favor of individual enterprise. Brandeis had supported President Woodrow Wilson's 1912 campaign promise of "the new freedom," whereby small operators would flourish through government reform of business, banking, and tariffs. The longtime justice saw the rise of chains as an abuse of corporate privilege and not as the result of increasingly efficient business and distribution methods. Brandeis's efforts to regulate and control the excesses of large-scale conglomerates drove him during much of his political and personal life. "The small man needs the protection of the law," Brandeis proclaimed in a 1915 statement to the House Committee on Interstate and Foreign Commerce regarding unrestricted competition, but he warned, "the law becomes the instrument by which he is destroyed." This truism would come to pass in the 1930s, when independent grocers demanded federal legislative solutions to the ongoing chain problem.[59]

Small business found perhaps its greatest supporter in Wright Patman, a US congressman from Texas. A committed Democrat and longtime supporter of New Deal–era reforms, Patman had grown up in rural northeast Texas surrounded by the kinds of small local stores that chains threatened. Elected to the House in 1928, Patman took an active role in national politics, introducing a 1929 bill that would have paid World War I veterans an early "bonus" for their service, believing "cash turned loose now would give new business life to every community in the United States." In 1932, he led the movement to impeach Treasury Secretary Andrew Mellon for his mismanagement of federal banking during the onset of the Great Depression. Brandeis's anti-corporation stance on chain stores greatly influenced Patman's own views. The Texan not only had read Louis D. Brandeis's *Other People's Money and How Bankers Use It* (1914), a collection of scathing anti-monopoly essays, but had also crossed paths multiple times with the justice as the two joined in the battle against chains. Patman's sentimentality toward rural America, however, influenced much of his political and personal defense of independent retailers, despite opposition from those who saw local merchants more and more as an outmoded segment of the economy.[60]

Patman's first opportunity to help small business at the federal level came in 1928 when independent retail grocers called on the Federal Trade Commission (FTC) for an investigation of corporate chain practices. In its 1928 resolution, the National Association of Retail Grocers focused on the economic and social consequences of continued chain expansion and consolidation, citing "unfair methods of competition in commerce or agreements, conspiracies, or combinations in restraint of trade." A committee of seven investigators headed by Patman began its query by looking into the so-called superlobby of chain organizations that reportedly held sway over market and business conditions. Patman's probe revealed that large-scale chain organizations like A&P had received special "allowances" from manufacturers for their purchases, much the same as Boston Wholesale Grocers' Association members and department stores had in the nineteenth century. Discounts included 3 percent to 10 percent from meat processors such as Armour and Swift and manufacturers like General Foods and Del Monte. In addition, A&P received nearly $6 million in advertising concessions from these and other firms. Other grocery chains benefited as well, including Safeway, Kroger, Gristede Brothers, and National Tea, all major organizations with a growing market presence.[61]

Patman's committee concluded that chains had used their size to influence trade prices, securing buying advantages to which independents had little access. Legislative efforts such as the Sherman (1890) and Clayton (1914) antitrust acts, which endeavored to curb such monopolistic practices, had failed to protect independent grocers. The Clayton Act in particular strove to end the kinds of cartels and agreements that groups like the BWGA had used to control buying and selling prices. Yet a loophole in the Clayton Act had continued to allow for competitive price discrimination, provided it was performed "in good faith to meet competition." This proviso effectively destroyed the measure's power to shield small businessmen from the kinds of agreements that chains (and wholesale organizations) used to gain price and market advantages. An insider cautioned, "The survival of independent merchants, manufacturers, and other businessmen" was "seriously imperiled" by the price discrimination uncovered in Patman's investigation.[62]

The committee's inquiry coincided with the 1933 passage of the National Industrial Recovery Act (NIRA), a New Deal program designed to stimulate economic recovery through job creation and price regulation. The National Recovery Administration (NRA) and its Food and Grocery Code helped curb chains' competitive edge by mandating that all retail grocers add at least a 6 percent premium to the wholesale prices they paid for goods sold in their

By the 1930s, when this independent grocer rested behind his store counter and motto, chain methods had begun transforming retailing from a focus on personalized service to systematized self-service. Author's collection.

stores. Wholesalers in particular welcomed NRA regulation for its tendency to establish higher manufacturers' prices, giving them greater profits. Chains, however, watched the price advantages they once received for their bulk purchases vanish, putting them on near-equal footing with local retailers. Their concerns were short lived, however. By 1935, the NRA came under the gun from critics like Brandeis who believed the act restrained competition and fair trade despite the protections it appeared to afford small businesses. The Supreme Court declared the act unconstitutional in May 1935, enabling chain stores to resume their competitive buying and price wars with independent retailers.[63]

In the wake of the NRA's demise and the FTC's investigation, several trade organizations submitted legislative proposals designed to check chains' buying advantages by replacing the NRA's price codes and amending the Clayton Act. A bill submitted to Patman by the United States Wholesale Grocers' Association caught the congressman's attention. Wholesalers, who once had focused their antagonisms on retail buying syndicates, now joined with independent retailers to fight chains and the elimination of distribution intermediaries through vertical integration. Working with Arkansas Democratic senator Joseph T. Robinson, Patman refined the wholesalers' measure, penned by the association's general counsel, H. B. Teegarden, and introduced it to Congress in 1935 as the Robinson-Patman Act. Both congressmen sought to resolve price discrimination by suggesting measures that would temper chains' purchasing power and rebalance competition. This they believed would give small businesses equal opportunity to receive the prices and concessions granted to large-scale buyers, especially in the grocery industry.[64]

In June 1936, Congress passed and President Roosevelt signed the Robinson-Patman Act, effectively closing the Clayton Act loophole while providing independent dealers some protection from chain organizations. Patman declared the Act "the Magna Carta of free, independent business enterprise in America." Grocers and other small merchants believed Patman's words were more than just talk. Many who interpreted the Act read it not as a way to level the competitive playing field as Patman intended, but as an anti-chain measure, designed to stop the spread of large-scale chain stores into local communities. Small-town newspapers across the country reported on the bill, suggesting that passage of the act would "rid our communities of the chain system of doing business," as one Pennsylvania editorial claimed. The paper further indicated, "If we the people of these United States want to stay on the right side of the track, we must get together and wage a vigorous and relentless war upon parasitical invaders of the local field."[65]

Although independent merchants and concerned citizens overwhelmingly supported the Robinson-Patman Act, many incorrectly assumed that the bill would abolish the kind of quantity concessions from which chains benefited. Over in Indiana, onlookers claimed the bill would "forbid 'quantity discounts' [and] lower prices obtained by the chain and mail-order concerns on order for large amounts of goods." Days after Congress passed the statute, the *Port Arthur News* in Texas ran a New York columnist's interpretation of the bill. "The law aims at ending price advantages deriving from quantity purchases which chains enjoy over independent competitors," the New Yorker declared. The journalist conceded, however, that "several sections of the measure are vague and open to various interpretations."[66]

In truth and in practice, both the Indiana and Texas papers (along with many others) had misconstrued Patman's bill, leading independent grocers and others to place greater faith in the measure's ability to push back chains while protecting the integrity of small business than it actually intended. Although the act contained stipulations regarding quantity discounts, it did not remove them, as some small businessmen alleged or wished. It continued to allow volume discounts to buyers, but limited them to "economic differences in cost." As long as a seller could demonstrate a "difference or savings in handling costs" with regard to shipping, advertising, or warehousing, he was free to give volume discounts to some buyers over others.[67]

In hearings prior to the bill's passage, Democratic senator Alben Barkley, later vice president under Harry S. Truman, questioned the effect such a measure would have on a "small merchant with a little store," who "has to pay for what he buys [at] a larger unit price than is paid by his larger competitor." Fellow party member and Kentuckian Senator Marvel Logan responded, "There is no way by legislation to afford protection to the less fortunate or less efficient merchant under a condition such as that." He continued:

> We may go as far as we can to protect him, but if there be one merchant who is efficient, who saves by discounting his bills, and desires to use that savings by passing it on to the public, the man who cannot secure such advantages is apt to go under sooner or later, and we cannot help him by law. . . . We cannot prevent efficiency; we cannot stop progress.[68]

What Logan and others laid bare was that the new criterion for small business had shifted from the "self-reliant personal independence" of nineteenth-century merchants to measures of "efficiency" brought about by twentieth-century corporate chains. This new definition of American enterprise, which fully encapsulated chain store methods, pushed outside the boundaries of government protection those small businessmen who conducted trade without benefit of economies of scale and scope. Despite Wright Patman's claim that the Robinson-Patman Act was "the Magna Carta" of small business enterprise, the bill, much like state laws, offered little refuge for local merchants. Independent proprietors who operated a single store without joining a voluntary chain stood in the way of "progress" for their inability to match the economic efficiencies of large-scale operators. In this way, both state and federal governments gave legal clearance not only to reward corporate and voluntary chains' efficiency with volume discounts but also to acknowledge "bigness" as the model of American retail enterprise.

Although lawmakers doubtlessly sought to protect the integrity of free, independent enterprise, they ultimately had little interest in saving so-called wasteful small businesses. In a November 1936 speech, Patman made plain that "the inefficient small merchant will not be protected by this bill. It is not a shelter or an umbrella over them. The small merchant will have to succeed in the best way he can. . . . We do not want to reward the small merchant." Neither Wright Patman nor Congress intended to overturn chains' business methods. As long as chains represented greater economy for the trade and for consumers, federal regulators would do little to stop their growth. "We do not want to do anything that will retard cleverness and greater efficiency," Patman maintained.

While the Texas congressman was convinced that it was "against public interest for a national chain-store concern to continue to operate in this Nation," he nevertheless had difficulty reconciling chains' efficiency with

independent merchants' business methods and practices, which did not con-
form to Patman's economic definition of a successful enterprise. He continued
to maintain that small businessmen would "not only be destroyed" but also
"their country will be destroyed" if chains continued to operate unchecked.
Although Patman and his supporters acknowledged independent merchants'
contributions to local communities, they nevertheless failed to understand
fully the ways in which small businessmen had not only created and sustained
national trade, but also contributed to chain methods. In this way, both passage of the Robinson-Patman Act and state regulations unintentionally priv-
ileged chain store methods, leaving independent merchants confused as to
what they had gained or lost.[69]

Three years after passage of the Robinson-Patman Act, a survey of
New York independent store owners confirmed the bill's ambiguous intentions and effects. When asked, "How should the Robinson-Patman Act benefit
the merchant?" 30 percent of the grocery, drug, hardware, dry goods, and other
tradesmen responded, "Don't know." Another 11 percent had "Never heard of
it," while 7 percent believed that it "Should put chain stores out of business."
Many independent merchants evidently still had little knowledge about how
the Robinson-Patman Act proposed to help small retailers despite considerable discussion in trade journals and local newspapers. Consumers polled
likewise knew little about the measure and its objectives. Nearly 62 percent
of New Yorkers queried not surprisingly had "Never heard" of the Robinson-
Patman Act, with a small percentage believing the bill "Favors chain stores."
Yet when asked where they purchased their groceries, more than 60 percent
claimed that they still preferred independent stores to chains, with the overwhelming majority suggesting that people should shop independents "to
encourage them to stay in business," despite charging customers "somewhat
higher prices."[70]

The 1939 US Retail Census supported New York consumers' general
responses. Grocery chains actually lost ground in the years following passage
of the Robinson-Patman Act. Between 1929 and 1939, the total number of grocery stores operated by chain organizations dropped from 53,466 to 40,159.
Sales dipped slightly too, with chains taking only 36.8 percent of total grocery
sales, down from 39.1 percent in the same period. Meanwhile, the number of
independent stores, spurred in part by their participation in voluntary chains,
grew from just over 307,000 in 1929 to 387,000 ten years later. While the
Robinson-Patman Act may have played a minor part in the decline of chain
stores in this period, helping some independent grocers keep pace with chain
store buying and selling, the Depression, along with the development and
growth of supermarkets are more likely explanations.[71]

Making Big even Bigger

In 1930, former A&P clerk and Kroger chain manager Michael J. Cullen took independent grocery stores and the trade to new levels. In a detailed letter to the president of Kroger, Cullen sought financial support for his idea of opening retail outlets "monstrous in size," forty feet wide and approximately 150 feet deep for six thousand square feet of selling space, ten times the size of the average independent or chain store. Cullen promised to sell "300 items at cost and another 200 items at 5 percent above cost," a system and store he believed shoppers "would break my front doors down to get in." While Cullen's proposition garnered only silence from Kroger, this did not dissuade the innovative grocer from putting his plan into action using $15,000 of his own money. By 1932, his eight New York stores made nearly $6 million in grocery sales alone, and Cullen quickly franchised the approximately $30,000 system; four years later, 1,200 outlets operated in eighty-five cities nationwide. The immediate success and magnitude of King Kullen stores and several imitators such as Big Bear, forced chains like A&P once again to look to independent grocers like Cullen for fresh ideas.[72]

A&P responded by closing and consolidating many of its economy stores and opening supermarkets instead. In Buffalo, New York, the company shut down 227 stores between 1934 and 1937, taking the city's total chain outlets from 417 to 190; in their place, A&P opened fourteen new supermarkets. The story was the same in Chicago, where the company closed 430 of its smaller economy stores and opened thirty-five supermarkets. In total, A&P shuttered more than 21 percent of its stores in four years, replacing them with more than two hundred supermarkets. Other chains followed, with corporations like American Stores replacing many of its smaller outlets with larger operations. The shift to supermarkets enabled chains to realize even greater economies of scale and also reduce some of the anti-chain tax burden by decreasing store numbers.[73]

Corporate chains' efforts to remake their organizations in the 1930s further extended to improving their public image. The anti-chain movement coupled with Wright Patman's FTC investigation had scared chains, especially within smaller communities where they had gained a foothold over local retailers. Many corporate firms engaged in widespread public relations campaigns to improve their position with consumers and bolster their acceptance as community-based businesses. The prolonged battle between independent and chain grocers had provoked chain organizers to promote their stores not only as model retail enterprises but also as civic organizations. The National Chain Store Association proposed a series of resolutions designed to publicize chains' community and charitable contributions. It also encouraged store employees to participate in "all recognized community activities," while pushing managers to join local chambers of commerce and contribute to community chest funds.[74]

Meanwhile, chain executives like Albert H. Morrill, president of the Kroger Grocery and Baking Company, and F. H. Massman, vice president of the National Tea Company, had taken to the road on national speaking tours, talking with local consumers and community leaders about the benefits of chain stores and their commitment to local responsibilities. Responding in 1930 to reports that chains "remove money from the community," Merrill stated that his company had begun "conducting a campaign to make the branches greater independent units in localities in which they conduct their business." In one promotional drive, Merrill offered $3,000 in prizes to Kroger employees for "the best slogan representing the meaning of the company to the public." By the end of the 1930s, such efforts had begun to pay off, making it more difficult for independents to claim America's neighborhoods as their particular business domain.[75]

Employing sophisticated public relations tactics, chains made important strides in convincing consumers and civic leaders that they could serve community interests. A&P in particular fought hard to overcome bad press following the FTC's superlobby investigation. In a marketing blitz, A&P declared that the company was "prepared to spend a substantial sum of money" to tell "our story to all the American people." A&P executives employed aggressive advertising campaigns, drawing on "every medium available," along with donating money to a number of consumer organizations. In addition, the firm hired Carl Byoir, a well-connected public relations executive, to counter both the negative publicity stirred up by Patman's investigation and the continued spread of state chain store taxes. Byoir enlisted the support of both the labor and consumer movements to build a bulwark of nationwide pro-chain support funded by A&P.[76]

Other grocery chains such as Safeway inserted themselves into independent grocers' earliest commercial relationships, working with area farmers to increase distribution of produce and meat through chain stores. In 1936, Safeway president Lingan A. Warren emphasized his firm's "Farmer-Consumer" campaign goals in a half-page newspaper advertisement. "It is self evident that we have good reason for wanting to aid farmers," Warren declared, "since 35 percent of Safeway's retail business is with farmers." The chain leader denounced the "old system" of distribution used by independent retail and wholesale grocers as the reason farmers had experienced a decline in "real wages," as opposed to New Deal efforts to limit crop production and raise market prices. Warren further persuaded farmers (and consumers) that the marketing and distribution methods used by chains "pay more money back to the farmer by widening his markets." In publicizing their community relations campaigns, Safeway, A&P, Kroger, and other chains began to make significant inroads into communities, reaching consumers in new ways and on a level independent grocers found increasingly difficult to answer on their own.[77]

Redefining Small Business in the Corporate Age

Chains' public relations marketing helped change perceptions of their stores and their methods. In the years following passage of the Robinson-Patman Act, introduction of anti-chain legislation declined precipitously. Between 1938 and 1940, only 118 state chain tax bills were introduced (down from 849 between 1931 and 1937), only one of which was passed into law. Mississippi newspapers claimed in 1939 that where once there were "nation-wide efforts" to tax chains, "there is increasing evidence that the nation is veering away from the 'punitive tax' recourse." When Wright Patman attempted to pass an amendment to the Robinson-Patman Act that would tax chains far more heavily than in the past (termed by many as a "Death Sentence Bill"), two million women reportedly stood ready to protest. Patman based the new measure on his belief that independent merchants had "gained the good will of the American people" and that "the people have recognized honesty and fairness" in locally owned businesses. Yet a 1939 *Fortune* magazine survey found that nearly 50 percent of those questioned "wanted the chains left alone," while only 6.3 percent "favored putting chains out of business." The tide of negativity toward chain stores clearly had shifted, making chain store methods increasingly accepted as the prevailing retailing form in America.[78]

What little protection independent grocers had in the Robinson-Patman Act came from its support of cooperative ventures. While the measure had outlawed coercive "agreements" between chains and manufacturers, it sanctioned voluntary chains and cooperative buying and selling among independent grocers as a way to match corporate chains' efficiency and economy, much like Wisconsin's tax measure. "Cooperative retailers who buy in wholesale quantities comparable to the volume purchases of chains, and with the same economy of methods," Patman insisted, "are entitled to the same scale of discounts and proportionally equal allowances." As a result, the boon of cooperatives that emerged in the 1930s to take advantage of volume discounts persisted, as independent grocers continued adapting to the new definition of small business.[79]

Ultimately, chains' increased acceptability among consumers, combined with the ambivalent nature of the Robinson-Patman Act, provoked unanswerable questions about the future of independent grocers. The controversy over chain stores and the rise of anti-chain arguments seemed only to raise greater awareness of chain store methods, spurring increased talk about "efficiency" and "bigness" as hallmarks of business acumen and expertise. Independent grocers' long-standing authority built around the pairing of innovativeness and community now seemed problematic once chains had redefined the model of small business enterprise and entrepreneurship as a standardized, corporate system. Albert Morrill, Lingan Warren, and Clarence Saunders replaced the image of the avuncular storekeeper to become the new faces of the grocery trade, their growing presence through print and radio advertising making chain owners and operators public figures. In 1950, George and John Hartford, owners of A&P, appeared on the cover of *Time* magazine, a gold chain framing the brothers' image. Chain executives' money and resources helped propel these men and their stores into the spotlight and brought them into homes across the country. Neighborhood grocers, with little access to the same financial and media resources, lacked for outlets outside of voluntary chains to promote their services on the same scale.[80]

By the 1940s corporate chain stores could claim new authority as archetypes for American business enterprise, but they did so only because independent grocers' long history of innovativeness had made possible the development of modern grocery retailing. Nearly every method chains claimed as particular to their stores had been pioneered and implemented by independent grocers, albeit with varying degrees of success. Chains made vertical integration, self-service, and cash-and-carry the industry standard, but it was small grocers who had first dared to attempt these new paths. While corporations answered the chain store "question" on the national level, declaring victory in mass media, the debate was always local in nature. Neighborhood grocers battled not only to stake their claim over retailing but also to emphasize that the central role they had and continued to play in local commerce was not to be overshadowed by cheap prices and bigger stores. For these small businessmen, it was not a matter of "the past crying out against the present," as some have characterized, but rather the present warning the future.[81]

Conclusion

Looking Backward, Moving Forward

A 2005 press release from Carnegie Mellon University announced a new study devoted to "every local retailer's worst nightmare: a new mega-store . . . opening just up the street." Walmart, the nation's largest department store had also positioned itself as the country's largest food retailer. The "supercenter" had overtaken supermarkets to become the latest model for retailing in the twenty-first century. Executives nationwide nervously watched as Walmart drove a shocking number of companies out of business and threatened even more. Looking for ways to counter the "Walmart effect," business analysts and scholars pursued efforts to prevent the eradication of supermarkets by an even bigger corporate form.[1]

The grocery trade had come full circle. In the post–World War II era, chains slowly gave way to supermarkets as the dominant retailing form for selling food in America. These massive, suburban-based stores became the new "local grocers," serving consumers and communities. According to the 2012 US Businesses Census, conducted every five years, over 42,000 supermarket firms operated more than 66,000 stores across the United States. Meanwhile, grocery stores (a category distinct from supermarkets and defined as "establishments primarily engaged in retailing a general line of food products") outpaced supermarkets in both numbers and net sales, with 65,000 firms conducting trade in 91,000 stores. While supermarkets now dominate commercial and popular perceptions about modern grocery retailing, independent stores (along with local and regional chains) persist.[2]

The overall picture, however, is grim. Nearly thirty grocery chains (regional and national) filed for bankruptcy protection between 1993 and 2003, the majority citing competition from Walmart as the leading factor in their potential failures. Walmart's $53 billion in annual grocery sales earned from 1,258 supercenters enabled the company to undercut retail prices, charging 8 percent to 27 percent less than chains like Kroger or Safeway. The super-power undersold its competition by earning the kinds of volume discounts from manufacturers and growers that the Robinson-Patman Act protected, along with other economic measures enjoyed by large-scale corporations such as economies of scale and scope. Much like independent grocers in the 1920s, supermarket chains now wondered how they could compete with the corporate behemoth. In December 2010, even A&P, once the largest and most dreaded grocery chain in America, filed for bankruptcy, the victim of "falling revenues, a leveraged balance sheet, legacy costs, and unfavorable supply relationships," according to its refinancing officer. Five years later in July 2015, A&P declared bankruptcy yet again, citing increased competition from companies like Walmart and Whole Foods and $2.3 billion in liabilities.[3]

Walmart's success epitomizes not only the current apex in bigness and efficiency but also the success of retailing and distribution as the nation's primary economic driving forces. Chains' organizational structure made possible Walmart's strategy of selling more for less in both rural towns and globally. As a result, it has become a template business, a firm that establishes new standards of operational, political, and social influence that others follow. Walmart's focus on retailing, though, makes it unique among other template companies, which include the Pennsylvania Railroad, US Steel, and General Motors. As an archetype for modern-day capitalism, Walmart's exploitation of retail and information technology and logistics has enabled retailing to triumph over manufacturing, a first in the history of American enterprise. But its growth and low prices have come at a cost to local economies and to its workers, with minimum wages, a lack of advancement opportunities, and temporary employment all standard practices. Walmart exerts its worldwide influence by farming out production to cheaper labor markets in Asia and extending its stores into the same region in the hunt for new consumers. History generally has been unkind to template firms, however. Most have succumbed to business, economic, political, and social changes, making it difficult for these big conglomerates to sustain their positions at the top. It is prudent, therefore, to consider how long Walmart can continue its unchecked expansion. Recent setbacks along with changes in company leadership and strategy suggest that the organization may be preparing for yet another retail revolution.[4]

Walmart is both the antithesis of small local business and its progeny. Without question, the company represents everything independent grocers

feared and of which they forewarned: concentrated capital, the loss of neighborhood businesses, and transient employees instead of community-minded
owners. The contrast is apparent; but it is equally important to recognize
that even the world's largest retailer still engages in the language and methods of local retailing. Sam Walton, after all, made his name and his money
in southern towns and crossroads communities where neighborhood shops
once dominated. Even though Walton's corporate strategy echoes the catalog giant Montgomery Ward by supplying affordable manufactured goods
to farming and rural populations, his company's public identity and customer services emphasize down-home hospitality. The "Walmart paradox,"
as some have called it, allows the company to rule worldwide retailing while
maintaining through its cheap prices and accessibility that it stands for Main
Street principles. Walmart's welcoming senior-citizen army of greeters, in
other words, has just as much to do with stamping the image of the avuncular corner grocer onto a faceless corporation as it does with mass distribution and consumption; one is not exclusive of the other. In capitalism's
ever-evolving systems, the local continues to guide not just the national but
the global as well.[5]

Searching for strategies to combat Walmart's market supremacy, supermarkets also have looked backward. Chains such as Kroger, Publix, Safeway,
and Giant Eagle have taken a closer look at the "small community grocery
store" as a future retailing model. At 14,000 square feet, Giant Eagle "Express"
stores take up less than one-sixth the size of a typical supermarket. Undeniably
larger than nineteenth-century shops, these "smaller" forms, many hope, will
"re-create some of the effect . . . of a village feel," as one Pittsburgh, Pennsylvania,
resident anticipated. Others, eager for a return to the fabled nostalgia of the
"corner grocer," believe such places will fulfill a "craving people have for traditional grocery stores in their neighborhoods, where they might run into
friends while picking up something to make for dinner." Past tendencies to
build "ever larger stores," in the words of one journalist, were predicated on
the notion "that consumers want choice above all." Most supermarkets stock
between thirty thousand and forty thousand products. Yet shoppers spend on
average only twenty-two minutes in a grocery store, leading many to think that
"we are moving into an era when people want less assortment," shattering
long-standing assumptions about consumer behavior and driving the shift to
more compact footprints.[6]

The recent move to build smaller, community-centered stores marks
one aspect of local retailers' continued influence on American business.
Even Walmart acknowledged this course in 2012 by opening the first of
its "Neighborhood Markets" (about 25 percent the size of the company's
Supercenters). The following year, it proposed opening eighty of these

supermarket-sized outlets nationwide, with plans to have more than five hundred in operation by 2016. "Our small format provides a competitive advantage that allows us to rapidly fill in new markets and compete more effectively with grocery, dollar and drugstore competition," Walmart CEO Bill Simon maintained. Combining consumers' longing for the past with current business and market shifts, corporations once again have drawn inspiration from neighborhood grocers' methods. These new spaces made headlines in 2008 when the *New York Times* reported that the average grocery store size decreased in recent years despite more than two decades of expansion in supermarket buildings. Acknowledging small grocers' persistence, the *Times* recognized, "small grocery stores have been around forever, and some old-time neighborhood markets still exist." Of the nearly 65,000 grocery firms in operation in 2012, more than 40,000 (or 62 percent) employed fewer than five workers—small businesses indeed. While many look back wistfully on the corner grocer, others have found and continue to find in them the inspiration and path forward. "Small is the new big," one twenty-first-century industry insider insisted.[7]

Giant Eagle's first Express store, located in Harmarville, Pennsylvania, represents the industry's new focus on more compact footprints. In a return to pre-suburban supermarket days, a company spokesman claimed the format offered "The potential to better service our customers in the smaller or more urban communities where they live and work." Photo © Germaine Williams 2014.

Not all returns to the past have been successful, however. In 1997, Webvan sought to "revolutionize" the grocery trade by offering home delivery to online shoppers. Started by Louis Borders (of Borders bookstores), Webvan combined the time-honored personal service with modern automated warehouses and computerized ordering and scheduling. Webvan promised to deliver groceries to customers' doors for about the same cost as picking them up at the store. By 2001, though, Webvan was a colossal failure, having lost nearly $1.2 billion in investments. Although the company had little trouble attracting first-time customers, it could not generate repeat orders. When polled, Webvan clients admitted that "they liked the service but found that it required too much planning to decide in advance what to order," a response not unlike that of nineteenth-century grocery catalog shoppers.

Other delivery services, however, have thrived in the wake of Webvan's crash, including East Coast companies FreshDirect and Peapod, and Instacart, a grocery shopping courier business found in major metropolitan markets nationwide. In 2013, Amazon introduced Amazon Fresh, promising same-day delivery of local products, prepared meals, and specialty grocery items to its online customers. Meanwhile, dozens of regional chains likewise began offering e-commerce options including online shopping in addition to home delivery. Even Walmart jumped on the bandwagon, launching Walmart To Go in 2011, giving shoppers the option of picking up online orders at a store or requesting residential drop-off. Once the bane of economizing chains and shoppers, independent grocers' personalized amenities have once again become modern and progressive.[8]

Supermarket chains too have refocused attention on personal service as a way to recapture the market. Using new information technologies—swipe cards, online apps, and social media—that track consumers' buying practices, they have begun concentrating on customer spending habits to understand buyers' needs better and to encourage loyalty. Regulars can earn discounts on gasoline, food, and services when they concentrate their spending dollars with one retailer. This business model, used for decades by retail organizations, builds on notions of trust brokering by cultivating commercial relationships and promoting value through quality and satisfaction assurances—nineteenth-century commercial intimacy gone twenty-first-century digital.[9]

Community. Service. Loyalty. These same terms and ideas that once pegged neighborhood retailers as "old fashioned" have become signposts of modern American retailing. While chain stores, supermarkets, and super-centers in succession supplanted small businesses as dominant forms of retail enterprise, their pioneering techniques are universal today. Walk into any con-temporary supermarket and illuminated glass cabinets showcase cakes, pies, and meats in bakery and deli departments; cash registers and checkers ring up our purchases; merchandising analysts do the work of traveling salesmen, negotiating buying opportunities and marketing deals, while serving as the "primary point of contact in building and maintaining vendor relationships." Whole Foods, the nation's leading organic grocer, emphasizes that its "business is intimately tied to both the neighborhoods and the larger global community" it serves. More supermarkets are carving out social spaces where hipsters now play checkers, listen to live music, or attend wine tastings. Meanwhile, wholesale grocers still distribute produce, canned goods, and boxed foods from commercial centers and warehouses to the countless rural and urban supermarkets, chain stores, and shops that comprise today's complex retail landscape. Nineteenth-century roots anchor today's marketing and distribution. Smallness and innovation endure as a profitable business model: The Corner Grocery, Inc.[10]

Small business's path through industrial capitalism may have differed from that of big business, but it was just as innovative and modern. Local businessmen confronted many of the same competitive, economic, and technological challenges encountered by Andrew Carnegie, John D. Rockefeller, and Frank Woolworth. Yet American industrialization was built as much on food manufacturing, production, distribution, and retailing as on industrial goods, and perhaps more so, since nearly every American had dealings with their neighborhood storekeeper. Like the nation's manufacturing leaders, independent grocers crafted solutions centered on efficiency, scale, and price controls, but they also focused on service, style, and community to differentiate themselves in the market. They rarely sought to monopolize trade, drive others from the marketplace, or cultivate mammoth enterprises. Instead, they fashioned methods that enabled them to benefit from broader infrastructural changes without abandoning local ties, turning social concepts of community into commercial profitability. It was a powerful combination that chain moguls recognized and sought to duplicate in their stores, acknowledging that for most Americans, capitalism operated (and continues to operate) on the local level.

The nation's rapid advance to mass distribution and marketing took place because of independent retail and wholesale grocers, not despite them. Industrial capitalism came of age in the countless neighborhood shops and warehouses that stood adjacent to the factories, rail yards, and refineries that made up nineteenth-century enterprise. Its activities rang out with the chime of every cash register bell, bled onto every salesman's order book, traveled in every wholesaler's wagon, and spilled out of every cracker box. Historians' continued emphasis on "bigness" has eclipsed the significance of this work, in effect leading us to situate conceptions of modern business almost solely within the frameworks of large-scale enterprise. Shifting attention to small business and constructing more-inclusive narratives that encompass the range of proprietorships, firms, and corporations represented in American commerce complicates the stories we tell about the past and expands our understanding not only of modern business but also of capitalism and its many varieties and intricacies. Though few nineteenth-century grocers would have identified as captains of industry, all would have called themselves businessmen or businesswomen.

Notes

INTRODUCTION

1. Weston P. Truesdell, "Prosperous Go-Ahead San Leandro," *Oakland* (CA) *Tribune*, December 23, 1896, 17.

2. "B[udd].T. Scott," *Fresno* (Calif.) *Republican Weekly*, March 1, 1895, 7.

3. "Interesting Queries," *New England Grocer* 50, no. 20 (April 11, 1902), 37; Godfrey M. Lebhar, *Chain Stores in America, 1859–1962* (New York: Chain Store Publishing Corporation, 1952), 63–67.

4. Most influential among these works are those of business historian Alfred D. Chandler, whose "organizational response to fundamental changes in processes of production and distribution" became the paradigm for multitudes of organizational syntheses and firm studies focused on explaining corporate consolidation at the turn of the nineteenth century. See Alfred D. Chandler Jr., *Strategy and Structure: Chapters in the History of Industrial Enterprise* (Cambridge, MA: MIT Press, 1962); Alfred D. Chandler Jr., *The Visible Hand: The Managerial Revolution in American Business* (Cambridge, MA: Harvard University Press, 1977); Alfred D. Chandler Jr., *Scale and Scope: The Dynamics of Industrial Capitalism* (Cambridge, MA: Belknap Press, 1990).

5. Richard White, *Railroaded: The Transcontinentals and the Making of Modern America* (New York: W.W. Norton, 2011), xi–xxxiv; Philip Scranton, *Endless Novelty: Specialty Production and American Industrialization, 1865–1925* (Princeton, NJ: Princeton University Press, 1997), 3–24; Richard R. John, "Train of Catastrophes," *Reviews in American History* 41, no. 1 (March 2013), 106.

6. William Leach, *Land of Desire: Merchants, Power, and the Rise of a New American Culture* (New York: Vintage Books, 1993); M. M. Zimmerman, *The Supermarket: A Revolution in Distribution* (New York: McGraw-Hill, 1955), 9; Marc Levinson, *The Great A&P and the Struggle for Small Business in America*

(New York: Hill and Wang, 2011), 8; Richard S. Tedlow, *New and Improved: The Story of Mass Marketing in America* (New York: Basic Books, 1990), 182–186; 214.

7. Robert H. Wiebe, *The Search for Order, 1877–1920* (New York: Hill and Wang, 1967), 1–10.

8. Robert D. Johnston, *The Radical Middle Class: Populist Democracy and the Question of Capitalism in Progressive Era Portland, Oregon* (Princeton, NJ: Princeton University Press, 2003), 3–17; Alan Trachtenberg, *The Incorporation of America: Culture and Society in the Gilded Age* (New York: Hill and Wang, 1982), 3–10; Olivier Zunz, *Making America Corporate, 1870–1920* (Chicago: University of Chicago Press, 1990), 1–10; Gerald Carson, *The Old Country Store* (New York: Oxford University Press, 1954). Carson's take on country grocers acknowledges their important commercial contributions but misses their link to modern business.

9. Mansel G. Blackford, "Small Business in America: A Historiographic Survey," *Business History Review* 65, no. 1 (Spring 1991), 10; Mansel G. Blackford, *A History of Small Business in America* (New York: Twayne, 1991), ix–xi; Burroughs Adding Machine Company, *The Rise of Richard F. Brune, Grocer* (Detroit, MI: Burroughs Adding Machine Co., 1915), 15, 38; Scott A. Sandage, *Born Losers: A History of Failure in America* (Cambridge, MA: Harvard University Press, 2005), 1–21.

10. John Russell Bartlett, *Dictionary of Americanisms* (Boston: Little, Brown, 1859), 101; C[harles] H. Slack advertisement, *American Grocer* 30, no. 15 (October 11, 1883), 1153; Lewis Austin Storrs, *Koheleth* (New York: G.W. Dillingham, 1897), 38.

11. "Can We Afford to Be Clean?" *Women's Home Companion* 35, no. 1 (January 1908), 17; Glenn Porter and Harold Livesay, *Merchants and Manufacturers: Studies in the Changing Structure of Nineteenth-Century Marketing* (Baltimore, MD: Johns Hopkins University Press, 1971); Lewis E. Atherton, *The Frontier Merchant in Mid-America* (Columbia: University of Missouri Press, 1971).

12. Joseph A. Schumpeter, *Capitalism, Socialism, and Democracy* (New York: Harper, 1950, 1976), 83; Levinson, *The Great A&P*, 250, 262–263; Vicki Howard, "Department Store Advertising in Newspapers, Radio, and Television, 1920–1960," *Journal of Historical Research in Marketing* 2, no. 1 (2010), 61–85. Howard notes that twentieth-century local businesses often capitalized on the nostalgic image of "mom and pop" by cultivating a sense of place.

13. Thomas J. Schlereth, "Countury Stores, County Fairs, and Mail-Order Catalogues," in *Consuming Visions: Accumulation and Display of Goods in America, 1880–1920*, ed. Simon J. Bronner (New York: W. W. Norton, 1989), 349; Diane E. Wenger, *A Country Storekeeper in Pennsylvania: Creating Economic Networks in Early America, 1790–1807* (University Park: Pennsylvania State University Press, 2008), 3; James M. Mayo, *The American Grocery Store: The Business Evolution of an Architectural Space* (Westport, CT: Greenwood Press, 1993), 75. Mayo's architectural exploration of grocery stores acknowledges proprietors as "business pioneers."

14. Chase and Sanborn advertisement, "The Old Fashioned New England Grocery," cardboard poster in author's possession, ca. 1940.

15. R. E. Gould, *Yankee Storekeeper* (New York: Wittlesey House, 1946), 130; Carson, *The Old Country Store*, 189; Laurence A. Johnson, *Over the Counter and*

on the Shelf: Country Storekeeping in America, 1620–1920 (Rutland, VT: Charles E. Tuttle, 1961).

16. Philip Scranton, *Proprietary Capitalism: The Textile Manufacture at Philadelphia, 1800–1885* (Cambridge: Cambridge University Press, 1983), 414–422.

17. Porter and Livesay, *Merchants and Manufacturers*, 215; "Transportation—Its Bearing upon the Future of New York," *American Grocer* 14, no. 19 (November 6, 1875), 505.

18. Women and African Americans, while difficult to locate within the grocery trade, have not been overlooked in the business history literature. See Angel Kwolek-Folland, *Incorporating Women: A History of Women and Business in the United States* (New York: Twayne, 1998); Wendy Gamber, *The Female Economy: The Millinery and Dressmaking Trades, 1860–1930* (Urbana: University of Illinois Press, 1997); Edith Sparks, *Capital Intentions: Female Proprietors in San Francisco, 1850–1920* (Chapel Hill: University of North Carolina Press, 2006); Juliet E. K. Walker, *The History of Black Business in America: Capitalism, Race, Entrepreneurship* (New York: Prentice Hall, 1998); Robert E. Weems, *Black Business in the Black Metropolis: The Chicago Metropolitan Assurance Company, 1925–1985* (Bloomington: Indiana University Press, 1996).

CHAPTER 1

1. John Darby, "Prospectus," *American Grocer* 1, no. 1 (September 1869), 16, 49; Ralph B. Draughon Jr. and Delos Hughes, *Lost Auburn: A Village Remembered in Period Photographs* (Montgomery, AL: New South Books, 2012), 49; "Darby's Prophylactic Fluid," advertisement, *American Farmer*, April 1, 1869, n.p.; Frank Hastings Hamilton, ed., *Surgical Memoirs of the War of the Rebellion*, vol. 2 (Cambridge, NY [Mass?]: Riverside Press, 1871), 449; C. E. Latimer, "Diseases of the Maxillary Sinus," *Dental Cosmos* 12, no. 1 (January 1870), 8; Laurence A. Johnson, *Over the Counter and on the Shelf: Country Storekeeping in America, 1620–1920* (Rutland, VT: Charles E. Tuttle, 1961), 39–40; G. F. Kirkman, "Christmas Time and the Grocers," *American Grocer* 1, no. 4 (November 1, 1869), 71.

2. Mansel G. Blackford, *A History of Small Business in America* (New York: Twayne, 1991), xi–xx; Diane E. Wenger, "Delivering the Goods: The Country Storekeeper and Inland Commerce in the Mid-Atlantic," *Pennsylvania Magazine of History and Biography* 129, no. 1 (January 2005), 46; Diane E. Wenger, *A Country Storekeeper in Pennsylvania: Creating Economic Networks in Early America, 1790–1807* (University Park: Pennsylvania State University Press, 2008); Lewis E. Atherton, *The Southern Country Store, 1800–1860* (Baton Rouge: Louisiana State University Press, 1949), 1; William Cronon, *Nature's Metropolis: Chicago and the Great West* (New York: W.W. Norton, 1991), 92.

3. George P. Rowell and Company, *American Newspaper Directory* (New York: George P. Rowell, 1872), 119.

4. W. J. Rorabaugh, *The Alcoholic Republic: An American Tradition* (New York: Oxford University Press, 1979), 3–22; "Michigan Temperance Advocate," *Journal of the*

American Temperance Movement 4, no. 10 (October 1840), 151; Blackford, *A History of Small Business in America*, 6; Leonard Bacon, *A Discourse on the Traffic in Spirituous Liquors* (New Haven, CT: B. L. Hamlen, 1838), 4.

5. Paul E. Johnson, *A Shopkeeper's Millennium: Society and Revivals in Rochester, New York, 1815–1837* (New York: Hill and Wang, 1978), 3–14; *The Revised Statutes of the State of Indiana* (Indianapolis: Douglass & Noel, 1838), 581–586; *The Laws of the Territory of Iowa* (Burlington, IA: J. H. McKenny, 1840), 27; Bacon, *A Discourse on the Traffic in Spirituous Liquors*, 52.

6. Hayden, Upham, and Company, advertisement, *The Liberator*, July 23, 1831, 1; "Whether Are Country Groceries of Real Utility?—And How Far May They with Propriety Be Restricted," *The American Farmer, and Spirit of the Agricultural Journals of the Day (1838–1850)* American Periodical Series, August 7, 1839, 1, 11.

7. "The City Council v. C. D. Ahrens," in James A. Strobhart, ed., *Reports of Cases Argued and Determined in the Court of Appeals and Court of Errors of South Carolina* 4 (Columbia, SC: A. S. Johnston, 1850), 241–258; "Mayor and Aldermen of Columbia v. Beasly," in *Reports of Cases Argued and Determined in The Supreme Court of Tennessee during the Years 1839–1840* (Nashville: J. George Harris, 1841), 232–241; *Reports on the Subject of a License Law by a Joint Special Committee of the Legislature of Massachusetts* (Boston: Wright and Potter, 1867), 531; Maureen Ogle, *Ambitious Brew: The Story of American Beer* (New York: Harcourt, 2006), 25.

8. "Sheriff's Sale of Store Goods," *Delaware County* (Media, PA) *American*, December 23, 1857, 1.

9. Cronon, *Nature's Metropolis*, 104–109, 62.

10. Harriet Connor Brown, *Grandmother Brown's Hundred Years, 1827–1927* (Boston: Little, Brown, 1930), 99–101.

11. Milo Milton Quaife, ed., *The Early Day of Rock Island and Davenport: The Narratives of J. W. Spencer and J. M. D. Burrows* (Chicago: R. R. Donnelley, 1942), 183–184; Cronon, *Nature's Metropolis*, 105; Gerald Carson, *The Old Country Store* (New York: Oxford University Press, 1954), 71–72.

12. Ford and Drouillard advertisement, *Gallipolis* (Ohio) *Journal*, April 21, 1853, 4.

13. George Washington Williams, *History of the Negro Race in America, 1619–1880*, vol. 2 (New York: G. P. Putnam's Sons, 1883), 140; Martin R. Delany, *The Condition, Elevation, Emigration and Destiny of the Colored People of the United States* (1852; rpt., Baltimore: Black Classic Press, 1993), 97; Samuel T. Wilcox advertisement, *Williams' Cincinnati Directory and Business Advertiser, 1850–51* (Cincinnati: C. S. Williams, 1850), 105; Juliet E. K. Walker, "Black Entrepreneurship: An Historical Inquiry," *Essays in Economic and Business History* 1 (1983), 38.

14. Susan Strasser, *Satisfaction Guaranteed: The Making of the American Mass Market* (New York: Pantheon, 1989), 39; Johnson, *Over the Counter*, 31–33.

15. Brian P. Luskey, *On the Make: Clerks and the Quest for Capital in Nineteenth-Century America* (New York: New York University Press, 2010), 62–65, 72–79; "Wanted," advertisement, *New York Sun*, May 8, 1866, 3; "Wanted," advertisement, *Richmond* (VA) *Daily Dispatch*, October 1854, 3; David R. Roediger, *The Wages of*

Whiteness: Race and the Making of the American Working Class (New York: Verso, 1991), 95–163.

16. Luskey, *On the Make*, 1–20; unsigned letter to the editor, *New York Daily Tribune*, November 15, 1850, 7; "Wanted" advertisement, *Daily Cincinnati Press*, April 18, 1859, 3.

17. Luskey, *On the Make*, 54–82, 215; "As Clerk in a grocery," advertisement, *New York Daily Tribune*, December 16, 1850, 1; "The Late Stephen Whitney," *New York Daily Tribune*, February 17, 1860, 8; "Stephen Whitney," *Brattleboro Vermont Phoenix*, February 25, 1860, 2; "The Late Stephen Whitney," *Western Reserve* (Warren, OH) *Chronicle*, March 7, 1860, 1.

18. "Wanted," advertisement, *Evening Star* (DC), February 1856, 3; "Wanted," advertisement, *Daily Richmond* (VA) *Dispatch*, February 22, 1853, 3; "Wanted," advertisement, *Daily Richmond* (VA) *Dispatch*, November 15, 1855, 2; "Boy," *New York Daily Tribune*, October 8, 1851, 1; Luskey, *On the Make*, 215–216.

19. "Suggestions to Vincennes Merchants," *Vincennes* (IN) *Weekly Western Sun*, January 23, 1869.

20. Figures compiled from a survey of grocers from Boston, Massachusetts; Cedar Rapids, Iowa; and Vicksburg, Mississippi, listed in R. G. Dun and Company, *The Mercantile Agency and Reference Book* 67 (January 1885).

21. "Reckless Methods of Doing Business," *American Grocer* 15, no. 26 (June 24, 1876), 737.

22. "Failures and Assignments," *American Grocer* 30, no. 15 (October 11, 1883), 1141; "Failures," *New England Grocer* 17, no. 23 (November 20, 1885), 33; [Joseph F.] Fowlkes, "Co-Operative Stores," First Meeting, National Negro Business League, 1900, *Records of the National Negro Business League* (Bethesda, MD: University Publications of America, 1995), 188.

23. "Nehemia Dozy and His Old-Fashioned Store," *American Grocer* 5, no. 9 (February 26, 1876), 228; "George Washington Dusenbury," letter to the editor, *American Grocer* 16, no. 16 (October 14, 1876), 571, emphasis in original; Arwen Palmer Mohun, "Laundrymen Construct Their World: Gender and the Transformation of a Domestic Task to an Industrial Process," *Technology and Culture* 38, no. 1 (January 1997), 101; "The Old Way and the New," *American Grocer* 16, no. 17 (October 21, 1876), 620.

24. Mohun, "Laundrymen Construct Their World," 101; "The Old Way and the New," *American Grocer* 16, no. 17 (October 21, 1876), 620.

25. Richard B. DuBoff, "Business Demand and the Development of the Telegraph in the United States, 1844–1860," *Business History Review* 54, no. 4 (Winter 1980), 461; J[ames] B. Hovey, letter to the editor, *American Grocer* 15, no. 13 (March 25, 1876), 343; H. K. and F. B. Thurber and Company, letter to the editor, *American Grocer* 15, no. 14 (April 1, 1876), 371.

26. Alfred D. Chandler, *The Visible Hand: The Managerial Revolution in American Business* (Cambridge, MA: Harvard University Press, 1977), 285–314; Strasser, *Satisfaction Guaranteed*, 82–83.

27. Susan B. Carter, "National Income Originating and Persons Engaged in Wholesale and Retail Trade: 1869–1929," Table De1-13 in *Historical Statistics of the United States, Earliest Times to the Present: Millennial Edition*, ed. Susan B. Carter, Scott Sigmund Gartner, Michael R. Haines, et al. (New York: Cambridge University Press, 2006); George Rogers Taylor, *The Transportation Revolution* (New York: Rinehart, 1957), 138–148; Glenn Porter and Harold Livesay, *Merchants and Manufacturers: Studies in the Changing Structure of Nineteenth-Century Marketing* (Baltimore: Johns Hopkins University Press, 1971), 214–227.

28. G. A. Eckerley advertisement, *Memphis* (TN) *Public Ledger*, January 2, 1869, 4; D. K. Irwin advertisement, *Wheeling* (WV) *Daily Intelligencer*, June 30, 1870, 3; Thomas J. Schlereth, "Country Stores, County Fairs, and Mail-Order Catalogues: Consumption in Rural America," in *Consuming Visions: Accumulation and Display of Goods in America, 1880–1920*, ed. Simon J. Bronner (New York: W. W. Norton, 1989), 350–351; G. F. Kirkman, "Opening a Store," *American Grocer* 2, no. 4 (March 28, 1870), 60–62.

29. William Leach, *Land of Desire: Merchants, Power, and the Rise of a New American Culture* (New York: Pantheon Books, 1993), 40.

30. "The City," *Forth Worth Daily Gazette*, January 7, 1886, 3; "City News," *Cairo* (IL) *Bulletin*, October 1, 1875, 3; Farley and Hofman, Rochester Show Case Works catalog (Rochester, NY: Farley and Hofman, ca. 1882), 2–19.

31. Thomas H. B. Parks, Improvement in Removable Tops for Show-Cases, US Patent 195,529, filed June 11, 1877, and issued September 25, 1877; William Henry Lockwood, Improved Ventilating Show-Case, US Patent 77,389, filed April 28, 1868; Hans A. Winden, Improvement in Grocers' Sample-Cases, US Patent 183,614, filed March 14, 1876, issued October 24, 1876.

32. Zachariah R. Traver, Design for a Grocer's Can-Stand, US Patent 9,152, filed November 29, 1875, issued March 21, 1876; G. F. Kirkman, "Arrangement of a Grocery Store," *American Grocer* 2, no. 8 (April 25, 1870), 143–144; Farley and Hofman, Rochester Show Case Works catalog, 15; William Volkland, Improvement in Store-Counters, US Patent 166,043, filed March 29, 1875, issued July 27, 1875.

33. Ira Clizbe, letter to the editor, *American Grocer* 15, no. 8 (February 19, 1876), 202.

34. Charles Kerr, ed., *History of Kentucky*, vol. 3 (New York: American Historical Society, 1922), 327; William F. Reinhardt and Brother, letter to the editor, *American Grocer* 15, no. 12 (March 18, 1876), 343; Leach, *Land of Desire*, 62.

35. Pamela Walker Laird, *Advertising Progress: American Business and the Rise of Consumer Marketing* (Baltimore: Johns Hopkins University Press, 1998), 24–25; Leach, *Land of Desire*, 54–70; Karal Ann Marling, *Merry Christmas! Celebrating America's Greatest Holiday* (Cambridge, MA: Harvard University Press, 2000), 82–120.

36. "Chips," *Salt Lake Herald*, November 4, 1880, 3; "City and County News," *Wichita* (KS) *City Eagle*, May 11, 1876, 3; "St. Valentine's Day," *Charleston* (SC) *Daily News*, February 14, 1872, 3; "Two Beautiful Heads," *Frankfort* (KY) *Weekly Roundabout*, December 27, 1879, 4; "Brief Reference," *Sacramento Daily Record-Union*, June 8, 1880, 3; Leach, *Land of Desire*, 62.

37. Laird, *Advertising Progress*, 110; Jackson Lears, *Fables of Abundance: A Cultural History of Advertising in America* (New York: Basic Books, 1994), 113–133; "Metropolitan Tea Company," *Knoxville Daily Chronicle*, March 19, 1871, 4; William C. Edwards, ed., *The Lincoln Assassination: The Rewards Files*, microfilm transcription, 152; "Where to Buy Groceries," *National Republican* (DC), September 21, 1876, 4.

38. "The Boss," *Salt Lake Herald*, December 16, 1880, 3; George D. Pyper, *Stories of Latter Day Saint Hymns,Their Authors and Composers* (Salt Lake City: Deseret News Press, 1939), 35. George Manwaring was a well-known member of the Church of Jesus Christ of Latter-day Saints, authoring several hymns; Leach, *Land of Desire*, 55–57; [Harry Harman?], *Window Dressing for Grocers* (Chicago: Charles S. Thomas, 1896), 19–21, 65–74.

39. "Miscellaneous News Items," *New Bloomfield* (PA) *Times*, June 10, 1879, 4; Elphonzo Young's advertisement, *National Republican* (DC), June 19, 1880, 4; "Local News," *Stark County* (Canton, OH) *Democrat*, August 5, 1880, 5; Richard R. John, *Network Nation: Inventing American Telecommunications* (Cambridge, MA: Belknap Press, 2010), 218–220.

40. "A Look About," *New England Grocer* 40, no. 1 (December 4, 1896), 32.

41. Diary of Edmund A. Fuller, June 16, 1875, vol. 3, n.p., February 17, 1874, vol. 3, n.p., and January 23, 1878, vol. 4, n.p., Fuller Family Collection, Maine Historical Society, Portland, Maine (hearafter Fuller diary). Fuller first writes about "marking goods" in 1874 and continues the practice throughout much of his time in business.

42. Cronon, *Nature's Metropolis*, 81–93.

43. Ira Mayhew, *A Practical System of Book-keeping by Single and Double Entry* (Boston: Sanborn, Carter, Bazin, 1851); "Wanted," advertisement, *New York Daily Tribune*, October 1842, 3; Blackford, *A History of Small Business in America*, 9.

44. Carson, *The Old Country Store*, 93; James D. Norris, "One-Price Policy among Antebellum Country Stores," *Business History Review* 36, no. 4 (Winter 1962), 455–458.

45. C. Y. Moyer, *The Business Manual; A Complete Guide in All Mercantile and Legal Transactions and Reference Book for Every Day Use* (Chicago: Union Publishing House, 1890), 169; Carson, *The Old Country Store*, 94–95.

46. "The Old-Fashioned and the Modern Way of Doing Business Contrasted," *American Grocer* 16, no. 18 (October 28, 1876), 665–666; "Cash," letter to the editor, *American Grocer* 19, no. 10 (February 28, 1878), 594; Edith Sparks, *Capital Intentions: Female Proprietors in San Francisco, 1850–1920* (Chapel Hill: University of North Carolina Press, 2006), 163; Blackford, *A History of Small Business in America*, 9.

47. Gary John Previts and Barbara Dubis Merino, *A History of Accountancy in the United States: The Cultural Significance of Accounting* (Columbus: Ohio State University Press, 1998), 115–131; Chandler, *The Visible Hand*, 39; Fuller diary, March 18, 1874, vol. 1, n.p.; Fuller diary, April 17 and 21, 1874; August 4 and 18, 1874; January 14, 1875, vol. 3, n.p. Fuller's ledgers do not survive but likely were retained by the Maine Supreme Judicial Court when he was required to submit them as evidence during a lengthy lawsuit he was party to in the late 1880s and early 1890s.

48. "Country Merchants," *American Grocer* 3, no. 8 (August 20, 1870), 179; W. A. Woolson, letter to the editor, *American Grocer* 16, no. 11 (September 9, 1876),

348; Jacob H. Hoffmann, letter to the editor, August 17, 1875, *American Grocer* 14, no. 15 (October 9, 1875), 395; Fuller diary, December 11, 1875, vol. 3, n.p.; August 10, 1874, vol. 2, n.p.; February 12, 1868, vol. 1, n.p.; Stephen Mihm, *A Nation of Counterfeiters: Capitalists, Con Men, and the Making of the United States* (Cambridge, MA: Harvard University Press, 2009), 305–359.

49. Woolson, letter to the editor, 348; "Many Readers," letter to the editor, *American Grocer* 15, no. 4 (January 22, 1876), 90.

50. Response to "Many Readers," letter to the editor, *American Grocer* 15, no. 4 (January 22, 1876), 90.

51. "Many Readers," 90; Jacob H. Hoffmann, letter to the editor, *American Grocer* 14, no. 15 (October 9, 1876), 395; Fuller diary, December 11, 1875, vol. 3, n.p.; August 10, 1874, vol. 2, n.p.; February 12, 1868, vol. 1, n.p.; W[illiam] H. Home, letter to the editor, *American Grocer* 16, no. 17 (October 21, 1876), 620.

52. Fuller diary, November 16, 1874, December 15, 1874, and March 1, 1875, vol. 1, n.p.; Bruce H. Mann, *Neighbors and Strangers: Law and Community in Early Connecticut* (Chapel Hill: University of North Carolina Press, 1987); [Victor] A. Tulane, "Building Up a Grocery Business," Fifth Annual Convention, National Negro Business League, 1905, *Records of the National Negro Business League* (Bethesda: MD: University Publications of America, 1995), 80.

53. Frederick B. Goddard, *Giving and Getting Credit: A Book for Business Men* (New York: Baker and Taylor, 1895), 26–27; Young, letter to the editor, 315; Scott A. Sandage, *Born Losers: A History of Failure in America* (Cambridge, MA: Harvard University Press, 2005), 70–98.

54. Gazzam Collection Agency advertisement, in Horace Greely, *The Tribune Almanac and Political Register for 1871* (New York: Tribune Association, 1871), 189; McKillop, Walker and Company, *Mercantile Register of Reliable Banks and Attorneys* (New York: McKillop, Walker and Company, 1882), n.p.; "Collection Agencies," *American Grocer* 14, no. 19 (November 6, 1875), 505; Fuller diary, August 4, 1874, vol. 1, and September 18, 1877, vol. 4, n.p.

55. Young, letter to the editor, 315.

56. Cronon, *Nature's Metropolis*, 211–213, 319.

57. Albert Welles, "Domestic Poultry," *De Bow's Review* 15, no. 5 (November 1853), 508–509; "Egg Market," in *Niles' National Register* 11, no. 14 (December 4, 1841), 224; A. M. Dickie, "Our Poultry Interests," in *First Annual Report of the Pennsylvania Board of Agriculture* (Harrisburg: Lane S. Hart, 1878), 141–142; A. M. Dickie to US Commissioner of Agriculture, in *Information in Relation to Disease Prevailing among Swine and Other Domestic Animals* (Washington, DC: US Government Printing Office, 1878), 8.

58. Maine Board of Agriculture, *Eighteenth Annual Report of the Secretary of the Maine Board of Agriculture for the Year 1873* (Augusta: Sprague, Ownen & Nash, 1873), 224; Fuller diary, January 21, 1874, vol. 1, n.p.; Susanne E. Freidberg, "The Triumph of the Egg," *Comparative Studies in Society and History* 50, no. 2 (March 2008), 406–407; Arthur H. Cole, "Agricultural Crazes: A Neglected Chapter in American Economic History," *American Economic Review* 16, no. 4 (December 1926), 634–637.

59. Fuller's egg book (used in combination as a cash journal) is the only account-ing ledger that survives from his business; Fuller diary, August 28, 1874, and April 7, 1875, vol. 1, n.p.

60. Winifred B. Rothenberg, "The Market and Massachusetts Farmers, 1750–1855," *Journal of Economic History* 41, no. 2 (June 1981), 283–314; Stephen Kern, *The Culture of Time and Space, 1880–1918* (Cambridge, MA: Harvard University Press, 1983), 111; Fuller diary, November 18, 1883, vol. 7, n.p.; McCracken and Company, letter to the editor, *American Grocer* 15, no. 4 (January 22, 1876), 90.

61. O[wen] Kelly and Son, letter to the editor, *American Grocer* 15, no. 4 (January 22, 1876), 90; Frederick Watts, *Report of the Commissioner of Agriculture for the Year 1874* (Washington, DC: US Government Printing Office, 1875), 273–274.

62. Cronon, *Nature's Metropolis*, xvii–xix, 104–109.

63. "Instruction for Packing and Shipping Eggs," *American Grocer* 15, no. 4 (January 22, 1876), 97; "On Preserving Eggs," *Journal of Horticulture, Cottage Gardener, and Country Gentleman* 36, old series (1866), 94; Cronon, *Nature's Metropolis*, 122–127; Archie Cunning trade card, undated, box 5, "Food," Warshaw Collection of Business Americana, National Museum of American History, Archives Center, Smithsonian Institution; Freidberg, "Triumph of the Egg," 400–423.

64. *Devereaux, Receiver of the Atlantic and Great Western Railroad v. Buckley and Company*, in John Henry Truman, John Allan Mallory, Herbert A. Shipman, et al., eds., *The American Railway Reports: A Collection of All Reported Decisions Relating to Railways*, vol. 21 (New York: J. Cockcroft, 1880), 72–77.

65. *Devereaux, Receiver of the Atlantic and Great Western Railroad v. Buckley and Company*, 72–77.

66. P. J. Meisch to Andrew Schoch, March 31, 1923, microfilm reel 1, Andrew Schoch Grocery Company Business Records, Minnesota Historical Society Manuscript Collection, St. Paul, MN.

67. Tulane, "Building Up a Grocery Business," 78–79.

68. Tulane, "Building Up a Grocery Business," 78–83.

69. Fuller diary, October 10 and 15, 1883, vol. 7, n.p.

70. P[eter] H. Felker, *The Grocers' Manual* (New York: American Grocer Publishing Association, 1879), 138–143, 186–193, 288–307.

71. James Ritty, Improvement in Cash Register and Indicator, US Patent 221,360, filed March 26, 1879, and issued November 4, 1879.

CHAPTER 2

1. "The Grocers Come to the Front," *(NCR) Perfected* 1, no. 3 (1886), 13.

2. "The Problem of Grocery Fixtures," *Grocery World* 35, no. 12 (March 23, 1903), 28–29.

3. James R. Beniger, *The Control Revolution: Technological and Economic Origins of the Information Society* (Cambridge, MA: Harvard University Press, 1986), 1–27; JoAnne Yates, *Control through Communication: The Rise of System in American Management* (Baltimore: Johns Hopkins University Press, 1989), esp. chapter 1;

William Fielding Ogburn, *Social Change with Respect to Culture and Original Nature* (New York: B.W. Huebsch, 1922), 200–213.

"Grocers' Check Book," *American Grocer* 36, no. 1 (July 7, 1886), 20.

4. The National Cash Register Company (hereafter NCR) ledger that forms the archival foundation for this chapter lists only one department store client from 1885 to 1887, located in Denver, Colorado. Agent's and Commissions Ledger (1884–1887), serial number 1182-4241, National Cash Register Archive, Montgomery County Historical Society, Dayton, Ohio (hereafter NCR Archive); James W. Cortada, *Before the Computer: IBM, NCR, Burroughs, and Remington Rand and the Industry They Created* (Princeton, NJ: Princeton University Press, 1993), 65; Eric von Hippel, *Democratizing Innovation* (Cambridge, MA: MIT Press, 2005), 4.

5. Cortada, *Before the Computer*, esp. chapter 2; Lars Heide, *Punched-Card Systems and the Early Information Explosion, 1880–1945* (Baltimore: Johns Hopkins University Press, 2009); Robert Kee, "Data Processing Technology and Accounting: A Historical Perspective," *Accounting Historians Journal* 20, no. 2 (December 1993), 197–198.

6. Max Weber, *The Protestant Ethic and the Spirit of Capitalism* (New York: Routledge Classics, 2001), 120–121; Gary John Previts and Barbara Dubis Merino, *A History of Accountancy in the United States: The Cultural Significance of Accounting* (Columbus: Ohio State University Press, 1998), 4–5.

7. NCR advertisement, "70 Per Cent of the Merchants," *San Jose* (CA) *Evening News*, December 28, 1887, 3.

8. Research for this chapter centers on a one-volume ledger detailing 2,948 sales records (1884–1887) from the National Cash Register Company. While the ledger contains accounts from 1884, their numbers are scant and the information incomplete. Currently, only one additional ledger listing a few sales from 1884 is available in the collection. Information in this ledger, however, lacks many of the details from the later ledger, recording only when and to whom the machine was sold and where it was shipped along with incomplete remarks about sales terms; therefore, it was not used in my analysis. I instead chose to utilize the more complete data from 1885 to 1887, the first years in which John H. Patterson took control of the organization. Sales records from 1887, however, also are incomplete, ending sometime in July, Agent's and Commissions Ledger (1884–1887), NCR Archive.

9. Regina Lee Blaszczyk, *Imagining Consumers: Design and Innovation from Wedgwood to Corning* (Baltimore: Johns Hopkins University Press, 2000). While no African Americans or women grocers are represented in the data, women do appear in connection with a few other trades, most notably with hotels and boardinghouses.

10. "A Busy Place," *Newport* (RI) *Mercury*, November 17, 1883, 1; "The Problem of Grocery Fixtures," 29.

11. Richard L. Crandall and Sam Robins, *The Incorruptible Cashier,* Volume 1: *The Formation of an Industry, 1876–1890* (New York: Vestal Press, 1988), 29.

12. Cortada, *Before the Computer*, 64–66; Miles Alarm Cash Drawer advertisement, *Petersburg* (VA) *Index*, August 24, 1872, 6; "Miles Alarm Cash Drawer," *Charleston* (SC) *Daily News*, September 27, 1871, 3; "Miles Alarm Till Manufacturing Company," *Daily Columbia* (SC)*Phoenix*, September 2, 1873, 2.

13. "The Sins of the Old Cash Drawer," *Grocery World* 36, no. 1 (September 7, 1903), 181–186.

14. "The Cash Recording Machine," *Scientific American*, 38, no. 7 (February 16, 1878), 95; Crandall and Robins, *Incorruptible Cashier*, 29; James Ritty, Improvement in Cash Register and Indicator, US Patent 221,360, filed March 26, 1879, and issued November 4, 1879.

15. Samuel Crowther, *John H. Patterson: Pioneer in Industrial Welfare* (Garden City, NJ: Doubleday, Page, 1923), 58, 82.

16. "An Ingenious Thief," *San Francisco Morning Call*, August 27, 1891, 3; "How Kork Got in Trouble," *Fort Worth Gazette*, September 27, 1891, 4; "Graduates Los Angeles Business College," *Los Angeles Daily Herald*, February 1, 1890, 3; Crowther, *Patterson*, 13; "The Grocers Come to the Front," 13.

17. "The Grocers Come to the Front," 12–13; Charles W. Wootton and Barbara E. Kemmerer, "The Emergence of Mechanical Accounting in the U.S., 1880–1930," *Accounting Historians Journal* 34, no. 1 (June 2007), 101–102.

18. Susan B. Carter, "National Income Originating and Persons Engaged in Wholesale and Retail Trade: 1869–1929," Table De1-13 in *Historical Statistics of the United States, Earliest Times to the Present: Millennial Edition*, ed. Susan B. Carter, Scott Sigmund Gartner, Michael R. Haines, et al. (New York: Cambridge University Press, 2006); Michael Zakim, "The Business Clerk as Social Revolutionary; or, a Labor History of the Nonproducing Classes," *Journal of the Early Republic* 26, no. 4 (Winter 2006), 567; "We Give It Up," *Frankford* (KY) *Roundabout*, July 29, 1893, 5.

19. "The Grocery Clerk's Hard Lot," *New York Evening News*, January 22, 1894, 4; John Higham, *Strangers in the Land: Patterns of American Nativism, 1860–1925* (New Brunswick, NJ: Rutgers University Press, 1955, 2004), 66; Brian P. Luskey, *On the Make: Clerks and the Quest for Capital in Nineteenth-Century America* (New York: New York University Press, 2010), 132–147.

20. Perry R. Duis, *The Saloon: Public Drinking in Chicago and Boston, 1880–1920* (Urbana: University of Illinois Press, 1983), 48; Jack Sullivan, "'Nasty Words' and Nifty Whiskeys," *Bottles and Extras* 17, no. 4 (October–December 2006), 68. Hannah and Hogg are referred to in revised editions of Theodore Dreiser's *Sister Carrie* as Fitzgerald and Moy's. Dreiser's original version, however, named Hannah and Hogg outright. See Theodore Dreiser, *Sister Carrie* (New York: Bantam Books, 1900, 1992), 35.

21. "Cash Always Balanced," *Omaha Daily Bee*, October 11, 1887, 8; "Six Questions," *Salt Lake Herald*, December, 25, 1887, 24; "The National Cash Register," *Washington* (DC) *Critic*, May 8, 1888, 4; Isaac F. Marcosson, *Wherever Men Trade: The Romance of the Cash Register* (New York: Dodd, Mead, 1945), 39; "Of Great Importance," *Washington* (DC) *Sunday Herald*, March 22, 1885, 4.

22. W. H. Babcock, "The Future of Invention," *Atlantic Monthly* 44, no. 262 (August 1879), 137; "The Hurry of Life," *Newport* (RI) *Daily News*, February 21, 1882, 2.

23. Yates, *Control through Communication*, 21–64; Jackson Lears, *Fables of Abundance: A Cultural History of Advertising in America* (New York: Basic Books, 1994), 1–13; Previts and Marino, *A History of Accountancy in the United States*, 160–166.

24. National Cash Register Corporation, "The Cash Register Era," in *NCR: Celebrating the Era, 1884–1984* (Dayton, OH: NCR Corporation, 1984), 5.

25. Crandall and Robins, *Incorruptible Cashier*, 65–101.

26. Joseph H. Crane, *How I Sell a National Cash Register*, unpublished manuscript, 1887, n.p., NCR Archive.

27. Crowther, *Patterson*, 151; R. G. Dun and Company, *The Mercantile Agency and Reference Book* 67 (January 1885), n.p.; Credit Report (1888) of A[lbert] J. Hussong, Ohio, vol. 140, p. 1266, R. G. Dun & Co. Credit Report Volumes, Baker Library Historical Collections, Harvard Business School, Cambridge, MA.

28. Northwestern Sleigh Company, *Wholesale Price List* (Milwaukee, WI: Northwestern Sleigh Company, 1889), 39; Kingman Golledge and Luther Cornwall credit ratings in, R.G. Dun and Company, *The Mercantile Agency and Reference Book* 67 (January 1885), n.p.; "Property Sales," *Washington* (DC) *Evening Star*, May 4, 1885, 1.

29. Information about Albert J. Hussong taken from 1910 U.S. Census, Dayton Ward 4, Montgomery, Ohio; and 1930 U.S. Census, Dayton Ward 4, Montgomery, Ohio, 3B.

30. "The Grocers Come to the Front," 12.

31. Yates, *Control through Communication*, 9–15; "A New System for Grocery, Hardware, Dry Goods & Other Stores," NCR advertisement, 1905, advertising files, NCR Archives.

32. Yates, *Control Through Communication*, 1–3.

33. Wootton and Kemmerer, "Emergence of Mechanical Accounting," 98–100; Ross Thomson, "Learning by Selling and Invention: The Case of the Sewing Machine," *Journal of Economic History* 47, no. 2 (June 1987), 433.

34. Marcosson, *Wherever Men Trade*, 60; "Complaints," *N.C.R.* 2, no. 34 (July 15, 1889), n.p.

35. JoAnne Yates, "Business Use of Information and Technology during the Industrial Age," in *A Nation Transformed by Information: How Information Has Shaped the United States from Colonial Times to the Present*, ed. Alfred D. Chandler Jr. and James W. Cortada (New York: Oxford University Press, 2000), 115; "The Grocers Come to the Front," 12; Beniger, *Control Revolution*, 173.

36. E. P. Thompson, "Time, Work-Discipline, and Industrial Capitalism," *Past & Present*, no. 38 (December 1967), 56–97.

37. Crane, *How I Sell a National Cash Register*, n.p.; James Ritty and John Birch, Cash Register and Indicator, US Patent 271,363, filed February 15, 1882, and issued January 30, 1883; Crandall and Robins, *Incorruptible Cashier*, 75.

38. Henry E. Blood, unpublished salesman's manual, [1889], n.p., NCR Archives.

39. Max Weber, *The Theory of Social and Economic Organization*, trans. A. M. Henderson and Talcott Parsons (New York: Free Press, 1947), 186–202; Andrew Schoch Company, general ledger, vol. 6 (1890–1895), microfilm reel 6, Andrew Schoch Grocery Company Business Records, Minnesota Historical Society Manuscript Collection, St. Paul, Minn.

40. Crane, *How I Sell a National Cash Register*, n.p.

41. NCR, "The Cash Register Era," 23; JoAnne Yates, "Co-Evolution of Information-Processing Technology and Use: Interaction between the Life Insurance and Tabulating Industries," *Business History Review* 67, no. 1 (Spring 1993), 4–5, 48; Marcosson, *Wherever Men Trade*, 60; "The Grocers Come to the Front," 12.

42. Of the 2,947 registers sold between 1885 and July 1887, 933 had modified keyboards, Agent's and Commissions Ledger (1884–1887), NCR Archive.

43. *Leading Manufacturers and Merchants of New Hampshire* (New York: International Publishing, 1887), 177.

44. Crandall and Robbins, *Incorruptible Cashier*, 118, 163; "Display of Inventions," *The N.C.R.* 11, no. 19 (October 1, 1898), 510.

45. Yates, *Control through Communication*, 120–123; "Pierce System," *The N.C.R.* 1, no. 12 (April 1, 1888), 4.

46. Von Hippel, *Democratizing Innovation*, 96.

47. Beniger, *Control Revolution*, 260–261; "Personal," *Ottawa* (IL) *Free Trader*, October 8, 1887, 4; Matthew Sobek, "Detailed Occupations—Males: 1850–1990 [Part 1]," Table Ba1440-1676 in *Historical Statistics of the United States, Earliest Times to the Present: Millennial Edition*, ed. Susan B. Carter, Scott Sigmund Gartner, Michael R. Haines, et al. (New York: Cambridge University Press, 2006); Matthew Sobek, "Detailed Occupations—Females: 1860–1990 [Part 1]," Table Ba1721-1957 in *Historical Statistics of the United States, Earliest Times to the Present: Millennial Edition*, ed. Susan B. Carter, Scott Sigmund Gartner, Michael R. Haines, et al. (New York: Cambridge University Press, 2006); Susan Porter Benson, *Counter Cultures: Saleswomen, Managers, and Customers in American Department Stores, 1890–1940* (Urbana: University of Illinois Press, 1986), 31–74.

48. Johan Schot and Adri Albert de la Bruheze, "The Mediated Design of Products, Consumption and Consumers in the Twentieth Century," in *How Users Matter: The Co-Construction of Users and Technologies*, ed. Nelly Oudshoorn and Trevor Pinch (Cambridge, MA: MIT Press, 2003), 230; Crandall and Robins, *Incorruptible Cashier*, 88.

49. Crowther, *Patterson*, 90–92; Walter A. Friedman, *Birth of a Salesman: The Transformation of Selling in American History* (Cambridge, MA: Harvard University Press, 2004), 122.

50. O[liver] C. Collins, letter to the editor, June 29, 1886, *American Grocer* 36, no. 1 (July 7, 1886), 20; *The Empire State, Its Industries and Wealth: Also an Historical and Descriptive Review of the Industries and Wealth of the Principal Cities and Towns* ... (New York: American Publishing and Engraving Co., 1888), 161; Credit Report (1879) of Oliver Collins, New York, vol. 100, p. 149, R. G. Dun & Co. Credit Report Volumes, Baker Library Historical Collections; United States and Foreign Advertising and Collection Company, "Commercial Phone, and the Advertisers and Collectors' Chart," vol. 9, no. 1 (September 1885), http://fulton.nygenweb.net/people/debtors1. html; National Manufacturing Company advertisement, *American Grocer* 31, no. 1 (January 3, 1884), 39.

51. Robert M. Fogelson, *Bourgeois Nightmares: Suburbia, 1870–1930* (New Haven, CT: Yale University Press, 2005), 60–66.

52. "McQuaid's Big Market Grocery Store," advertisement, *Des Moines Daily News*, February 18, 1898, 8. The 1889 Creston, Iowa, city directory lists approximately 4,800 names, including twenty-three grocers of varying sizes and combinations, *Creston, IA, 1890* (Creston, IA: Nixon Waterman, 1889).

53. "Our Statement!" *San Jose Evening News*, December 23, 1887, 6.

54. "Six Years' Experience of a Storekeeper," *N.C.R. Hustler* 9, no. 71 (October 1892), 1–2.

55. "Six Years' Experience," 1–2.

56. NCR bookkeepers noted which machines shipped on "consignment," either to agents or business owners, with no salesman's commission recorded in these cases; Friedman, *Birth of a Salesman*, 122; Bovie, Pitrat, and Company advertisement, *Gallipolis* (OH) *Journal*, September 9, 1880, 3.

57. Friedman, *Birth of a Salesman*, 105–111.

58. Credit Report (1883–1889) of C[harles] F. Eastlack, New Jersey 7, p. 159, and J[ames] R[ufus] Eastlack, New Jersey, vol. 7, p. 261, R. G. Dun & Co. Credit Report Volumes, Baker Library Historical Collections; "Oscar Adams Eastlack," *DVRBS*, http://www.dvrbs.com/people/camdenpeople-OscarAEastlack.htm; "Camden Grocer in Trouble," *Philadelphia Inquirer*, January 7, 1906, 6.

59. *Annual Report of the Commissioner of Patents by the United States Patent Office* (Washington, DC: US Government Printing Office, 1870), 170; Charles F. Eastlack, Improvement in Cattle Pump, US Patent 79,217, filed June 23, 1868; Dan McConnell, "Oscar Eastlack Listed as Owner of Initial Vehicle to Operate on City's Cobbled Streets during Century Turn," *Camden* (NJ) *Courier Post*, January 29, 1938, n.p., http://www.dvrbs.com/PEOPLE/CamdenPeople-OscarAEastlack; Credit Report (1889) of J[ames] R[ufus] Eastlack, New Jersey, vol. 7, p. 261, R. G. Dun & Co. Credit Report Volumes, Baker Library Historical Collections.

60. Crandall and Robins, *Incorruptible Cashier*, 82.

61. Kathleen Franz, *Tinkering: Consumers Reinvent the Early Automobile* (Philadelphia: University of Pennsylvania Press, 2005), 2.

62. "Jottings," *New England Grocer* 40, no. 1 (December 4, 1896), 11.

63. Herman Cordts to NCR, testimonial letter, January 21, 1893, in "Opinions of New York and Brooklyn Storekeepers," Advertising Scrapbook #510, 1892–1900, and Joseph S. Campbell to Oscar Groshell, testimonial letter, August 8, 1902, "Competition Files," box 8, folder 7, NCR Archives; Alfred D. Chandler, *The Visible Hand: The Managerial Revolution in American Business* (Cambridge, MA: Harvard University Press, 1977), 404; Joseph A. Litterer, "Systematic Management: Design for Organizing Recoupling in American Manufacturing Firms," *Business History Review* 37, no. 4 (Winter 1963), 369–391.

64. Clarence Saunders, Self-serving Store, US Patent 1,242,872, filed October 21, 1916, and issued October 9, 1917.

65. "A Retired Traveler's Views," unsigned letter to the editor, *American Grocer* 14, no. 18 (October 30, 1875), 477.

CHAPTER 3

1. Portions of this chapter appeared originally as Susan V. Spellman, "Trust Brokers: Traveling Grocery Salesmen and Confidence in Nineteenth-Century Trade," *Enterprise & Society* 13, no. 2 (June 2012), 276–312. Samuel Iseman

to Simon Strauss, December 17 and 18, 1890, Simon Strauss Papers, South Caroliniana Library, University of South Carolina, Columbia, SC (hereafter Strauss Papers).

2. Pamela Walker Laird, *Pull: Networking and Success since Benjamin Franklin* (Cambridge, MA: Harvard University Press, 2006), 54; Scott A. Sandage, *Born Losers: A History of Failure in America* (Cambridge, MA: Harvard University Press, 2005), 161; Jonathan Barron Baskin, "The Development of Corporate Financial Markets in Britain and the United States, 1600–1914: Overcoming Asymmetric Information," *Business History Review* 62 (Summer 1988), 200–201.

3. Walter Friedman, *Birth of a Salesman: The Transformation of Selling in America* (Cambridge, MA: Harvard University Press, 2004), 56–87; Roy Church, "Salesmen and the Transformation of Selling in Britain and the US in the Nineteenth and Early Twentieth Centuries," *Economic History Review* 61, no. 3 (August 2008), 695–725; Michael French and Andrew Popp, "Ambassadors of Commerce": The Commercial Traveler in British Culture, 1800–1939," *Business History Review* 82, no. 4 (Winter 2008), 789–814; Roman Rossfeld, "Suchard and the Emergence of Traveling Salesmen in Switzerland, 1860–1920," *Business History Review* 82 (Winter 2008), 735–759.

4. Philip Scranton, *Endless Novelty: Specialty Production and American Industrialization, 1865–1925* (Princeton, NJ: Princeton University Press, 1997), 8–9; Glenn Porter and Harold C. Livesay, *Merchants and Manufacturers: Studies in the Changing Structure of Nineteenth Century Marketing* (Baltimore: Johns Hopkins University Press, 1971), 159–160, 214; Alfred D. Chandler, *Scale and Scope: The Dynamics of Industrial Capitalism* (Cambridge, MA: Belknap Press, 1990), 28–31; Marc Levinson, *The Great A&P and the Struggle for Small Business in America* (New York: Hill and Wang, 2011), 90.

5. Susan Strasser, *Satisfaction Guaranteed: The Making of the American Mass Market* (New York: Pantheon Press, 1989), 19–20; P[eter] R. Earling, *Whom to Trust: A Practical Treatise on Mercantile Credits* (Chicago: Rand McNally, 1890), 238.

6. "Thirty Years' Change in the Jobbing Grocery Business," *Grocery World* 36, no. 6 (August 10, 1903), 8; Porter and Livesay, *Merchants and Manufacturers*, chapters 8 and 9; Baker and Lowrey quoted in Porter and Livesay, *Merchants and Manufacturers*, 216.

7. John Russell Bartlett, *Dictionary of Americanisms: A Glossary of Words and Phrases, Usually Regarded as Peculiar to the United States* (Hoboken, NJ: Wiley, 1848, 2003), 123.

8. Timothy Spears, *100 Years on the Road: The Traveling Salesman in American Culture* (New Haven, CT: Yale University Press, 1995), 97–101.

9. "The Loss and Gain of Drumming for Custom," *Hunt's Merchants' Magazine* 33, no. 3 (March 1855), 389–390.

10. Quoted in Bartlett, *Dictionary of Americanisms*, 123–124.

11. Friedman, *Birth of a Salesman*, 65; Laird, *Pull*, 189–190.

12. Claude S. Fischer, *America Calling: A Social History of the Telephone to 1940* (Berkeley: University of California Press, 1992), 23; Tom Schachtman, *Absolute Zero*

and the Conquest of Cold (New York: Mariner Books, 2000), 112; William Cronon, *Nature's Metropolis: Chicago and the Great West* (New York: W.W. Norton, 1992), 331; "Does It Pay to Employ 'Drummers'?" *American Grocer* 4, no. 8 (February 25, 1871), 235.

13. H. K. Thurber & Co., letter to the editor, *American Grocer* 4, no. 11 (March 18, 1871), 334. Thurber conducted his trial for several months in 1870 before sharing his opinions in 1871; "Drummers," *American Grocer* 4, no. 9 (March 4, 1871), 267; "Do Drummers Pay," *American Grocer* 4, no. 9 (March 4, 1871), 271.

14. *The History of Austin Nichols & Co., Inc., 1855–1955* (n.p.: [1955]), 1–2, box 2, "Food," Warshaw Collection of Business Americana, National Museum of American History, Archives Center, Smithsonian Institution (hereafter Warshaw Collection).

15. "Does It Pay to Employ 'Drummers'?," 235; "Do 'Drummers' Pay," 271.

16. "Do 'Drummers' Pay?," *American Grocer* 4, no. 12 (March 25, 1871), 363; Friedman, *Birth of a Salesman*, 1–13.

17. "Does It Pay to Employ 'Drummers'?," 235; "Observer," anonymous letter to the editor, *American Grocer* 4, no. 14 (April 8, 1871), 429; H. K. Thurber & Co. advertisement, *American Grocer* 4, no. 1 (January 7, 1871), 694.

18. H. K. Thurber & Co., letter to the editor, 334; Porter and Livesay, *Merchants and Manufacturers*, 2, note 2; Church, "Selling in Britain," 720; Joseph Nimmo Jr., *Report on the Internal Commerce of the United States* (Washington, DC: US Government Printing Office, 1881), 205–206.

19. "Observer," 429.

20. "Big Dick Thompson," *Gentry* (AR) *Journal-Advance*, June 16, 1905, 3; "Adams," *North Adams* (MA) *Evening Transcript*, March 31, 1899, 3; Announcements, *Mexia* (TX) *Evening News*, February 1, 1899, 1; "James Egan," *Vinita* (Indian Territory) *Indian Chieftain*, July 4, 1889, 3; "What the Reporter Caught," *Freeport* (IL) *Daily Journal and Republican*, May 17, 1884, 1; "Rowland Items," *Lumberton* (NC) *Semi-Weekly Robesonian*, April 5, 1901, 1; "They Made the Snow Fly," *Boston Daily Globe*, February 13, 1892, 4.

21. Samuel Iseman to Simon Strauss, November 20 and December 18, 1890, Strauss Papers.

22. Friedman, *Birth of a Salesman*, 5; "City Sales," November 1899, "Country Sales," December 1899, and Unknown to Franklin MacVeagh, June 8, 1899, box 35, folder, "Business File Wholesale Groceries, 1899–1900," Franklin MacVeagh Papers, Manuscript Division, Library of Congress (hereafter MacVeagh Papers).

23. "Do 'Drummers' Pay," 271; Harvard Bureau of Business Research, *Methods of Paying Salesmen and Operating Expenses in the Wholesale Grocery Business in 1918* (Cambridge, MA: Harvard University Press, 1919), 4–15; M[attheus] J. Bufka to Franklin MacVeagh, August 6, 1904, box 35, folder, "Business Files, Wholesale Grocery, 1902–1906," MacVeagh Papers; Contract between Franklin MacVeagh and Company and traveling salesmen, box 35, folder, "Business Files, Wholesale Grocery, April 1901," MacVeagh Papers; Nimmo, *Report on the Internal Commerce of the United States*, 208.

24. Pamela Walker Laird, *Advertising Progress: American Business and the Rise of Consumer Marketing* (Baltimore: Johns Hopkins University Press, 1998), 4–6;

Strasser, *Satisfaction Guaranteed*, 29–35; M. J. MacDonald to Franklin MacVeagh, February 12, 1900, box 25, folder, "Business Files, Wholesale Grocery, 1899–1900," MacVeagh Papers; Andrew F. Smith, *Pure Ketchup: A History of America's National Condiment* (Washington, DC: Smithsonian Institution Press, 2001), 42–44, 95–97.

25. Strasser, *Satisfaction Guaranteed*, 39–42; Franklin MacVeagh to [D. T.] Haskett, December 29, 1908, box 35, folder, "Business Files, Wholesale Grocery, 1907–1914," MacVeagh Papers; Donna R. Gabaccia, *We Are What We Eat: Ethnic Food and the Making of Americans* (Cambridge, MA: Harvard University Press, 1998), 55–63.

26. Barnett A. Elzas, *The Jews of South Carolina: From the Earliest Times to the Present Day* (1905; repr., Spartanburg, SC: Reprint Company, 1983), 256; *Claflin & Co. v. Iseman* [No number in original], Supreme Court of South Carolina, 23 S.C. 416; 1885 S.C., September 17, 1885, Decided.

27. Joseph S. Iseman to James Iseman Sr. et al., February 23, 1984, and James M. Iseman Jr. to Joseph S. Iseman, October 14, 1983, Iseman Family Collection, 1961–1996, Jewish Heritage Collection, College of Charleston, Charleston, SC.

28. Lizzie Iseman to Leopold Strauss, March 12 and May 14, 1878, and contract of sale between Leopold Strauss and S. M. Call, February 14, 1887, Strauss Papers; Simon Strauss advertisement, *Bennettsville* (SC) *Marlboro Democrat*, January 31, 1890, 4.

29. Robert F. Dalzell Jr., *Enterprising Elite: The Boston Associates and the World They Made Together* (Cambridge, MA: Harvard University Press, 1987), xii, 67; Naomi R. Lamoreaux, *Insider Lending: Banks, Personal Connections, and Economic Development in Industrial New England* (New York: Cambridge University Press, 1994), 25.

30. "Business in Charleston," *Manning* (SC) *Times*, April 15, 1891, 2; Sol Iseman advertisement, *Manning* (SC) *Times*, November 12, 1890, 4.

31. Samuel Iseman to Simon Strauss, November 25, 1890, Strauss Papers; Laird, *Pull*, 23.

32. Much work remains to be done on Jewish business history, especially in the realm of nineteenth-century trade. The problem of transparency in Jewish business methods and practices has undoubtedly made many business records and other potential sources scarce. See Rowena Olegario, "'That Mysterious People,' Jewish Merchants, Transparency, and Community in Mid-Nineteenth Century America," *Business History Review* 73, no. 2 (Summer 1999), 161–189; and Rowena Olegario, *A Culture of Credit: Embedding Trust and Transparency in American Business* (Cambridge, MA: Harvard University Press, 2006), 119–138.

33. Elzas, *Jews in South Carolina*, 241–259; Mark Granovetter, "The Strength of Weak Ties," *American Journal of Sociology* 78, no. 6 (May 1973), 1365; Cronon, *Nature's Metropolis*, 46–54.

34. "Suggestions to Vincennes Merchants," *Vincennes* (IN) *Weekly Western Sun*, January 23, 1869.

35. Sandage, *Born Losers*, chapter 4; Edward Neville Vose, *Seventy-Five Years of the Mercantile Agency, R.G. Dun & Co., 1841–1916* (Brooklyn, NY: R.G. Dun & Co., 1916).

36. Board and Dean billhead, December 9, 1863, box 2, folder, "Food," Warshaw Collection; Blake, Scott & Lee Co. to H. M. Leighton, February 5, 1907, box 2, folder 7,

"Food," Warshaw Collection; A. S. Burnell, Burnell's Commercial Agency credit rating book, Buchanan County, Iowa (Marshalltown, IA, 1887).

37. Samuel Iseman to Simon Strauss, November 30, 1890, and undated, Strauss Papers.

38. Lewis Atherton, *The Southern Country Store, 1800–1860* (Baton Rouge: Louisiana State University Press, 1949), 127–129; James H. Madison, "The Evolution of Commercial Credit Reporting Agencies in Nineteenth-Century America," *Business History Review* 48, no. 2 (Summer 1974), 164–186; Sandage, esp. chapters 5 and 6; Ross P. Seaton, "Wipe Out the Middle Man? You Can't," *Wholesale Grocery Review* 24, no. 6 (June 1924), 5; Laird, *Pull*, 51–91; Naomi R. Lamoreaux, Daniel M. G. Raff, and Peter Temin, "Beyond Markets and Hierarchies: Toward a New Synthesis of American Business History," *American Historical Review* 108, no. 2 (April 2003), 410–412.

39. Samuel Iseman to Leopold Strauss, undated, and February 10, 1891; Samuel Iseman to Simon Strauss, December 10 and 18, 1890, February 10, 1891, and undated, Strauss Papers.

40. Samuel Iseman to Simon Strauss, December 4, 1890, November 27 and 29, 1890, and undated, Strauss Papers; Walter Friedman, *Fortune Tellers: The Story of America's First Economic Forecasters* (Princeton, NJ: Princeton University Press, 2013), 1–11.

41. Friedman, *Birth of a Salesman*, 5; Church, "Selling in Britain," 699; Richard N. Langlois, "Chandler in a Larger Frame: Markets, Transaction Costs, and Organizational Form in History," *Enterprise & Society* 5, no. 3 (2004), 359–360; S. Hunerwadel to R. D. Hudson, December 25, 1908, and M[attheus] J. Bufka to S. Hunerwadel, December 28, 1908, box 35, file, "Business Files, Wholesale Grocery, 1907–1914," MacVeagh Papers; *Reports Containing all the Official Announcements and Decisions of the Interstate Commerce Commission*, August 23, 1890 (New York: L. K. Strouse, 1890), 98; Daniel M. G. Raff, "Wholesale trade margins of independent wholesalers, by type of business: 1869–1947," Table De475-481 in *Historical Statistics of the United States, Earliest Times to the Present: Millennial Edition*, Susan B. Carter, Scott Sigmund Gartner, Michael R. Haines, et al. (New York: Cambridge University Press, 2006); M[attheus] J. Bufka to Franklin MacVeagh, September 24, 1904, box 35, file, "Business Files, Wholesale Grocery, 1902–1906," MacVeagh Papers.

42. Friedman, *Birth of a Salesman*, 93; M. J. McDonald to Franklin MacVeagh, February 12, 1900, box 35, file, "Business Files, Wholesale Grocery, 1899–1900," MacVeagh Papers, emphasis in original; M[attheus] J. Bufka to Franklin MacVeagh, August 10, 1904, box 35, folder, "Business Files, Wholesale Grocery, 1902–1906," MacVeagh Papers.

43. Samuel Iseman to Simon Strauss, December 17 and 18, 1890, Strauss Papers. Harrell's case suggests new opportunities for business historians to consider the issues of segregation and racial policies from a supply-side perspective rather than as a consumer issue. While both "black" and "white" stores appeared in many towns, especially in the Jim Crow South, suppliers like Strauss appear to have sold to both. Whether race influenced price, quality, and terms remains uncharted.

44. Charles W. Willis, "On Keeping Promises," *New England Grocer* 66, no. 21 (April 8, 1910), 32; Dario Gaggio, "Pyramids of Trust: Social Embeddedness and Political Culture in Two Italian Gold Jewelry Districts," *Enterprise & Society* 7, no. 1 (March 2006), 19–58; Thomas Haskell, "Capitalism and the Origins of the Humanitarian Sensibility, Part 2," *American Historical Review* 90, no. 3 (June 1985), 547–566.

45. Jeremy Shearmur and Daniel B. Klein, "Good Conduct in a Great Society: Adam Smith and the Role of Reputation," in *Reputation: Studies of the Voluntary Elicitation of Good Conduct*, ed. Daniel B. Klein (Ann Arbor: University of Michigan Press, 1997), 30–33.

46. Samuel Iseman to Simon Strauss, December 17, 1890, Strauss Papers.

47. The term "strategic trust" is Eric Uslaner's, Eric M. Uslaner, *The Moral Foundations of Trust* (New York: Cambridge University Press, 2002), 24–25; Samuel Iseman to Simon Strauss, November 25, 1890, Strauss Papers.

48. Samuel Iseman to Simon Strauss, November 25, 1890, and Samuel Iseman to Leopold Strauss, December 31, 1890, Strauss Papers.

49. Frederick B. Goddard, *Giving and Getting Credit: A Book for Business Men* (New York: Baker and Taylor Company, 1895), 45.

50. Credit reports (1865–1877) of Bollman Brothers, South Carolina, vol. 6, pp. 17, 141, R.G. Dun & Co. Credit Report Volumes, Baker Library Historical Collections, Harvard Business School, Cambridge, MA; Ronald S. Burt, *Structural Holes: The Social Structure of Competition* (Cambridge, MA: Harvard University Press, 1992), 18–29.

51. W. H. Moseley to Simon Strauss, November 25, 1890; W. H. Commander to Simon Strauss, June 1891; Samuel Iseman to Simon Strauss, December 3, 1890, Strauss Papers.

52. Chee K. Ng, Janet Kiholm Smith, and Richard L. Smith, "Evidence on the Determinants of Credit Terms Used in Interfirm Trade," *Journal of Finance* 54, no. 3 (June 1999), 1120–1128; Benjamin S. Wilner, "The Exploitation of Relationships in Financial Distress: The Case of Trade Credit," *Journal of Finance* 55, no. 1 (February 2000), 154–155.

53. "Jottings: Maine," *New England Grocer* 39, no. 22 (October 30, 1896), 13.

54. R. G. Dun agents tracked few customers Iseman solicited. Those who appear in the surviving credit ledgers had estimated worth between $500 and $4,000 at any give time. See credit reports W. P. Dukes (1873–1876), South Carolina, vol. 12, pp. 119, 131, 139, and J. C. Piers [Peers] (1874–1880), South Carolina, vol. 12, p. 132, R. G. Dun & Co. Credit Report Volumes, Baker Library Historical Collections; Samuel Iseman to Simon Strauss, December 1, 1890, Strauss Papers.

55. Samuel Iseman to Simon Strauss, February 11, 1891, and December 1 and 3, 1890; Alexander Brooks to Simon Strauss, December 6, 1890, Strauss Papers.

56. J[oseph] M. St. Louis to R[ollin] A. Keyes, May 28, 1901, box 35, folder, "Business Files, Wholesale Grocery, 1901," MacVeagh Papers.

57. Richard S. Tedlow, *New and Improved: The Story of Mass Marketing in America* (New York: Basic Books, 1990), 186.

Max Weber would have attributed such valuations to "substantive rationality," a measure of market value that "cannot be measured in terms of formal calculation alone, but also involves a relation to the absolute values or to the content of the particular given ends to which it is oriented." In contrast, "formal rationality," in Weber's view, applied to "the extent of quantitative calculation or accounting which is technically possible and which is actually applied." Max Weber, *The Theory of Social and Economic Organization*, trans. Talcott Parsons (New York: Oxford University Press, 1947), 184–186.

58. Godfrey M. Lebhar, *Chain Stores in America, 1859–1950* (New York: Chain Store Publishing Company, 1952), 63; M[aurice] L. Toulme, "Wholesale Grocery Industry," *Journal of Marketing* 14, no. 2 (September 1949), 322–323.

59. Chandler, *Scale and Scope*, 28–31; Porter and Livesay, *Merchants and Manufacturers*, 218–219; Tedlow, *New and Improved*, 206–214.

60. Report 7 and 8, Committee to Reduce the Cost of Doing Business, February 13 and 16, 1923, box 38, folder 1, "Business Files, Wholesale Grocery, 1923," MacVeagh Papers.

CHAPTER 4

1. William J. Seaver, "The Root of All Evil," unattributed article, February 9, 1905, vol. 1, n.p., Boston Wholesale Grocers' Association Collection, Baker Library Historical Collections, Harvard Business School, Cambridge, MA (hereafter BWGA). All BWGA references pertain to Volume 1, an unpaginated collection of meeting minutes, except where noted. Rockefeller, quoted in Ron Chernow, *Titan: The Life of John D. Rockefeller* (New York: Random House, 1998), 148.

2. Naomi R. Lamoreaux, *The Great Merger Movement in American Business, 1895–1904* (New York: Cambridge University Press, 1985), 14–45; Alfred Chandler suggests that manufacturers in the 1870s took "the initial step to growth by way of merger" through associations, Alfred D. Chandler, *The Visible Hand: The Managerial Revolution in American Business* (Cambridge, MA: Harvard University Press, 1977), 315–339.

3. Ewald T. Grether, "Trends in the Wholesale Grocery Trade in San Francisco," *Harvard Business Review* 8, no. 4 (July 1930), 446–447. The number of national chain stores includes meat chains: see Susan B. Carter, Scott Sigmund Gartner, Michael R. Haines, et al., *Historical Statistics of the United States: Millennial Edition* 4 (New York: Cambridge University Press, 2006), 728; Roger Horowitz, *Putting Meat on the American Table: Taste, Technology, Transformation* (Baltimore: Johns Hopkins University Press, 2005), 33–35, 139–144. I define "chain store" as three or more stores in the same city under the same ownership, although there was no universally accepted definition, as chapter 5 will show.

4. William H. Bain, *Historical Address: Boston Wholesale Grocers' Association Fiftieth Anniversary* (Boston: T. R. Marvin, 1925), 7; "Regulating Prices of Sugar," *New York Times*, June 13, 1880, 10.

5. It is difficult to pinpoint when sugar became a "loss leader" in the grocery trade. Evidence indicates the practice had begun as early as the 1860s in England, suggesting a similar timeline in the United States. By the 1870s, however, the practice and problem had become sufficiently widespread as to exact substantial discussion about its effects on the trade. For a treatment of the situation in Great Britain, see F. G. Pennance and B. S. Yamey, "Competition in the Retail Grocery Trade, 1850–1939," *Economica* 22, no. 88 (November 1955), 303–317; E. M. Patterson, "Cooperation among Retail Grocers in Philadelphia," *American Economic Review* 5, no. 2 (June 1915), 280; Artemas Ward, *The Grocers' Hand-Book and Directory* (Philadelphia: Philadelphia Grocer Publishing Company, 1883), 294.

6. "Far-reaching Effect of Price Cutting," *Grocers' Review* 7, no. 5 (July 1898), 190, originally published in *Dry Goods Economist*.

7. Meeting of the association, December 13, 1906, BWGA; Bain, *Historical Address*, 10.

8. Alfred D. Chandler, *Scale and Scope: The Dynamics of Industrial Capitalism* (Cambridge, MA: Belknap Press, 1990), 393–427; Charles Postel, *The Populist Vision* (New York: Oxford University Press, 2007), 3–24.

9. William H. Becker, "American Wholesale Hardware Trade Associations, 1870–1900," *Business History Review* 45, no. 2 (Summer 1971), 179–200; James R. Beniger, *The Control Revolution: Technological and Economic Origins of the Information Society* (Cambridge, MA: Harvard University Press, 1986), 345; regular meeting minutes, May 12, 1898, BWGA.

10. Michael E. Porter, *On Competition* (Cambridge, MA: Harvard Business Review Book Series, 1998), 21–38; Ward, *The Grocers' Hand-Book*, 300. The *Boston City Directory* for 1874 lists sixty-five wholesale grocers, while the 1886 directory lists fifty wholesale grocery firms. Retail grocers who also identified as wholesalers likely account for the discrepancy between the increased BWGA membership despite the decline in number of wholesale grocers listed. Victoria Saker Woeste, *The Farmer's Benevolent Trust: Law and Agricultural Cooperation in Industrial America, 1865–1945* (Chapel Hill: University of North Carolina Press, 1998), 64; "The Wholesale Grocers," *Washington Evening Star* (DC), June 25, 1888, 4.

11. Ward, *The Grocers' Hand-Book*, 284; Thurber, Whyland & Co. to A[ugustine] C. Respess, July 10, 1890, box 16, folder 24, "Food," Warshaw Collection.

12. Meeting of the association, December 13, 1906, BWGA; Margaret Levenstein and Valerie Suslow suggest, "Cartels that control the distribution of goods, through a joint sales agency or some other mechanism, appear to be more stable," Margaret C. Levenstein and Valerie Y. Suslow, "What Determines Cartel Success?" *Journal of Economic Literature* 44, no. 1 (March 2006), 69.

13. Annual meeting minutes, November 11, 1897, BWGA; Richard Zerbe, "The American Sugar Refinery Company, 1887–1914: The Story of a Monopoly," *Journal of Law and Economics* 12, no. 2 (October 1969), 339–375; Levenstein and Suslow, "What Determines Cartel Success?" 69.

14. Annual meeting minutes, November 11, 1897, and meeting of the Association, December 13, 1906, BWGA.

15. Lamoreaux, *Great Merger Movement*, 163–165.

16. Hearings held before the Special Committee on the Investigation of the American Sugar Refining Company and Others, 62nd Congress, 2nd Session, 181 (1911), 1127, 1176; Zerbe, "American Sugar Refinery," 368; annual meeting minutes, November 10, 1898, BWGA; special meeting minutes, May 20, 1903, BWGA; executive committee meeting minutes, June 3, 1903, BWGA.

17. Woeste, *Farmers' Benevolent Trust*, 64; president's report at annual meeting of New England Grocers' Association, October 20, 1904, vol. 4, n.p., BWGA; Arthur Gilman, ed., *The Cambridge of Eighteen Hundred and Ninety-Six: A Picture of the City and Its Industries Fifty Years After Its Incorporation* (Cambridge, MA: Riverside Press, 1896), 358–359; regular monthly meeting minutes, May 9, 1901, annual meeting minutes, November 11, 1897, and regular monthly meeting minutes, February 14, 1901, BWGA.

18. Ward, *The Grocers' Hand-Book*, 296–300, originally printed in *Philadelphia Grocer*.

19. Annual meeting minutes, November 10, 1898, and annual meeting presidential address, November 14, 1901, BWGA.

20. Alfred Chandler suggests that for manufacturing firms, vertical integration was the "logical" end to the road, *The Visible Hand*, 316; "The Chain Store and the Buying Exchange," *Simmons' Spice Mill* 39, no. 2 (February 1916), 138; "The Buying Exchange," *Southern Merchant* 21, no. 49 (September 27, 1909), 13.

21. M. M. Zimmerman, *The Super Market: A Revolution in Distribution* (New York: McGraw-Hill, 1955), 11.

22. William Lewis Abbott, "Competition and Combination in the Wholesale Grocery Trade in Philadelphia" (Ph.D. diss., University of Pennsylvania, 1920), 17–19.

23. Milton Bucken, "How Western Retailers Fight Mail Order Schemes," *Grocery World* 39, no. 1 (January 2, 1905), 22b, 22d; B[urton] H. Allbee, "The Buying Exchanges of New York City," *Grocery World* 39, no. 12 (March 20, 1905), 29.

24. Wilford W. White, *Cooperative Retail Buying Associations* (New York: McGraw-Hill, 1930), 14–15; Grether, "Trends in the Wholesale Grocery Trade," 447.

25. Annual meeting minutes, October 13, 1904, BWGA; A[rchibald] L. Stark, "The Wholesaler and the Retailer: How Dependent Are They, Each upon the Other?" *New England Grocer* 65, no. 23 (October 22, 1909), 20.

26. The remaining percentage of manufactured food products was distributed to a variety of other retail outlets, including "country general stores," meat markets, restaurants, bars, and candy stores, Harold Barger, *Distribution's Place in the Economy since 1869* (New York: Columbia University Press, 1955), 132.

27. Special meeting minutes, June 12, 1902, and annual meeting presidential address, October 13, 1904, BWGA.

28. "New York Jobbers Want Manufacturers to Cease Selling Retailers," *Grocery World* 39, no. 7 (February 13, 1905), 28–29; Ellis L. Howland, "The Eliminating of Unfair Competition," *Southern Merchant* 21, no. 31 (May 24, 1909), 7.

29. Chandler, *The Visible Hand*, 225; "Fruit House Prices!" unidentified billhead, Ft. Wayne (IN), April 14, 1874, box 9, folder 24, "Food," Warshaw Collection

of Business Americana, National Museum of American History, Archives Center, Smithsonian Institution (hereafter Warshaw Collection); "The Wholesale Dealer as a Retailer," *American Grocer* 14, no. 10 (September 11, 1875), 253; B[enjamin] O. Hildreth, letter to the editor, *American Grocer* 13, no. 14 (October 2, 1875), 368; Ward, *The Grocers' Hand-Book*, 284.

30. Hildreth, letter to the editor, 368, "The Grangers Again," *American Grocer* 13, no. 3 (January 16, 1875), 67; Postel, *The Populist Vision*, 103–133.

31. Postel, *The Populist Vision*, 3–22, 104–105.

32. Postel, *The Populist Vision*, 130–131; Montgomery Ward Catalog, no. 13 (Spring and Summer 1875), 6; James M. Mayo, *The American Grocery Store: The Business Evolution of an Architectural Space* (Westport, CT: Greenwood Press, 1993), 94.

33. Howard R. Stanger, "From Factory to Family: The Creation of a Corporate Culture in the Larkin Company of Buffalo, New York," *Business History Review* 74, no.3 (Autumn 2000), 407–433; Howard R. Stanger, "The Larkin Clubs of Ten: Consumer Buying Clubs and Mail-Order Commerce, 1890–1940," *Enterprise & Society* 9, no. 1 (March 2008), 125–164; Patterson, "Cooperation among Retail Grocers," 289; E. M. Tousley, "What Cooperative Societies May Accomplish in Lowering Food Distribution Costs," *Annals of the American Academy of Political and Social Science* 50 (November 1913), 230.

34. William Leach, *Land of Desire: Merchants, Power, and the Rise of a New American Culture* (New York: Pantheon, 1993), 23; Macy's advertisement, *New York Times*, September 11, 1899, 5; "Brooklyn Grocers Protest," *New York Times*, November 15, 1894, 5.

35. "To Bait the Customers," *New York Times*, November 20, 1894, 3.

36. Meeting of the Association, December 13, 1906, BWGA.

37. "To Bait the Customers," 3; "Brooklyn Grocers Protest," 5.

38. Regular monthly meeting minutes, December 11, 1909, BWGA; Thomas C. Jenkins, billhead, October 16, 1896, box 9, folder 40, "Food," Warshaw Collection.

39. Abbott, "Competition and Combination," 13; Mayo, *American Grocery Store*, 94.

40. Special meeting minutes, October 26, 1905, and annual meeting presidential address, November 12, 1903, BWGA.

41. Special meeting minutes, June 12, 1902, BWGA.

42. "All Sugar Refiners Withdraw Price Guarantees," *Grocery World* 39, no. 1 (January 2, 1905), 8.

43. Patterson, "Cooperation among Retail Grocers," 289–290; Mid-winter meeting minutes, February 8, 1906, BWGA.

44. Special meeting minutes, October 26, 1905, special meeting minutes, June 12, 1902, meeting of the Association minutes, December 14, 1905, annual meeting minutes, November 10, 1898, and annual meeting presidential address, November 14, 1901, BWGA.

45. Report of the Committee of Five, December 7, 1905, BWGA.

46. "Men Who Feed Us," *Atlanta Constitution*, May 25, 1895, 5; "Southern Grocers Proceeded Against," *Galveston Daily News*, June 16, 1910, 1.

47. Testimony of Hinton G. Clabaugh in Senate Documents, 62nd Congress, 1st Session, April 4–August 22, 1911, 2496; *Clabaugh v. Southern Wholesale Grocers' Association* et al. No. 1,279, Circuit Court, N.D. Alabama, S.D. 181 F. 706; 1910 U.S. App., September 15, 1910.

48. Albert J. Churella, *The Pennsylvania Railroad: Building an Empire, 1846–1917,* vol. 1 (Philadelphia: University of Pennsylvania Press, 2012), 362–369.

49. Meeting of the association, December 13, 1906, BWGA, emphasis in original. Bain, *Historical Address,* 5, 10; annual meeting presidential address, October 13, 1910, BWGA.

50. Annual meeting presidential address, October 13, 1910, BWGA.

51. Abbott, "Competition and Combination," 77; White, *Cooperative Retail Buying Associations,* 193.

52. Martha L. Olney, "Credit as a Production-Smoothing Device: The Case of Automobiles, 1913–1938," *Journal of Economic History* 49, no. 2 (June 1989), 377–391; "The Credit System," *American Grocer* 4, no. 10, (March 11, 1871), 308.

53. Lewis E. Atherton, *The Frontier Merchant in Mid-America* (Columbia: University of Missouri Press, 1971), 18.

54. Abbott, "Competition and Combination," 76; regular monthly meeting minutes, February 14, 1901, and monthly meeting minutes, April 11, 1901, BWGA.

55. Barger, *Distribution's Place,* 81; Harvard Bureau of Business Research, *Bulletin No. 9,* "Operating Expenses in the Wholesale Grocery Business in 1916" (Cambridge, MA: Harvard University Press, 1917), 8; Harvard Bureau of Business Research, *Bulletin No. 19,* "Operating Expenses in the Wholesale Grocery Business in 1919" (Cambridge, MA: Harvard University Press, 1920), 9–15.

56. Abbott, "Competition and Combination," 75–77.

57. Wilbur Clayton Plummer, *Credit Extension and Business Failure: A Study of Credit Conditions and Causes of Failure among Grocery Retailers in Louisville, Kentucky* (Washington, DC: US Government Printing Office, 1929), 4; Edmund D. McGarry, *Mortality in Retail Trade* (Buffalo: University of Buffalo Bureau of Business and Social Research, 1930), 11, 90; Abbott, "Competition and Combination," 77.

58. "What Is 'Eliminated'?" *Bulletin of the National Wholesale Grocers' Association* 6, no. 4 (February 1921), 1; Barger, *Distribution's Place,* 77; M[aurice] L. Toulme, "Wholesale Grocery Industry," *Journal of Marketing* 14, no. 2 (September 1949), 322–323.

59. F. W. Hannahs, "Mission of the Wholesaler," *New England Grocer* 67, no. 2 (May 27, 1912), 10; Paul Terry Cherington, *The Advertising Book 1916* (New York: Doubleday, Page, 1916), 233; J. W. Millard, *The Wholesale Grocer's Problems: Costs, Customers, and Commodities,* United States Department of Commerce Distribution Cost Studies, no. 4 (Washington, DC: US Government Printing Office, 1928), 1.

60. Millard, *Wholesale Grocer's Problems,* 28; Marc Levinson, *The Great A&P and the Struggle for Small Business in America* (New York: Hill and Wang, 2011), 106.

61. Barger, *Distribution's Place,* 77.

CHAPTER 5

1. Frederick E. Croxton, *A Study of Housewives' Buying Habits in Columbus, Ohio, 1924* (Columbus: Bureau of Business Research, Ohio State University, 1924), 1; "Frederick Croxton, 91, Statistician and Author," *New York Times*, January 16, 1991, B9; "Marriages, Croxton-Harpster," *Ohio State University Monthly* 13, no.1 (October 1921), 42.

2. Croxton, *Study of Housewives' Buying Habits*, 3, 12–14.

3. Rowland Bertoff, "Independence and Enterprise: Small Business in the American Dream," in *Small Business in American Life*, ed. Stuart Bruchey (New York: Columbia University Press, 1980), 29; Mansel Blackford, *A History of Small Business in America* (New York: Twayne, 1991), xvi; James Truslow Adams, *The Epic of America* (New York: Little, Brown, 1931), 405.

4. *Louis K. Liggett Co. et al. v. Lee, Comptroller, et al.*, 288 U.S. 517 (1933); Godfrey Lebhar, *Chain Stores in America, 1859–1950* (New York: Chain Store Publishing Company, 1952), 130–132.

5. Thomas K. McCraw, *Prophets of Regulation* (Cambridge, MA: Belknap Press, 1984), 80–122; Arthur M. Schlesinger, *The Age of Roosevelt* (Boston: Houghton Mifflin Harcourt, 1957), 233.

6. Clarence Saunders, Self-serving Store, US Patent 1,242,872, filed October 21, 1916, and issued October 9, 1917; Clarence Saunders, *Piggly Wiggly: A System of Selling Merchandise* (Memphis, TN: [n.p.], 1917), n.p.; Lisa C. Tolbert, "The Aristocracy of the Market Basket: Self-Service Food Shopping in the New South," in *Food Chains: From Farmyard to Shopping Cart*, ed. Warren James Belasco and Roger Horowitz (Philadelphia: University of Pennsylvania Press, 2009), 180.

7. Sarah Elvins, *Sales and Celebrations: Retailing and Regional Identity in Western New York State, 1920–1940* (Athens: Ohio University Press, 2004), 92–98.

8. "Happenings of the Day," *Stuebenville (Ohio) Herald-Star*, July 1, 1918, 6.

9. "Cafeteria to Enlarge," *Syracuse (NY) Herald*, November 19, 1908, 10; Lowell Electric Light Corporation advertisement, *Lowell (MA) Sun*, July 11, 1914, 21; Christman's Self Service Grocery advertisement, *Marion (OH) Star*, March 8, 1916, 11; Tolbert, "Aristocracy of the Market Basket," 180.

10. Susan Strasser, *Satisfaction Guaranteed: The Making of the American Mass Market* (New York: Pantheon, 1989), 194–195; Tracey A. Deutsch, "Untangling Alliances: Social Tensions Surrounding Independent Grocery Stores and the Rise of Mass Retailing," in *Food Nations: Selling Taste in Consumer Societies*, ed. Warren Belasco and Philip Scranton (New York: Routledge, 2002), 159.

11. Robert Mueller, *A&P: Past, Present and Future* (New York: Progressive Grocer Magazine, 1971), 18; General ledger volume 7 (1895–1899), volume 8 (1899–1903), and volume 9 (1904–1911), and Stable Accounts, microfilm reels 5, 6, and 7, Andrew Schoch Grocery Company Business Records, Minnesota Historical Society Manuscript Collection, St. Paul, Minn.

12. "Economy in Retail Service," *National Wholesale Grocers' Association Bulletin* 3, no. 7 (May 1918), 17–18; William F. Willoughby, *Government Organization in War Time*

and After: A Survey of the Federal Civil Agencies Created for the Prosecution of the War (New York: D. Appleton, 1919), 105; "Some Suggestions for Installing Co-Operative Delivery Systems," *National Wholesale Grocers' Association Bulletin* 3, no. 1 (November 1917), 2; "Curtailed Delivery System Went into Effect Today," *Richmond* (VA) *News-Leader*, July 23, 1917, n.p., box 311, Records of National Council of Defense Commercial Economy Board, Record Group 62; National Archives at College Park, College Park, MD.

13. Scovel's Grocery advertisement, *Humeston* (IA) *New Era*, August 22, 1917, 4; Willoughby, *Government Organization*, 107; "Take a Basket and Bring Home Your Groceries," *Syracuse* (NY) *Herald*, August 16, 1917, 17; "Cash and Carry Plan," *National Wholesale Grocers' Association Bulletin* 4, no. 5 (March 1919), 5.

14. Croxton, "Study of Housewives' Buying Habits," 3; "The New Kind of Store," *Ladies' Home Journal* 34 (August 1917), 47.

15. Lendol Calder, *Financing the American Dream: A Cultural History of Consumer Credit* (Princeton, NJ: Princeton University Press, 1999), 211, 225; US Department of Commerce, *Census of Distribution Reports, Fifteenth Decennial Census*, vol. 1 (Washington, DC: US Government Printing Office, 1930), 72.

16. Charles F. Phillips, "Chain, Voluntary Chain, and Independent Grocery Store Prices, 1930 and 1934," *Journal of Business of the University of Chicago* 8, no. 2 (April 1935), 143–149; Marc Levinson, *The Great A&P and the Struggle for Small Business* (New York: Hill and Wang, 2011), 91–92, 107–108.

17. "We Aim to Please," *Sheboygan* (WI) *Journal*, May 10, 1927, 11; Christine Frederick, "Listen to this Sophisticated Shopper," *Chain Store Age* 1 (June 1925), 36, emphasis in original.

18. Lizabeth Cohen, *Making a New Deal: Industrial Workers in Chicago, 1919–1939* (New York: Cambridge University Press, 1990), 101–120; Myrtle Hatfield noted of Jewel stores in the 1930s, "It is the only grocery chain in Chicago which operates completely on the self-service plan," Myrtle Lohner Hatfield, "An Analysis of Some Grocery Store Practices from the Point of View of the Woman Buyer" (master's thesis, University of Chicago, 1936), 1, 47–61; John P. Nichols, *The Chain Store Tells Its Story* (New York: Institute of Distribution, 1940), 108.

19. Ernest R. Ham, "Carrying the Chain Store into the Home," *Chain Store Age* 2 (June 1926), 20–21, 51; National Tea Company advertisement, *Sycamore* (IL) *True Republican*, November 22, 1930, 7.

20. Elvins, *Sales and Celebrations*, 83–88; "Chain Stores versus Independent Merchant, Life Study Club Topic," *Warren* (PA) *Tribune*, March 28, 1928, 9; James Truslow Adams, *Our Business Civilization: Some Aspects of American Culture* (New York: Albert and Charles Boni, 1929), 18.

21. Henry S. Raab, "What Chain Stores Do for a Community," *Chain Store Age* 1 (August 1925), 43–44; Strasser, *Satisfaction Guaranteed*, 221–222.

22. Eloise Schaffer, "Our Community Builders," *Cumberland* (MD) *Evening Times*, January 31, 1930, 18; "Chain Stores versus Independent," 9.

23. Bertoff, "Independence and Enterprise," 38–39; Jesse Rainsford Sprague, "The Chain-Store Mind: Reflections of a Shopkeeper," *Harpers Magazine* 945 (February 1929), 357.

24. Rick Halpern, *Down on the Killing Floor: Black and White Workers in Chicago's Packinghouses, 1904–54* (Urbana: University of Illinois Press, 1997), 16–17; Roger Horowitz, *"Negro and White, Unite and Fight": A Social History of Industrial Unionism in Meatpacking, 1930–90* (Urbana: University of Illinois Press, 1991), 1–10; David B. Greenberg and Henry Schindall, *A Small Store and Independence* (New York: Greenberg, 1945), v.

25. Nichols, *Chain Store*, 227; J. George Frederick, "Big Business and the Little Man," *North American Review* 226, no. 4 (October 1928), 442.

26. Royal Copeland quoted in Lebhar, *Chain Stores*, 159, 48; Edwin J. Perkins, "The Entrepreneurial Spirit in Colonial America: The Foundations of Modern Business History," *Business History Review* 63, no. 1 (Spring 1989), 160–186; Bertoff, "Independence and Enterprise," 28–48.

27. "The Menace of the Chain Store," *Kellogg's Square Dealer* 4, no. 9 (September 1914), 1, 5; Tracey Deutsch, *Building a Housewife's Paradise: Gender, Politics, and American Grocery Stores in the Twentieth Century* (Chapel Hill: University of North Carolina Press, 2010), 73–103.

28. "Chain Stores in the Grocery Business," *J. Walter Thompson News Bulletin* 132 (September 1927), 6, 9–11.

29. Lebhar, *Chain Stores*, 114–114, 129; Nichols, *Chain Store*, 151.

30. Nichols, *Chain Store*, 134; "Kill 1933 Tax on Income of Chain Stores," *Milwaukee Journal*, June 4, 1935, 1; Jack Sherman, Application for Chain Store Occupational Tax Receipt, 1935, box 6, folder Se-Sl, Wisconsin Department of Taxation, General Property Taxation, Chain Store Tax Division Correspondence, 1933–1939, Wisconsin Historical Society, Madison, WI (hereafter WTC).

31. Harold McGugin, "Freedom or Monopoly: An Address on the Chain Store Menace," radio transcript, January 20, 1929, pamphlet in author's possession; Nichols, *Chain Store*, 148.

32. Frederick K. Hardy, "Taxation of Chain Retailers in the United States," *Journal of Comparative Legislation and International Law* 18, no. 4 (1936), 259; "Governor Asks for Further Relief in Property Taxes," *Milwaukee Journal*, June 4, 1931, 12; Wisconsin Tax Commission, Chain Store Tax Division to Green Bay Association of Commerce, January 2, 1934, box 3, folder Ga-Ge, WTC.

33. Markesan Quality Grocery to Wisconsin Tax Commission, September 20, 1937, box 4, folder M-Mas, WTC.

34. Wisconsin Tax Commission, Chain Store Tax Division to E[than] A. Cleasby, March 27, 1935, and E[than] A. Cleasby to Wisconsin Tax Commission, May 23, 1935, box 6, folder Se-Sl, WTC.

35. Wisconsin Tax Commission to Kaiser's Food Shop, March 2, 1936, and Carl A. Kaiser to Wisconsin Tax Commission, March 4, 1936, box 3, folder Ka-Kn, WTC.

36. Rose Lernor to R[ichard] C. Dubielzig, December 5, 1936 and Rose Lernor to R[ichard] C. Dubielzig, December 10, 1936, box 2, folder Fo, WTC.

37. G[rover] C. Gould to Wisconsin Tax Commission, February 20, 1934, and Wisconsin Tax Commission to the Daisy Market, February 23, 1934, box 2, folder

Da-Dy, WTC; Gilbert's Bazaar to Wisconsin Tax Commission, January 6, 1936, emphasis in original, box 2, folder Ga-Ge, WTC; Wisconsin Tax Commission to H. S. Dyer, February 16, 1939, box 2, folder Da-Dy, WTC.

38. Charles G. Daughters, *Wells of Discontent: A Study of the Economic, Social, and Political Aspects of the Chain Store* (New York: Newson, 1937), 117, 138–139; "Thirty-Three Groups File Lobby Expenses with State," *Sheboygan* (WI)*Press*, August 24, 1933, 17.

39. Raymond Scribner (for Sam Shniderman) to Wisconsin Tax Commission, March 2, 1934, and Wisconsin Tax Commission to Scribner, Cohen & Company, March 1, 1934, box 5, folder Sa-Sc, WTC.

40. Wisconsin Tax Commission to Kenneth Peisker, November 9, 1934, and Kenneth Peisker to Wisconsin Tax Commission, September 5, 1934, box 5, folder Pa-Pet, WTC; Gordon C. Corbaley, *Group Selling by 100,000 Retailers* (New York: American Institute of Food Distribution, 1936), 54.

41. Asa Strause to Wisconsin Tax Commission, January 30, 1934, box 5, folder Q & R, WTC; "Seattle Stores in National Movement," *Seattle Daily Times*, October 14, 1927, 19; "Red and White International Convention Draws Hundreds of Delegates to Seattle," *Seattle Daily Times*, September 24, 1929, 1.

42. Red and White advertisement, *Seattle Daily Times*, August 9, 1928, 15.

43. Elvins, *Sales and Celebrations*, 92–94; Contract between E. R. Godfrey & Sons Company and IGA members, [1930?], box 3, folder I, WTC; Hardy, "Taxation of Chain Retailers," 258.

44. James M. Mayo, *The American Grocery Store: The Business Evolution of an Architectural Space* (Westport, CT: Greenwood Press, 1993), 119–120; E. H. Gault, "Cooperation by Business Groups," *Journal of Marketing* 1, no. 4 (April 1937), 399–400; Corbaley, *Group Selling*, 62; Mueller, *A&P: Past, Present and Future*, 4.

45. "Quality Plus Advertising Gets Results," *National Wholesale Grocers' Association Bulletin* 6, no. 11 (October 1921), 13; Contract between E. R. Godfrey & Sons Company and IGA members.

46. Wilford L. White, *Cooperative Retail Buying Associations* (New York: McGraw-Hill, 1930), 86–91; "D.G.S. to Build Huge Warehouse," *Washington Herald*, January 31, 1937, n.p.; Robert J. Shepherd, *When Culture Goes to Market: Space, Place, and Identity in an Urban Marketplace* (New York: Peter Lang, 2008), 27; Isaac Jacobson quoted in Jacobson Scrap Book, research notes, September 1993, box 2, folder, "Mom & Pop Grocery: Jacobson Family," in Exhibit Files, "Half a Day on Sunday," Jewish Historical Society of Greater Washington, Washington, DC.

47. National Negro Business League, *Report of the Survey of Negro Business* (National Negro Business League, 1929), n.p.; White, *Cooperative Retail Buying Associations*, 91; Juliet E. K. Walker, *The History of Black Business in America: Capitalism, Race, Entrepreneurship*, vol. 1 (Chapel Hill: University of North Carolina Press, 2009), xii–xxiv.

48. National Negro Business League, *Report of the Survey of Negro Business*, n.p.; Robert R. Moton, speech transcript, August 1929, box 12, folder 1, Moton Family Papers, Library of Congress, Manuscript Collections Division (hereafter Moton Papers).

49. Albon L. Holsey, "The C.M.A. Stores Face the Chains," *Opportunity* 7 (July 1929), 210–213; Robert E. Weems, *Business in Black and White: American Presidents and Black Entrepreneurs in the Twentieth Century* (New York: New York University Press, 2009), 23–24; Jessie Carney Smith, "Colored Merchants Association," in Jessie Carney Smith, ed., *Encyclopedia of African American Business* (Westport, CT: Greenwood Press, 2006), 185–190; undated fragment, box 13, folder 2, Moton Papers.

50. Cohen, *Making a New Deal*, 148–149; A[tlanta] L. Brown-Lipscomb to Robert R. Moton, September 1, 1929, box 12, folder 3, Moton Papers.

51. Cheryl Lynn Greenberg, *Or Does It Explode? Black Harlem in the Great Depression* (New York: Oxford University Press, 1997), 114–139; Holsey, "The C.M.A. Stores," 213; Albon L. Holsey, "Let's Finish the Job in 1933," *The Negro Market* 1, no. 5 (December 1932), 1, box 12, folder 12, Moton Papers; Plan of the National C.M.A. Stores, Inc., 1931, box 12, folder 12, Moton Papers.

52. Report on C.M.A. Stock Subscriptions, November 16, 1931, box 12, folder 10, Moton Papers; Cohen, *Making a New Deal*, 152; Albon L. Holsey to Robert M. Moton, October 19, 1931, box 12, folder 9, Moton Papers; Albon L. Holsey to Robert R. Moton, July 20, 1931, box 12, folder 8, Moton Papers.

53. Robert M. Moton to Albon L. Holsey, March 5, 1931, box 12, folder 6, Moton Papers; Fred R. Moore to Albon L. Holsey, March 31, 1933, box 12, folder 13; Albon L. Holsey to Fred R. Moore, April 1, 1933, box 12, folder 13, Moton Papers.

54. Holsey, "Let's Finish the Job in 1933," 2–3; Albon L. Holsey to Robert M. Moton, emphasis in original, December 14, 1932, box 12, folder 12, Moton Papers; "C.M.A. Stores Point Way to Better Things," *New York Amsterdam News*, February 24, 1932, n.p., box 12, folder 11, Moton Papers; Cohen, *Making a New Deal*, 147–154; "What's Wrong with the C.M.A.?" *Pittsburgh Courier*, August 12, 1933, 10; Greenberg, *Or Does It Explode?* 138–139.

55. Undated fragment, box 12, folder 2, Moton Papers; Albon L. Holsey to Robert R. Moton, January 29, 1931, box 12, folder 5, and December 6, 1932, box 12, folder 12, Moton Papers; Albon L. Holsey to Robert R. Moton, April 1, 1933, box 12, folder 13, Moton Papers.

56. Tom Griffin to Albon Holsey, August 8, 1929, box 12, folder 3, Moton Papers; "What's Wrong with the C.M.A.," 10; Plan of the National C.M.A. Stores Inc., [n.d. 1932?], box 12, folder 12, Moton Papers.

57. Sprague, "Chain-Store Mind," 359; Frederick, "Big Business and the Little Man," 441, 444.

58. Phillips, "Chain, Voluntary Chain, and Independent Grocery Store Prices," 149.

59. Alfred Lief, ed., *Social and Economic Views of Mr. Justice Brandeis* (New York: Vanguard Press, 1930), 399.

60. Nancy Back Young, *Wright Patman: Populism, Liberalism, and the American Dream* (Dallas: Southern Methodist University Press, 2000), 30–76.

61. Lebhar, *Chain Stores*, 148–150, 186, 208.

62. Wright Patman, *Complete Guide to the Robinson-Patman Act* (Englewood Cliffs, NJ: Prentice Hall, 1938, 1963), 5–9.

63. Nichols, *Chain Store*, 159; Levinson, *Great A&P*, 167.

64. Nichols, *Chain Store*, 151, 198.

65. William D. Hubbard, editorial, *Indiana* (PA) *Weekly Messenger*, May 7, 1936, 5.

66. "Senate to Rush 'Fair Trade' Bill," *Hammond* (IN) *Times*, February 7, 1936, 53; James McMillin, "The National Whirligig," *Port Arthur* (TX) *News*, July 11, 1936, 8.

67. The FTC reserved the right to initiate quantity limits "in cases where there are so few purchasers of large quantities that one of them or a few of them may completely dominate and control the entire industry," Patman, *Complete Guide*, 15, 18.

68. Patman, *Complete Guide*, 338–341.

69. "Speech of Congressman Patman," November 17, 1936, n.p., and "Statement," box 1337A, folder "Releases, Robinson-Patman," Wright Patman Papers, Lyndon Baines Johnson Presidential Library, Austin, TX.

70. Louis Bader, "A Survey of Consumers' and Independent Store Owners' Reactions to Recent Price Legislation," *Journal of Marketing* 4, no. 1 (July 1939), 62, 67.

71. Bader, "Survey of Consumers and Independent Store Owners," 60; Lebhar, *Chain Stores*, 63.

72. M. M. Zimmerman, *The Supermarket: A Revolution in Distribution* (New York: McGraw-Hill, 1955), 32–35.

73. Zimmerman, *The Super Market*, 64–65; Levinson, *Great A&P*, 170–171.

74. T. Eugene Beattie, "Public Relations and the Chains," *Journal of Marketing* 7, no. 3 (January 1943), 250.

75. "Kroger Head Says Chains Will Grow," *Charleston* (WV) *Daily Mail*, April 1, 1930, 30; "Five City Residents Win Slogan Prizes," *Charleston* (WV) *Daily Mail*, August 6, 1930, 5. While Kroger identified several local winners, it did not release the winning slogans.

76. Beattie, "Public Relations," 251; Levinson, *Great A&P*, 167–193.

77. L. A. Warren, "Our Pledge to California Farmers," *Hayward* (CA) *Daily News*, October 28, 1936, 3.

78. "Chain Store Attacks Decline," *Greenwood* (MI) *Delta Democrat-Times*, June 11, 1939, 12; "Speech of Congressman Patman," n.p.; Beattie, "Public Relations," 253–255.

79. Patman, *Complete Guide*, 179–180.

80. Zimmerman, *The Super Market*, 31–53; Cover, *Time Magazine*, November 13, 1950.

81. Elvins, *Sales and Celebrations*, 104–105; Richard S. Tedlow, *New and Improved: The Story of Mass Marketing in America* (New York: Basic Books, 1990), 214.

CONCLUSION

1. "For Local Grocers, Understanding Customers Holds Key to Competing with the Wal-Marts," Carnegie Mellon University press release, October 7, 2005; Patricia Callahan and Ann Zimmerman, "Price War in Aisle 3—Wal-Mart Tops Grocery List with Supercenter Format," *Wall Street Journal* (Eastern edition), May 27, 2003, B.1;

Nelson Lichtenstein, ed., *Wal-Mart: The Face of Twenty-First-Century Capitalism* (New York: New Press, 2006), xi; Charles Fishman, *The Wal-Mart Effect: How the World's Most Powerful Company Really Works—and How It's Transforming the American Economy* (New York: Penguin Press, 2006).

2. US Census Bureau, "Statistics of U.S. Businesses: 2012: Supermarkets & Other Grocery (except convenience stores) United States," www.census.gov/econ/susb; US Census Bureau, "Statistics of U.S. Businesses: 2012: Grocery Stores United States," www.census.gov/econ/susb/.

3. Robert C. Blattberg, Karsten Hansen, and Vishal P. Singh, "Wal-Mart Supercenter versus the Traditional Supermarket: How Can a Local Grocery Store Survive?" *Kellogg Insight: Focus on Research*, Northwestern University, Kellogg School of Management, May 2, 2007, http://insight.kellogg.northwestern.edu/index.php/Kellogg/article/wal_mart_supercenter_versus_the_traditional_supermarket; Callahan, "Price War in Aisle 3," B.1; "A&P, Century-Old U.S. Grocery Store Owner, Files for Bankruptcy," *Bloomberg*, www.bloomberg.com/news/2010-12-12/a-p-grocery-store-owner-files-for-bankruptcy-as-competition-heightens.html; "A&P Bankruptcy Filing Indicates Likely Demise," *Wall Street Journal*, www.wsj.com/articles/a-p-files-for-chapter-11-bankruptcy-1437391572.

4. Nelson Lichtenstein, "Wal-Mart: A Template for Twenty-First-Century Capitalism," in *Wal-Mart: The Face of Twenty-First-Century Capitalism*, ed. Nelson Lichtenstein (New York: New Press, 2006), 3–30; Nelson Lichtenstein, *The Retail Revolution: How Walmart Created a Brave New World of Business* (New York: Picador, 2010), 11–45.

5. Susan Strasser, "Woolworth to Wal-Mart: Mass Merchandising and the Changing Culture of Consumption," in *Wal-Mart: The Face of Twenty-First-Century Capitalism*, ed. Nelson Lichtenstein (New York: New Press, 2006), 31–56; Bethany Moreton, *To Serve God and Wal-Mart: The Making of Christian Free Enterprise* (Cambridge, MA: Harvard University Press, 2010), 6–23.

6. Douglas Filaroski, "Publix, Others Build Smaller Grocery Stores," *Business Journal* (Tampa Bay, FL), October 3, 2003, n.p.; Teresa F. Lindeman, "Thinking Small Tight Economy Has Shoppers, Grocers Again Looking to Neighborhood Stores," *Pittsburgh Post-Gazette*, October 3, 2008, A.10; Blattberg et al., "Wal-Mart Supercenter versus the Traditional Supermarket," n.p.

7. Andrew Martin, "Miles of Aisles for Milk? Not Here," *New York Times*, September 10, 2008, A.1. The number of grocery stores and employees does not include "convenience" stores, which typically employ a smaller number of workers than supermarkets or grocery stores. "Convenience" stores form a separate category in the US Business Census, www.census.gov/econ/susb/ Wendy Toth and Dan Alaimo, Small Is the New Big," *SN: Supermarket News* 55, no. 20 (2007), 40–41; Lisa Liddane, "Walmart's Small Stores Take on Local Supermarkets," *Orange County Register* (Santa Ana, CA), November 6, 2012.

8. Saul Hansell, "An Ambitious Internet Grocer Is Out of Both Cash and Ideas," *New York Times*, July 10, 2001, A.1; Peapod, "Corporate Fact Sheet," www.peapod.com/corpinfo/companyFactSheet.jhtml; "Amazon Grocery Delivery Rolls into San Francisco,"

Associated Press, December 11, 2013, http://news.yahoo.com/amazon-grocery-delivery-rolls-san-francisco-192038000.html?soc_src=mediacontentstory.

9. Martin, "Miles of Aisles," A.1.

10. C & S Wholesale Grocers, *Jobs*, "Merchandising," accessed January 6, 2014, http://www.weselectthebest.com/jobs/openings/merchandising-analyst-9016; Whole Foods, "Core Values," www.wholefoodsmarket.com/mission-values/core-values.

Index